PARADIGM SHIFT:

Why International Students are so Strategic to Global Missions

JACK D. BURKE, PH.D. M.DIV.

WESTBOW
PRESS®
A DIVISION OF THOMAS NELSON
& ZONDERVAN

WestBow Press books may be ordered through booksellers or by contacting:

WestBow Press
A Division of Thomas Nelson & Zondervan
1663 Liberty Drive
Bloomington, IN 47403
www.westbowpress.com
1 (866) 928-1240

ISBN: 978-1-9736-5685-2 (sc)
ISBN: 978-1-9736-5686-9 (hc)
ISBN: 978-1-9736-5687-6 (e)

Library of Congress Control Number: 2019902861

Print information available on the last page.

WestBow Press rev. date: 03/14/2019

ENDORSEMENTS

My endorsement for *Paradigm Shift - Why International Students are so Strategic to Global Missions*:

What a timely and relevant resource with multidimensional information to empower those who reach out to international students. The author's depth of knowledge and experience provide unique insights to the leaders in the field. This excellent work comes to us at a time of global unrest characterized by transition, danger and opportunity. The mission to reach out to international students is a mission to impact the globe through positive learning and life experience which sends them back to their countries with a transformational ethos. A must read!

[signature]

Dr. Doug Shaw
President/CEO
International Students, Inc.

Dr. Burke is not against sending missionaries around the world; he simply wants us also to reach and use those from other countries who are studying in the United States and who will return to their nations already equipped with the language and the culture. He persuades with logic and his long personal experience.

Dr. Marvin D. Webster, past board member of CBInternational (now WorldVenture), CBHMS (now Mission Door), and Denver Seminary (Dr. Webster had a term of 3 years as Board Chair of both CBHMS and Denver Seminary.)

"Several decades ago, when I arrived as the Missions Pastor at Houston's First Baptist Church, one of the first leaders I met in the city was Jack Burke. He was a member of our church, and I quickly realized Jack was one of the top leaders in reaching international students in the world. Universities in the city welcomed him on campus because of his focus to love, care, and welcome international students. He and his wife had a fully developed strategy. His concepts could easily be adapted by churches to welcome students upon their arrival in America, establish friendships with matching sponsors, and provide a spiritual context for the international student to hear the Gospel. These short-term friendships turned into lasting relationships with individuals who became future leaders of the world from Asia, to India, to Africa and beyond. Often, our strategies are based on reaching across the world, nation, and city – in that order. Jack modeled for us the reverse by reaching international students in our *city* with the Gospel."

William Taylor, Leadership Team and Missions Pastor, Houston's First Baptist Church, HoustonsFirst.org

---

"You will be hard pressed to find anyone more qualified than Dr. Jack Burke to write a book that is a case for the strategic importance of ministry to international students. His book details the manner in which international students should be assisted while in the United States. Also, it lays out a vision for the importance of why Christian international students, when they return home, should be ready to share the joyous gospel message of hope and love. Nancy and I observed the ministry of Jack and D'Ann first hand for many years. Everything we saw was well done and extremely helpful. They were well respected by the entire Houston community and were recognized as leaders by every part of it. I honor them, admire them, and respect them."

Paul Pressler
Former Justice, Texas Court of Appeals
Former board member, So. Baptist International Mission Board (IMB) . . .
Former Board Chair, International Students Inc.(ISI)

The following are the International Student Ministry (ISM) leaders whom I certify that each endorsed and submitted their recommendations for WestBow Press to publish in my book, <u>Paradigm Shift - Why International Students are So Strategic to Global Missions</u>.. They are all professional peers. We share mutual respect personally and professionally.

Jack D. Burke, Ph.D., M.Div., M.S.
President, International Student Ministries Assistance, Inc
Director Emeritus, International Student and Scholar Services, University of Houston
Co-Founder, Association of Christians Ministering among Internationals (ACMI) Founder, NAFSA Christian Specific Interest Group (SIG)
Honorary Life Member of both ACMI and NAFSA: Association of International Educators

I can't think of anyone who knows more about international student ministry than Dr. Jack Burke. Throughout his decades of leadership at the University of Houston and his collaboration with various missions agencies, Dr. Burke has studied the strategies and practiced the tactics that lead to fruitful ministry among international students. Most of all, he has remained faithful to our Lord and passionate about the Great Commission.

Trae Vacek
Executive Director
Bridges International
713.545.6438 cell
tvacek@bridgesinternational.com

"Dr. Jack Burke brings a unique combination of experiences and understanding of international student ministry (ISM) to bear on this crucial subject. Not only did he work for decades in the international student office context, he's given leadership and ministered within the church-based side of ISM, and labored collaboratively with ISM agencies. With this breadth of ISM engagement, Jack passionately addresses the strategic role that international students have in fulfillment of the Great Commission, illustrated with examples and stories. If you want to learn more about this most timely opportunity in global outreach, and be challenged, read on!"

Dr. Beau Miller
Executive Director
Association of Christians Ministering Among Internationals (ACMI)

To call Dr. Jack Burke the "dean" of the worldwide international student ministry movement is no exaggeration. After more than 55 years of service, he has achieved pre-eminent stature amongst both foreign student advisers *and* international student ministers. No one comes close to him on the planet today. Thus, we should not only welcome this remarkable volume from an accomplished figure in the field of international student ministry, but we should *all* pay very close attention. Without question, this manifesto will be read by mission scholars and practitioners for decades to come. And it just may propel international student ministry into the forefront of the 21st century global mission movement. That will be none too soon.

Robert Osburn, PhD
Executive Director
Wilberforce Academy

"After hearing and seeing Dr. Burke's passion for serving international students in various contexts for nearly 40 years, I'm grateful for his vast treasure trove of written insights. While a multi-faceted vision for ministry among international students is clearly portrayed, it is particularly significant that this collection of the strategic components of international student ministry includes a high profile with numerous examples of the great influence and impact of returnees to their home country after studying abroad. For any person or ministry considering international student ministry, this is a must-read resource"

Leiton Chinn
Lausanne Catalyst for International Student Ministries,
Former President, ACMI.
Former NAFSA COMSEC National Team and Newsletter Editor; author of NAFSA publications on International Student Reentry

----

Dr. Jack Burke's book is a valuable addition to the growing body of literature on International Student Ministry. His 60 years-experience in the world of International Education gives him a unique perspective on the strategic nature of reaching international students. The stories of world changers today who were former international students at the University of Houston, where he directed the International Student and Scholars Office, demonstrate international students' impact and influence. This book is an urgent call to open our eyes, be involved and see how we can be a part of God's work in changing the world through international students.

Lisa Espineli Chinn
Former Director, Ministry to International Students, InterVarsity
Development Coach
3104 Streamhaven Dr., Indian Land, SC 29707
InterVarsity Christian Fellowship/USA
803.431.7679

One of the largest untapped mission fields in North America is a college or university where international students from all over the world are studying. These students will lead nations through government, academia, and various positions of power and influence in the upcoming years.

As a former international student led to our Lord by campus ministries, I started going to a national conference called ACMI (Association of Christians Ministering among Internationals) after being called to ministry. There I met Dr. Burke, one of the original visionaries behind the ACMI network. For close to two decades I've been inspired by his wealth of wisdom. I was inspired particularly by his models and stories involving partnerships with campus international student offices. With more than 60 years of information gathered in this book, Dr. Burke is a model, mentor, scholar, and practitioner. He is a pioneer with International Student Ministries across Southern Baptist leadership, but also well-respected across denominational lines.

Ed Moncada
International Student Strategist
Making Disciples Team
Missouri Baptist Convention

In my 35 years of ministry, I have not met a person more qualified to write this book. Dr. Jack Burke's credentials, experience, world travels, and passion for the foreigner on our land, puts him on the top of the honor list of those who have made a most significant contribution to the theory and practice of serving and caring for international students. This book is a must read even for the experienced Christian worker.

Blessings and thank you for your faithfulness over the decades.

Georges Houssney
President, Horizons International
(303) 442-3333
HorizonsInternational.org
EngagingIslam.org

Dr. Burke writes from a lifetime of distinguished service among international students and provides a much needed "jolt" to Christian leaders to seize the unique opportunity to complete the great commission through international student ministry. Dr. Burke presents a compelling case: Biblical, historically, statistically, and personally for the absolutely vital role that outreach to internationals should play in the life of every church, seminary, and University ministry in the USA. This book should be read by every Christian who wants to be a part of what God is doing to fulfill his commitment to bless all the nations. Hats off to Dr. Burke for providing such a needed resource."

Richard Mendola
Executive Director
International Friendships, Inc.
2500 N. High Street, Suite 200
Columbus, OH 43202
Phone: 614-294-2434 ext 205
Fax: 614-298-0434
www.ifiusa.org (student website)
www.ifipartners.org (volunteer/donor website)

In this book, Dr. Jack Burke offers a timely call to action: for churches and missions agencies to evaluate and redefine how we <u>do</u> missions. Christ continues to gift and to call <u>some</u> Christians to do "apostolic" ministry (traditional, cross-cultural, leave here to go there). But Christ commands <u>all</u> of his followers to practice hospitality: to show family love to strangers and foreigners. By welcoming international students on university campuses, ordinary Christians can make an extraordinary impact on future world leaders, academic, and culture shapers. Even modest-sized congregations can engage in cost-effective global-local missions. Cross-cultural friendships personalize church members' prayers and expand our vision for all world missions. I commend Dr. Burke's important contribution to the task of defining and doing missions biblically, and not only geographically.

RUF
INTERNATIONAL

Rev. J. Al LaCour, III
Coordinator, RUF International
WEB: <u>WWW.RUF.ORG/RUFI</u>
EMAIL: <u>alacour@ruf.org</u>
Twitter: @IntlBuzz
Skype: jalbuzz

"Dr. Jack Burke has a heart passion for the strategic opportunity to share the Gospel with the top thinkers from distant countries and cultures by taking advantage of the God given moment to develop relationships with the over 1 million international students at U.S universities. In this book, he shares the opportunity, and convincingly points us to invest our time, talents, and resources in this missions moment in time. His personal experience, as well as key stories of those taking the Gospel back to their homeland, inspire us all to get involved. This book will help you see the white harvest field, and hopefully begin to participate in the harvest."

Dr. Glen Osborn
Past President and Minister at Large
China Outreach Ministries
Author of *China In Our Midst*
Past Chair, ACMI Board

"The fingerprints of Dr. Jack Burke as a co-laborer with God can be seen all over the foundation that has been prepared for those who love and serve international students today. He is a trailblazer who has used his vision, wisdom, faith, and experience to open doors for those who would follow. Dr. Burke is a role model and an encourager. I am thankful to call him both a mentor and a friend."

Paula Parker
Director, International Friends Meet
Chair, ACMI Board
NAFSA Region XII Christian SIG Coordinator

To Whom It May Concern,

Always a man of vision and encouragement to international student ministry (ISM) leaders around the country, Dr. Jack Burke began mentoring me to pray and partner with other international student ministries when I first met him and D'Ann at the University of Houston in 1976 and then I watched him spearhead ACMI around the country. When God called me to move to Houston to begin in ISM with ISI, I had no clue where to start. Then I met Jack and saw his passion for international students and his determination to ask God for more and more workers to enter this expanding field of world mission. At that time there were less than 100,000 international students in the entire USA. 40 years later, the Spirit is drawing more than 1,000,000 to our doorsteps because of men of faith like Jack Burke. Without a vision to build a house of prayer for all nations, our churches die as ethnocentric versions of themselves rather than as the model we see in heaven.

Bob Culver
iFace/Interface Ministries, Past President
Atlanta, GA
404-444-6945, www.iface.org

I highly recommend Dr. Jack Burke's book, "Why International Students are so Strategic to Global Missions." In Acts 17:26, 27 God tells us that He is the one that determines the boundaries of man and His purpose is that man may seek after Him and find Him. God has expanded the boundaries of the International Student and brought them to a place where there are millions of Christians. There is no one that has more expertise, experience and recognized credentials to inspire, educate and lead us in successfully fulfilling the purpose of this great global mission field.

Norma Pickett
Former coordinator with her late husband, Jim, of Houston's First Baptist Church International Student Friendship Program; Assistant Volunteer Coordinator, International Friendship Program, University of Houston's International Student and Scholar Services Office

---

In the early 1900s the Student Volunteer Movement sent out tens of thousands of young missionaries from the "West" to plant churches worldwide. In the early 2000s this "student movement" has been symbolically reversed as hundreds of thousands of students have come to the West for higher education. The world at large is changing radically and with exponential rapidity, and so has Christian missions, with the emerging churches of the non-Western world growing spiritually as well as numerically, and increasing responding to Christ's call to "go into all the world" with the Gospel! All this change creates a staggering need for strong Biblical leadership in the worldwide Church. If God has brought the brightest and best of the nations to our "doorstep" in Western university communities, He must similarly be calling the church to welcome and love them in the name of Christ. Here is a book giving "meat" (inspiration and guidance) to the "bones" of these basic Biblical concerns. It comes to us at a strategic moment and possibly limited window of time we have left as concerned Christians to make our contribution to God's Kingdom purposes by reaching out to these international students in our midst!

Excellent job putting this book together, Jack!

Ned Hale, Former Director, Ministry to International Students, InterVarsity Volunteer, New College Madison and National Archivist, InterVarsity-USA
635 Science Drive
Madison, WI 53711-1099
608-334-5418 (mobile)

Since I have known you from 1982 ACMI at ISI Star Ranch, Colorado Springs, I have been impressed by your vision, compassion, and practical care to many international students and scholars. You and your wife have touched and ministered to many young and old lives of overseas folks who in turn have impacted their nations, cultures, and institutions. Myself, as a former international student for five years in the USA and then an ISM worker for over forty years in the USA and Canada, I thank God for you both spending a life time of service to internationals and in helping churches to wake-up and grasp this great global mission opportunity that God has been making available to them and bringing them right to our doorstep. Your labor of love with practical services touched many lives and became a good role model to a younger generation to dare get involved.

Thank you for all that you have done in this missions endeavor. Only Heaven can reveal them in due time and the Master Christ can reveal the final outcome with sparkling rewards in hand. I pray that this motivational book might become an inspiration to many in the younger generation to get involved and make a difference with more needy persons . Praise the Lord and press on.

Joseph Sabounji
Former Minister to Internationals
Park Street Church, Boston (Source: the book "Light to the Nations" p. 124)

The following are **ENDORSEMENTS** FROM
HIGHLY RANKED HIGHER EDUCATION CHRISTIAN
ADMINISTRATORS RESPONSIBLE FOR SPECIAL SERVICES TO:

- International students and scholars in prestigious universities
- Internationals who are either medical school students, research scholars, technicians in prestigious medical schools and/or hospitals

Over the years my mentor and friend Dr. Jack Burke has inspired generations of international students, scholars as well as professionals working in international offices.

Throughout his academic studies and his impressive career in higher education, the consistent theme that resonates is of his sincere heart for God and his calling to caring for internationals. From the time I was a freshman in college throughout my nearly 40 year career in international education I have observed his compassion and razor-sharp focus on serving the Lord through ministry to internationals – He was the inspiration for my career decision to work with internationals and he continues to inspire me to this day.

May this book also inspire you to catch the vision for what God has done in bringing internationals to our shores.

Anita Gaines, Director, International Student and Scholar Services, University of Houston; NAFSA Christian SIG Coordinator; former NAFSA Membership Chair; ACMI Conference plenary speaker 2018 and a co-editor of this book.

NOTE: Just ahead! International student enrollment at both Purdue University where Dr. Michael Brzezinski is Dean of International Programs and New York University where Thomas Sirinides is Director of International Student Services, **each has more than 10,000 international students enrolled. In fact, NYU has 15,000 international students enrolled now. What more can you ask for? Incredible opportunities begging for caring Christians who are concerned about global missions.**

Dr. Jack placed the concept of international student advising as a ministry to international students on the Christian map. Having followed this path for a large portion of my adult life, I can attest to the strategic importance and value of this work. This book is a must read for individuals interested in knowing how to appropriately share the love of Christ to international students studying in American university campuses.

Michael A. Brzezinski, Ed.D.
Dean, International Programs
Purdue University

For over half a century, Dr. Jack Burke has been an active member and leader in the professional field of international student advising and service, setting a high mark in terms of leadership, professionalism, service and devotion to the field. For over forty years, Jack has also been a founder, active member, and leader in the field of international student ministry, calling those of his own generation first, and now those who will follow after him to embrace this strategic, effective ministry as God's open door for the Gospel. I first encountered Jack in the 1980s when I was on staff with IVCF, and then again 15 years later as I was entering my current professional field. Jack has a unique history and gifting that pairs leadership in both the professional and ministry realms of international student work. I appreciate and respect him as a role model in each area. This book comes from Jack's deep devotion to, and passion for the calling of God to reach international students with the good news of Jesus Christ. I hope that through this book, many others will hear and heed the calling of God as Jack did in this strategic area of ministry.

Thomas Sirinides
Director for International Student Services, PDSO, RO*
Office of Global Services
New York University
383 Lafayette St.
New York, NY 10003
tsirinides@gmail.com
P: 212-998-4125

It is with great pleasure and honor that I endorse the book written by Dr. Jack Burke. I cannot think of anyone who has more educational and professional skills to write this book. Dr. Burke's leadership history as an Administrator for a Public University; an international renown Christian member of NAFSA: Association of International Educators; and, President of the International Student Ministries Assistance, Inc. are only a few of his professional leadership skills that enable him to write this book. Personally I have known Dr. Burke for over 35 years. Through these years, Dr. Burke has been a Christian mentor for me and many others in the field of international education. He provides us with the guidance, support, and faith to strengthen our relation with Christ and to use that skill to serve and guide our international students and scholars. I know that anyone who reads the book will benefit tremendously from Dr. Burke's expertise.

Rose Mary Valencia
Executive Director, Visa and Immigration Services Administration
Department; Academic & VISA Administration (AVA)
The University of Texas M.D. Anderson Cancer Center
Mid Campus Building (1MC)
7007 Bertner Avenue, 17th Floor (South Tower)
Houston, Tx 77030

A Christian leader described the campuses of the United States as the world on our doorstep. Dr. Jack Burke has led a movement to reach the world within these borders. For decades Jack and his wife D'Ann have recruited followers of Jesus to be ambassadors to the nations on these campuses. He has challenged and equipped each generation, whose foundation is Christ, to work within American Universities to offer hospitality and care to the international students and scholars. Leading by example, writing, speaking, and training, there are countless souls that have returned to their homes abroad changed by the love of God through those inspired to this calling. I was recruited by Dr. Burke in 1990 and have spent the last 27 years serving as an immigration specialist in the academic medical community.

Thank you for your love, your leadership and your faithfulness to this call.

Michele Stelljes, Supervisor, HR Immigration Services
Houston Methodist
HR Client Services
8100 Greenbriar Street, GB 162
Houston, TX 77054
Office: 832-667-6288 Mobile: 281-635-8727
Email: mmstelljes@HoustonMethodist.org

In the book of Acts, what do an Ethiopian government official, an Italian soldier, and Greek businesswoman all have in common? They all heard the good news while visiting a country away from their homeland. There are over a million international students here thousands of miles from their home who are quite possibly just a few miles from yours. Find herein, from the author's 60 years involvement with international students, how you can easily be involved in short-distance missions, sharing your lives with them, as well as the Good News, as you invite non-Christian students into your life and ministry.

Dale Hamilton
Program Coordinator
International Student and Scholar Services
University of Houston
Student Center North. Room 203
4465 University Dr.
Houston, TX 77204-3024
Phone: 1(713) 743-5077
Email: dhamilton@uh.edu

Shortly after university, I packed my bags and headed to Eastern Europe to work with a Christian organization. A year of language training and much agonizing effort was invested attempting to gain trust and credibility to *engage with locals* in meaningful conversations about the Gospel. Hard to quantify exactly, but I suspect I have more natural contacts on a monthly basis working with curious international students and scholars in my everyday work environment on campus than I had in my entire 3 years abroad. Internationals are here, interested and eager to *engage with locals.* (Me)

David Ayers, Ph.D.
Associate Dean, International Programs
Purdue University

Acknowledgments

I DEDICATE THIS BOOK to our Heavenly Father. I am extremely grateful and feel deeply honored that He would single me out to write this International Student Ministry challenge to the churches of this great land and the world.

*To my dear wife, **D'Ann**, you should receive the grand prize for encouragement, patience, love, plus for your helpful advice, editing and proof-reading throughout the past five years that I have been working on this book. I couldn't have done this without your help, my beloved team-mate and best friend.*

To D'Ann's and my close friend, **Anita Gaines**, the University of Houston's Director of International Student and Scholar Services (ISSS) Office, and Coordinator of the national NAFSA Christian SIG, I cannot begin to tell you how much I appreciate your coming to Idaho from Houston on several occasions to proof-read and edit the book. With your experience as a speech writer for certain university administrators and faculty your help was invaluable. Also, to another good friend, **Jane Dunham**, I am so glad to have a former U. of H. ISSS Office professional staff member and English major from Cornell University, an Ivy League University, on my team. It was helpful that your experience included working for the southeast Texas presbytery (a regional body of Presbyterian congregations) for eight years, writing and editing their monthly newsletter and newspaper page. I appreciate your coming from Austin, Texas to Boise to help with the editing and proof-reading of the book. I wish to thank also **Paula Parker**, ACMI Board Chair, Director of the ISM, "International Friends Meet," and NAFSA Christian SIG Region XII Coordinator, for your careful, thoughtful read of the manuscript, making corrections when necessary and providing appropriate feedback. Not to be overlooked is **Stefan Johnsson** for his voluntary help in solving some perplexing computer problems.

To those who are in church ministries to international students; also presidents, executive directors of international student ministry (ISM) organizations past/present I salute you. I appreciate the way in which many of you demonstrated your enthusiastic support for this book through your endorsements and/or articles sent. It is easy to recognize you are the leadership God has provided for international student ministry to move forward.

I appreciate all others who submitted articles or gave me a word of encouragement during the many years of writing this book. I want you to know that's the fuel God used to keep me going. One in particular is **Norma Pickett,** a very close friend and volunteer church leader who has walked lock-step with D'Ann and me in ISM for decades, as did her beloved husband **Jim** before the Lord called him home. To **Leiton Chinn,** past President of ACMI, and the one bearing the name of ACMI's highest award, also **Lisa Espineli Chinn,** ISM's #1 popular speaker, you both deserve my highest respect. Among the endorsements received I appreciate that of **Dr. Beau Miller,** ACMI'S Executive Director, and also for his highly analytical and strategic article.

Before closing I wish to extend my deepest appreciation for University of Houston distinguished Christian international student alumni, **Sam Tin** and **Patrick So** from Hong Kong, and **Suyin** (pseudonym) from Singapore. What you wrote for this book will make it easy for Christians to see how Christian international students returning home from America can make an impact for Christ in their own countries and regions of the world. Also, thank you **Sam and Irene** for your friendship, encouragement, and loyal support through the many decades of our ministry. This book would not have been possible without your support.

Preface

THE PRIMARY REASON FOR writing this book to you and others in our nation's Christian community is to present the strategic importance for international students and scholars to come under the umbrella of global missions. Your author has deep convictions about the need for a paradigm shift in global missions now that we have such a tremendous resource in global missions. That is the one million plus international students coming from practically every country on the face of the earth! Recognizing that these future world leaders God has brought to our nation's campuses have the potential for creating an impact upon their own nations for Christ should stretch our imaginations as Christians to the unparalleled opportunity that is ours. We need to come to grips with the reality that having such rapid growth over the past decade of international students on our nation's campuses is not just a coincidence. God works in mysterious ways and this has to be one of them. We, the Christian community of this great land, need to get with God's program and focus on identifying, recruiting, training and equipping Christian international students for their return to their homelands. They have the potential for becoming much more effective and efficient missionaries to people in their own countries than those coming from other nations whose language, culture, and world views are completely different. One of the unique features this book has to offer is to provide illustrations of Christian international students who have returned home to accomplish feats for God, on a scale traditional foreign missionaries would never have thought possible. So the documentation is here.

Further, missions by returned Christian international students can be done and has been done more economically than by present traditional methods.[1] *Reason for the reduced cost is quite obvious. In K.P. Yohannan's book,* Revolution in World Missions[2] *you will read the cost comparison of traditional versus indigenous missions. By comparison indigenous missions which international student missions is considered a part of, costs much, much less.* <u>Churches and denomination leaders, you should be tapping into your global missions budget to support ministries to international students attending local colleges and universities.</u> *After all, reaching international students from other nations should come under global missions. God has brought international students, many being Christians, to our nation's colleges and universities. They are potential missionaries. Our part is to provide the specialized Biblical, theological, re-entry training, and follow-up encouragement needed for their return home. Fortunately, the traditional missionary's need for expensive and time-consuming language and culture training does not appear on the international student's list of needs in preparation for the return trip to their part of the world. For most students the matter of raising funds for the cost of returning to their respective homelands is not an issue either*

Although I have much to say about how international student ministry (ISM) should be carried out, this book does not go into any depth of the how's of ISM. Suffice it to say we should be taking every opportunity to meet the special needs of international students whether or not they are Christians. Through the loving kindness, thoughtfulness, hospitality and sharing one's faith, many internationals have become followers of Jesus. These students want the qualities of the Biblical "fruits of the spirit" which they see in Christians who love the Lord and want to share their faith with others. Acts of love opens doors for followers of Jesus to share their faith. Included in these acts of love is being a good listener when the student expresses what is important to him or her, including their own religious beliefs.

In this book you will find what is being done in the ministry for international students, who is doing it, where it is being done, and many more reasons why than what you have just read. This book is a <u>case for why we as Christians should consider a ministry for international students a current best method in today's world for carrying out the Great Commission.</u> *(I say current because there are other nations that are trying their best to attract international students to study in their countries. Yes, attracting international students to study in one's country or one's university has become highly competitive in the global market of higher education.) Right now, America is #1 in attracting international students to its shores for higher education. We desperately need to take advantage of this window of opportunity while it is still open.*

This book rests its case on missions to the nations as being best carried out through Christian international students upon their return home. To gain a head start it helps if the students have leadership qualities and have a reasonable amount of Biblical and theological training. It has been my experience that these are the ones who are best qualified to share the gospel with people in their respective nations in every respect—logically, more effectively, more efficiently, and certainly most economically. Another way of putting it is International Student Ministry should be central to today's global missions challenge and practice.

My experience in international student ministry has come from being involved in leadership, both inside the university 30 years as the administrative director in charge of services to international students and more than 30 years of experience outside the university as a volunteer leader working with churches and parachurch ministries to international students. (A brief account of my credentials to write this book may be found toward the end of the book.) This total adding up to more than 60 years has led me to share this vision with you.

This book will answer the following questions.

- Why have international students and scholars become so strategically important to the global ministries of churches, parachurch organizations, denominations, theological seminaries, Christian universities, Bible colleges, and mission agencies to fulfill the Great Commission?
- Who are some of the Christian international students who have returned to their countries as "movers and shakers" for Christ?
- Why is there need for a paradigm shift in global missions to move international students to the center of global missions focus?
- Why is it so important for our nation's Christian community to be involved in outreach ministries to the more than one million international students and scholars who are enrolled or doing scholarly research in our nation's colleges and universities?
- Why are international students and alumni so vitally important to our nation's strategic global interests? How many are here? Why

do they come? Where do they come from? What universities do they attend and what are their fields of study?

- What is currently being done by churches and Christian parachurch organizations for outreach ministries to international students? Who is doing it and what is the contact information for these organizations?
- What is currently being done by Christians who work for universities with international students? What ministries are involved in preparing <u>Christian</u> international students for effective ministry upon their return home? What yet needs to be done? Why is the professional Association of Christians Ministering among Internationals (ACMI) so important to organizations and individuals involved in ministry to international students?
- Why is NAFSA: Association of International Educators, a 10,000 member secular organization, important to those involved with ministry to international students? Also, why is NAFSA's Christian Specific Interest Group (SIG) regional and national meetings so important for Christians who work in higher education?
- Who was involved (and what did they do) during the post World War II period which propelled ministering to international students into a movement on the global missions scene?
- What makes the author so uniquely qualified to write this book?

Scriptures used by the author in this book are from the New International Version (NIV). The other Scriptures, all cited by Dr. Robert (Bob) Taussig found in Chapter 17, are from the NIV, King James Version, and the Common English Bible (CEB), as noted.

Contents

**Why a Book that so Passionately Promotes a
Ministry for International Students?**

*Paradigm shift in global missions needed now that we have such a
tremendous resource God has brought to our very own shores.*

Chapter

EXCITING NEWS FOR GLOBAL MISSION STRATEGISTS AND ALL OTHER MISSION-MINDED CHRISTIANS

Press Release
IIE Releases Open Doors 2016 Data
International Students in U.S. Top One Million for the First Time© 2016 Institute of International Education, Inc. All rights reserved. INSTITUTE OF INTERNATIONAL EDUCATION, IIE and OPENING MINDS TO THE WORLD are trademarks or registered trademarks of Institute of International Education, Inc. in the United States and other countries.

THE WORLD IS FLOODING our campuses with many international students, the United States remains the number one destination for students who seek a global education. In Fall 2016, according to IIE's Press Release of the publication Open Doors, the number of international students in the United States increased by 7.1% to reach an all-time high of 1,043,839 students when including those signed up for optional practical training.

To help churches throughout America realize the missions implication of IIE's Fall 2016 press release, think of it this way. America, the country that has the largest number of Christians, attracts by far more international students than any other country on planet earth. Further, it is safe to assume most of these students coming from all over the world are non-Christian. It is the strong reputation of American higher education that continues to attract international students to come to the United States. Enhancing that reputation are centers throughout the world spawned by the U.S. Department of State that publicize the variety of institutions of higher education and locations from which international students may choose.

Mission Board leaders, church ministers, mission pastors, Christian higher education leadership and mission professors, and all other mission-minded Christians, listen up! From a global missions perspective look at the following unparalleled opportunities for global missions God has brought by a tsunami wave of future world leaders to our very own shores. To become fully engaged in global missions you need to look no further than your local college campus.

A strategic look at enrollment data and personal application of that data

When I caught the vision for the great opportunity there was to impact the world for Christ through Christian international students was fall 1953, the fall I began my theological studies at Fuller Theological Seminary. Then there were only 33,675 international students in the United States.[3] In fall 2016 Open Doors reports the international student enrollment topped off at 1,045,839 when including those signed up for optional practical training. That's record-breaking having more than one million international students! It only takes the international student enrollment of the top three universities in 2016 to more than match the total number of international students of all American universities when I first caught the vision of the need for ministry to international students. With these skyrocketing figures, it is tragic that so many Christian leaders in our great country have not yet caught the vision. The following data is from the 2016 OPEN DOORS publication's Fast Facts.

You will be amazed at the impressive enrollment data of these international students which appears in the Fact Sheet of the Open Doors 2016 publication. **For updates of this data and trends in future years, go to IIE's website – www.iie.org/opendoors**. Also, you will find IIE's Open Doors 2015 article, "U.S. Trends: International Students in the United States" of great interest in which the lead article notes, "The number of international students in the United States increased by 10% in 2014/15, the highest rate of growth in 35 years.[4] The article topics of special interest are "Which students are driving the growth, international students' academic interests, and the impact of international students." The 2017 update is found in the next few pages.

UPDATE 2017: Following are excerpts of the Institute of International Education produced Open Doors 2017 update]

Open Doors 2017 Executive *Summary*

CONTACT:
Sharon Witherell, IIE, switherell@iie.org
U.S. Department of State, ECA-Press@state.gov

About Open Doors: Open Doors is a comprehensive information resource on international students and scholars studying or teaching at higher education institutions in the United States, and U.S. students studying abroad for academic credit at their home colleges or universities. The research is supported by a grant from the Bureau of Educational and Cultural Affairs at the U.S. Department of State.

International Students in the United States

Overview: The number of international students enrolled in U.S. higher education increased by 3.4 percent to 1,078,822 students in 2016/17, with almost 35,000 more students than the prior year in the country on non-immigrant student visas. This marks the eleventh consecutive year that Open Doors reported expansion in the total number of international students in U.S. higher education. In 2016/17, there were 85 percent more international students studying at U.S. colleges and universities than were reported a decade ago.

International students represent just over five percent of the more than 20 million students enrolled in U.S. higher education for the third year, up from three to four percent earlier in the decade. This increase is due to both the growing numbers of international students and small declines in the number of American students enrolled in U.S. higher education since the total U.S. higher education enrollment reached its peak in 2012/13.

Places of Origin: For the third year in a row, the largest growth was in the number of students from India, primarily at the graduate level and in optional practical training (OPT). China remains the top sending country, with almost twice the number of students in the U.S. as India, but India's rate of growth outpaced China's.

Students from the top two countries of origin—China and India—now represent approximately 50 percent of the total enrollment of international students in the United States. Despite a decrease of 3.8 percent, South Korea moved up to the third leading place of origin, after dropping to fourth place the previous year. The number of students from fourth leading host Saudi Arabia decreased by 14.2 percent. After these top four countries, no country represents more than three percent of the total international students in the United States. Canada remains the fifth leading place of origin, with the number of students increasing very slightly to 27,065.

Each of the top 25 places of origin had more than 7,000 students in the United States. There were increases in the number of students from 18 of the top 25 places of origin, including China, India, Canada, Vietnam, Taiwan, Mexico, Iran, Nigeria, Nepal, Germany, Kuwait, France, Indonesia, Venezuela, Malaysia, Colombia, Spain, and Bangladesh. Bangladesh 9.7% and moved up to #25, while Thailand had a continued decrease and moved out of the top 25 list. Nigeria (up 9.7 percent) and Nepal (up 20.1 percent) showed particularly strong increases.

Students from Iran, the eleventh leading place of origin, increased by 3 percent to 12,643, still significantly lower than the peak of more than 50,000 Iranian students in the United States in 1979/80. From 1974/75 to 1982/83, Iran was the top sender of international students to the United States.

Japan, United Kingdom, and Turkey saw very slight decreases of less than two percent each. South Korea once again saw a decline from the previous year (down 3.8 percent), and Hong Kong decreased by 4.7 percent. The factors driving these declines likely include a mix of global and local economic factors, and in some cases expanded higher education opportunities at home and declining populations. Saudi Arabian students in the United States decreased by 14.2 percent to 52,608 from its previous high of over 61,000, largely due to changes in the Saudi government scholarship program, now approaching its 14th year. The largest drop was among students from Brazil who declined 32.4 percent to 13,089 students. This decrease can be attributed to the conclusion of the Brazil government's Scientific Mobility Program, which previously sponsored many Brazilian students' U.S. studies.

Host States: The internationalization of campuses across the United States continues, with nearly all of the top 25 host universities and all of the top ten states hosting more international students than in the prior year. California hosted 156,879 international students, followed by New York, Texas, Massachusetts and Illinois. All but nineteen states and U.S. territories saw increases in international enrollments in 2016/17. Host Campuses: For the fourth year in a row, New York University hosted the largest number of international students. The University of Southern California remains the second leading host. These two universities were followed by Columbia University, Northeastern University, Arizona State University, and University of Illinois at Urbana-Champaign. Combined, the top 25 campuses hosted 22.4 percent of all international students in the United States. In 2006/07, there were 156 institutions that hosted 1,000 or more international students, while the new Open Doors reports 250 institutions hosting 1,000 or more international students in 2016/17.[5]

Farrugia, C., R. Bhandari, J. Baer, C. Robles & N. Andrejko (2017). *Open Doors 2017 Report on International Educational Exchange.* New York: Institute of International Education.

Prior to my retirement, when I was a university director of International Student and Scholar Services, if you had 2,000 international students you were assured a spot in the top 20 universities enrolling international students. Now to be in the top 20 one has to have well over four times that number. Yes, times have changed and we need to take advantage of opportunities presented by these large numbers. As an example, Dr. Michael Brzezinski, Dean of International Programs at Purdue University, who got his start in my office at the University of Houston, has for more than two decades been responsible for services to an international student enrollment that in recent years exceeds 10,000, almost half being from China. There are also many other universities whose numbers are well above 10,000.

Countries where missionaries and returning trained Christian international students are both desperately needed.

Christian international students and traditional foreign missionaries are both needed especially in countries where the percentage of Christians is low. The most effective, of course, being well-trained and equipped Christian international students returning to their countries of origin. The church's job is to recruit and train as many of these students as possible. Let's face it, the reason traditional missionaries are still needed is, as Jesus said "The harvest is plentiful, <u>but the workers are few</u>. Ask the Lord of the harvest, therefore, to send out workers into his harvest field." (Luke 10:2) (Author underlined)

In the following chart notice all the countries that are listed with less than 10% Christians that have students in the US. When you see the chart with the number of countries with less than 2% it makes you want to weep. Even worse is to see countries listed with less than 1%. As a solution to the problem we have tried the traditional approach of sending missionaries to these countries for hundreds of years. Don't you think it's high time that we try to reach them with "insiders?" That's Christian well-trained international students returning from America and other countries who are fellow citizens, speak the same language (without accent), understand the same culture, are well-connected, and are destined to be future leaders of their own countries.

2016

Country of Origin of International Students*		% Country that is Christian**
China	328,547	5.1
India	165,918	2.5
Saudi Arabia	61,287	4.4
Taiwan	21,266	5.5
Japan	19,334	1.6
Vietnam	16,579	8.2
Turkey	10,821	0.4

Iran	10,194	0.2
Nepal	8,155	0.5
Indonesia	7,920	9.9
Thailand	7,341	0.
Malaysia	6,822	9.4

83%*** United States has largest Christian population in the world

*www.iie.org/opendoors/factsheet 2016

**Christianity by Country, Wikipedia, 2010

*** **"Poll: Most Americans Say "They're Christian," by analysis – by Gary Langer, 7/18/2016; abcnews.go.com/us/story?id=90356**

Other countries from which fewer international students come that have less than 10% Christian:** Afghanistan (.02%), Algeria (2%), Bangladesh (0.4%), Burma (Myanmar 7.9%), Cambodia (1.0%), Egypt (5.1%), Gambia (4.2%), Iraq (3.0%), Israel (3.5%), Jordan, (6.0%), Laos (2.2%), Libya (2.7%), Morocco (1%), Pakistan (1.6%), Sri Lanka (7.5%), Sudan (1.5%), Syria (2%), Tunisia (0.2%), Yemen (0.2%)

*Christianity by country, Wikipedia, 2010

Reviewing these countries with such a small percentage being Christian we have to do a reality check. You will recall the phrase used in the Navy, "all hands on deck." Well, this is a situation where both returning Christian international students and traditional missionaries are desperately needed. Besides the traditional missionaries, there are missionaries' kids who often are referred to as MK's, now as adults, are also needed. Many MK's as most of you know speak the language of the people better than their parents. I have a couple of nephews, John and Dale Burke, who are good examples. John, a theological seminary graduate whose wife is from Argentina, teaches in Spanish periodically at the seminary level in Colombia. Dale as a Christian "witnessing" businessman does some of his secular work in Mexico where he grew up speaking Spanish.

2

Chapter

MISSIONS STRATEGY UPDATE NEEDED TO MEET CHALLENGES AND OPPORTUNITIES OF GLOBALIZATION

What is Globalization?

ACCORDING TO ONE DEFINITION, "Globalization is a process of interaction and integration among the people, companies, and governments of different nations, a process driven by international trade and investment and aided by information technology. This process has effects on the environment, on culture, on political systems, on economic development and prosperity, and on human physical well-being in societies around the world."[6]

Ways we can picture globalization

- United Nations
- World Trade Organization (WTO)
- World Bank

- World Council of Churches
- International Monetary Fund (IMF)
- Multinational corporations
- Global mutual funds on the stock market
- Global climate change
- Multi-country alliances: European Union, NATO
- NAFSA: Association of International Educators
- International law
- Manufactured goods: Look at the labels on your clothing. It's more likely to say "China" than from any other country.
- Look at the flow of cars on the city streets. It is common to see a high percentage are foreign cars - Japan, Korea, Germany, France and Sweden are examples.
- The same goes for electronic equipment inside your house or apartment – much is made outside the USA.
- Food and drink – Coca Cola perhaps was the first to discover global marketing, now Mac Donald's can also be found in cities throughout the world; many specialty restaurants can be found that cater to the tastes of any nationality.
- Communications: I-phones, Email and text messages, global phone calls by satellite
- Foreign language studies on the increase.
- Intercontinental flights
- Intercontinental ballistic missiles
- Foreign travel on the increase
- Payment by Credit Card acceptable in many nations

All goes to show, we live in a "shrinking world."

Now what should be our response as mission-minded Christians to the fact that we live in a dangerous world, a world that is globally interdependent, and that we as Americans live in a country that is #1 in its attraction to students from all over the world desiring to study at our universities? Do you think all of this came about by chance? Or, do you see God in His sovereignty at work in drawing international students like a magnet to a country where 80% are considered to be Christians?

The central purpose of this book is to make Christians like you and your church aware that we have the future leadership of the world attending our nation's colleges and universities. The new missions' strategy no longer should focus only on "over there" because so many are "over here." It may be for only four years, time enough to earn a bachelors or graduate degree. Being away from the constraints of the home environment, if these future world leaders are ever going to experience the love of Christ and hear the gospel message, there could not be a better time than now. Who is going to take this message to them? This is a people-to-people approach. This means that all of us as Christians have a responsibility. We as the church can no longer afford to duck that responsibility. Going on short-term mission trips, as important as they may seem as a priority, needs to be compared with taking advantage of the low-cost opportunity of befriending international students who are on our very doorstep from the same countries where mission trips are designed to go. No trips to the airport. Just follow the instructions of the church coordinator of the international friendship program, the directions of a parachurch staff person in your area who works with international students, or a Christian who works in a campus International Student Office. Whichever way, you will find out how to make contact with international students.

It worked for me. The first international student I met at the University of Oregon became a life-long friend. Before graduation, he knew exactly how to become a follower of Jesus, before heading to medical school in Brussels, Belgium and as a doctor to his home town, Baghdad, Iraq.

In his own research in the area of Globalization, Dr. Douglas Shaw, President of International Students Incorporated (ISI), wrote that the "world economy has become porous beyond imagination. Existing transnational alliances, treaty organizations, and long-standing boundaries are now fading in significance. The word 'Europe' now refers to a single, economic commonwealth. The same global upheavals which are forcing international business to become so fast-paced and responsive, demand that we 'spreaders' of the gospel do the same." Then Dr. Shaw, who is of Asian descent himself, referred to an article in "Asian Partners International" which makes the claim that "eighty percent of nations with unreached people groups are now closed to traditional missions[7]. [One by one, developing nations turn away Western families believed to be Christian missionaries.] Global trends like the resurgence of fundamentalist Islam, anti-American sentiment, and rampant spiritual darkness make Christian evangelism the most dangerous practice across vast swaths of the planet. All around us glare the signs of a world that has transformed many of yesterday's mission paradigms into noble but unworkable relics of a former era."[8]

PURPOSE OF BOOK

My book's main purpose is to focus on a strategy to carry out global missions in a dangerous world, which an increasing number believe to be through a relatively untapped resource, Christian international students, upon their return home. There are many reasons which will be cited elsewhere. But for now suffice it to say Christian international students are the most acceptable form of Christian witness to the people in their home countries. After returning to their homelands international students in general are often the ones who become their respective nation's future leadership.

In this book you will meet Christian international students who returned home armed with the gospel and specialized training. They became effective ambassadors for Christ in their own homelands.

- You will also find Biblical precedence for Christian internationals who returned home as leaders and effective witnesses for Christ. It makes a lot of sense for us to support ministries which reach out to international students and train those who are Christians in preparation for their return to their homelands. It is proving to be the most logical, effective and efficient way to conduct global missions. Besides that, it is the most economical way. All it takes from us is to do the following:
- Identify the Christian international students in our nation's colleges as soon after their arrival as possible.
- Encourage and be supportive of them in their search for a church (it could be a church that serves their own language groups), campus Christian community group, and Christian friendship family.
- Train and equip them with a good understanding of the scriptures and specialized training for re-entering their society before they return to their homelands.
- Identify seekers - those who openly want to find out what Christianity and the Bible are all about. For those who make a commitment to be followers of Christ, help them in the same

way we do those who arrive on campus as Christian international students.

- What about the traditional approach of sending foreign (in our case American) missionaries to the mission field? Although there is still a place for the traditional approach, we must come to grips with the reality that the world is fraught with dangers and obstacles for them to be safe and effective. **By comparison, trained Christian international students returning to their homelands have many advantages and therefore far greater chances of accomplishing the mission successfully, and even at less expense since they are mostly self-supporting, than does the traditional approach.** Any objective, open-minded and clear-thinking missions-minded Christian should be able to come easily to this conclusion through the reading of this book.

Through this book I would like to believe that I am talking to many who are responsible for planning strategies of how best to share the "good news" about Jesus' life, purpose of his death and His resurrection especially to those coming from countries where Christians are a relatively small minority.

3

Chapter

CHALLENGES POSED BY THE GREAT COMMISSION

Converts to Christ Among Foreign Nationals After Pentecost Were Ready for the Mission Back Home

REGARDING DECISIONS AS TO who could best represent Christ in taking the gospel to other countries, we should be reminded of the scripture in Isaiah 6:8 where Isaiah said "Then I heard the voice of the Lord saying, Whom shall I send? And who will go for us?" Paul the Apostle, a former international student, was one of those who could have answered Isaiah's call, though centuries later, "Here am I, Send me!"

The disciples soon found that the Lord made the impossible possible on the Day of Pentecost when people from countries of the known world came to Jerusalem to celebrate the Day of Pentecost and heard the "good news" from Peter miraculously in their own languages.

As cited elsewhere, among those who returned to their home countries with changed lives and the gospel was the Ethiopian who was in charge of Queen Candace's Treasury, the Roman centurion and "those with him" who were stationed as guards at the foot of the cross who upon witnessing the way Christ died and the "earthquake and all that happened . . . [they] were terrified and exclaimed, 'surely he was the Son of God!'" (Matt. 27:54)

Parenthetically there were other Roman centurions who made decisions to follow Christ also. One who upon meeting Jesus in Capernaum sought Jesus' help to heal his servant who was at his house "paralyzed and in terrible suffering." Although Jesus offered to go to his house the centurion said that was not necessary. "Just say the word and my servant will be healed." Jesus was so impressed with the centurion's faith that he said "I have not found anyone in Israel with such great faith." (Matt. 8:5-10) Then Jesus said to the centurion, "Go! It will be done just as you believed it would. And his servant was healed at that very hour." (Matt. 8:13) Also, there is the miraculous account of the meeting between Peter and the Roman Centurion from the Italian Regiment, whom we would call today a "seeker." When Peter who after being escorted to Cornelius' house in another town explained the scriptures, Cornelius and people with him, in a truly miraculous event, became followers of Christ and were baptized. (Acts 10: 34-48.

Through the centuries many have ventured out to distant lands with nothing but a heart for God and desire to take the "good news" about Jesus to foreign people in distant lands. You will find an explanation of some of these heroes of the faith elsewhere in this book.

Today, 2000+ years since Christ ascended into heaven, in many ways it still seems impossible when you look at nations with populations showing such low percentages of Christians.

However, the tables are rapidly turning. As has been pointed out before, the Lord has sent us a potential solution to the problem of lack of "manpower" by flooding our nation's colleges and universities with international students from nations around the world. In fact, the nation's colleges and universities now are serious about recruiting international students for reasons which will be explained later. They come from diverse religious backgrounds, including Christian. The interesting thing is that many come from 10-40 window countries that are closed to missionaries. For Christian mission strategists to overlook that fact is beyond comprehension. Even among international students there should be some prioritizing for outreach. A perfect example is Cito Cruz, formerly an international student himself, who at one time was in charge of missions and international student ministries at McLean Bible Church in McLean, Va. Cruz has emphasized in his presentations at ACMI conferences, "We should seek to train the <u>Christian</u> international students on our nation's campuses first. It's our Jerusalem." Cruz went on to say something to the effect "This way we can gain a head start in preparing Christian international students to be effective witnesses for Christ upon return to their homelands."

Let's take a moment to revisit the Day of Pentecost. Can't you just imagine the scene on that special day when Jews from 17 nations or geographic entities gathered together in Jerusalem? When Peter got up to preach, for him to be understood the Holy Spirit came upon those who were followers of Jesus who were sharing the gospel to disparate masses of people. Miraculously every one heard the gospel preached in his own native language. For those who made their living as fishermen or collecting taxes, carrying out this command seemed impossible. Why did this command seem so impossible to all disciples left behind? Dr. John R. Bisagno, delivered the most dynamic sermon[9] I have ever heard on reasons why it appeared so impossible to the followers of Christ to fulfill the Great Commission. In that Sunday sermon delivered to two audiences totaling close to 5,000 here were the points for his reasons why this appeared to be a "mission impossible." It was:

- Physically impossible
- Geographically impossible
- Numerically impossible
- Financially impossible
- Socially impossible
- Legally impossible
- Logistically impossible

Dr. Bisagno ended his sermon by pointing out four First Baptist Church leaders who best exemplified ministries which church members should get involved with during the coming year. I am deeply grateful for his backing that Sunday morning by naming me as one of four church leaders that the thousands who were attending should contact.

In my wife D'Ann's and my case it was the Friendship Family Program which brought members of the church into a friendship relationship with international students from all over the world who were attending the University of Houston. Although the administrative work was done by a corps of Christian volunteers who came to a community room at my office, D'Ann was the University of Houston Volunteer Coordinator of the Program as well as at Houston's First Baptist Church which supplied the largest number of friendship families of any church or any other organization in the city. Norma Pickett followed D'Ann as the initial First Baptist Church Friendship Family Program Coordinator. She was assisted by her husband Jim. Norma served as the Coordinator for most years prior to my retirement. The Picketts received the university ISSS Office's "D'Ann Burke Volunteer of the Year Award." Through the years the Picketts became like members of the office family they were so well respected for their dedication. The work has continued under the guidance of Houston First Baptist's Marie and Hal Downing who recently were honored with a 20th year anniversary celebration for being in charge of the program. They too had previously received the university office's highest honors through recognition given.

Shortly you will read about **Paul's conversion and how he, a former international student from the Roman province, Cilicia, took time out for training to become equipped for missionary service. Paul returned to his homeland as a missionary. He held Roman citizenship, the same citizenship as the Gentiles whom he was called to serve, spoke the same language, and understood the same culture.** And look at all that he accomplished as a former international student in serving the Lord.

Therefore, we have to be careful that we don't think of ourselves as being the first generation to come up with the idea of Christian international students being the most effective missionaries to their own homelands. One needs only to look at the life of Paul the Apostle as an example.

Indigenous Missions Thriving

As mentioned in the Preface, K.P. Yohannan in his book, Revolution in World Missions, reinforces this theme regarding the indigenous missionary movement. Every reader should know who K.P. Yohannan,[10] is. Let me introduce him. Dr. Yohannan is a noted authority on foreign missions in Asia. "Dr. Yohannan is the founder and international director of Gospel for Asia. He is the author of more than 200 books and is also an internationally known speaker and missionary statesman. Speaking on his behalf in the introductory section of his book, Revolution in World Missions, were Erwin Lutzer, Senior Pastor, Moody Church, Chicago, IL; Skip Hetzig,

Senior Pastor, Calvary of Albuquerque, Albuquerque, NM; George Verwer, Founder and former International Director, Operation Mobilization; Luis Bush, Director, World Inquiry; among others. Dr. Yohannan credits John Haggai as a mentor who served as a great inspiration to him at the beginning of his ministry."

Yohannan's viewpoint about the effectiveness of Western missions is revealed in the following explanation. "I knew Western missions alone could not get the job done. Because my own nation [India] and many others were closed to outsiders, we had to turn to the national believers. Even if Western missionaries somehow were permitted back, the cost of sending them would be in the billions each year. National evangelists could do the same for only a fraction of that amount." Yohannan continued driving home his message by saying "Despite a valiant rear guard action by many outstanding evangelical leaders . . ., it has been impossible for the Western missionary movement to keep up with exploding populations and the new political realities of nationalism in the Two-Thirds world. Most Christians in North America still conceive of missions in terms of blond-haired, blue-eyed white people going to the dark-skinned Two-Thirds World nations.

In reality, all that changed at the end of World War II when the Western powers lost political and military control of their former colonies. When I stand before North American audiences in churches and missions conferences, people are astonished to hear the real facts of missions today." Yohannan added, "**The frontline work of mission in Asia has been taken over almost completely by indigenous missionaries. <u>And the results are outstanding.</u>** (Author underlined) Believers are shocked to learn that national missionaries are starting hundreds of new fellowships every week in the Two-Thirds World, [and] that thousands of people a day are [starting] fellowships every week in the Two-Thirds World, [and] that thousands of people a day are coming to Christ, . . Examples cited are India, which no longer permits Western missionary evangelists. More church growth and outreach is happening now than at any point in our history . . . China . . . over 500,000 underground churches reportedly have sprung up . . . responsible authorities place [the estimated number] around 50 million . . . all this happened under the spiritual direction of the indigenous church movement."

Yohannan compares the financial cost for a mission organization in supporting a missionary on the field with an economically modest budget for supporting indigenous missions. "In his research as to what is the cost for a mission organization supporting a John Doe missionary on the field, according to Yohannan "one mission organization estimates it costs around $80,000 per year to keep a missionary couple in India. When factoring in inflation, it could easily be much higher now for a traditional missionary organization.[11]

I'm sure you have gathered by now that the main purpose for this book is to focus on a strategy to carry out global missions in this dangerous world. After returning to their homelands international students in general are the most effective and often the ones who become their respective nation's future leadership. In this book you will meet Christian international students who returned home armed with the gospel and specialized training. They became effective ambassadors for Christ in their own homelands.

You will also find Biblical precedence for Christian internationals who returned home as leaders and effective witnesses for Christ.

4

Chapter

WHY PAUL THE APOSTLE, A FORMER NON-CHRISTIAN INTERNATIONAL STUDENT, WAS "CALLED" TO RETURN TO HIS HOMELAND AS A MISSIONARY

FOR STARTERS, LET'S TAKE a look at the way the Lord introduced Ananias, the Christian leader in Damascus, to the traumatic "calling" which the notorious Saul (later renamed Paul) had just experienced. In his introduction of Saul, here were the Lord's instructions to Ananias: "**Go! This man [Paul] is <u>my chosen instrument to carry my name before the Gentiles and their kings</u> and before the people of Israel. I will show him how much he must suffer for my name.**" (Acts 9:15-16) (Author added bold print and underlining.)

Why Paul? Once you strip away Paul's hatred and violent terrorist attacks toward Christians, could it be that Paul once saved was a perfect fit to take the Gospel message back to his homeland? After all, not everyone was equipped to be God's spokesperson to the "Gentiles" in the Roman world, and as the Scriptures also stated, to "their kings and before the people of Israel." (Acts 9:15)

Here are plausible reasons for his calling to return to his homeland:

1. **Paul was well educated.** He had traveled from Cilicia, a Roman Province, to Jerusalem to study under Gamaliel. (The distance Paul traveled took longer than any international student takes in traveling from his country to the USA today. In today's world Paul would have been **classified as an international student.**) Gamaliel, a Pharisee and teacher of the law, had an impeccable reputation. He "was honored by all the people." (Acts 5:30)

    To study under Gamaliel was equivalent in today's world to saying that he studied under a famous professor at Harvard or at another prestigious university.

2. **Paul held Roman citizenship.** Having been born a Jew Paul had credentials to be accepted in the Jewish society. Having as his home base, Tarsus, a city located in Cilicia, a province of the Roman world, gave Paul Roman citizenship. (Acts 9:11)

3. **Having Roman citizenship brought Paul certain privileges.** That meant he could travel throughout the Roman world with the privileges of a citizen. Since the message he and Barnabas brought to the Jews was rejected, **Paul said "we now turn to the Gentiles.** For this is what the Lord has commanded us: 'I have made you a light for the Gentiles, that you may bring salvation to the ends of the earth.'" (Acts 13:46-47)

    In being Roman citizens Paul and Silas had privileges that went beyond what was available to other disciples. For example, when the Roman magistrates discovered that Paul and Silas were <u>Roman citizens</u> after they had been beaten and thrown into prison - the magistrates "were alarmed. They came to appease them and escorted them from the prison." (Acts 16:37-38).

    Before Paul's conversion, there were attempts to reach Gentiles for Christ but nothing on the scale of Paul's three missionary journeys. I like what the NIV Life Application Study Bible commentator said about Paul, "God did not waste any part of Paul – his background, his training, his citizenship, his mind . . ." (Life Application Study Bible, p. 2331, published by Tyndale House Publishers, Wheaton Illinois, Zondervan, 2005)

4. **Native language was Greek, needed for travel in the Roman Gentile world and had a good cultural understanding of the area.** Paul being born in the province Cilicia could speak fluent Greek to the Gentiles. Being born a Jew and a student under Gamaliel he could speak Aramaic to those in Israel. He was bilingual. Paul displayed his cultural understanding and sensitivity when he spoke to the Athenians at the Areopagus when he said "Men of Athens I see that in every way you are very religious . . ." (Acts 17:22-23) Also, in wanting to take Timothy with him on a journey he circumcised Timothy "because of the Jews who lived in that area, for they all knew that his father was a Greek." (Acts 16:3)

5. **Excellent Writing Ability.** Paul wrote 13 books of the New Testament, most Biblical books written by a single author.

6. **Strong leader with deeply held religious convictions.** When he first surfaced in the scriptures Paul (then called Saul) was present at the death by stoning of Stephen. "The witnesses laid their clothes at the feet of a young man named Saul." (Acts 7:58) Before his conversion Paul went to the high priest and asked him for letters to the synagogues in Damascus, so that if he found any there who belonged to the Way, whether men or women, he might take them as prisoners to Jerusalem. Paul was not alone on the trip. There were men traveling with him. (Acts 9:1-7)

In reviewing the Book of Acts, one can see that **Paul met with the leadership of society.** To name a few there was the high priest Ananias, the chief priests and the Sanhedrin, Governors Felix and Festus, King Agrippa, Tertullus, the high priest's lawyer, and the commander who freed Paul from prison. During their first missionary journey to Cyprus (where Barnabas was from), Paul and Barnabas met with the Pro-Consul Sergius Paulus, "an intelligent man" who had "sent for Barnabas and Paul because he wanted to hear the word of God." (Acts 13:7) The Pro Consul became a believer "for he was amazed at the teaching about the Lord." (Acts 13:12)

7. **Dedication and perseverance displayed in suffering and hardship.** In reading the long list of hardships, pain and suffering which Paul endured (2 Corinthians 6:3-10) to get the Gospel out to the ends of the earth, it doesn't take a rocket scientist to figure out that going abroad to do missionary work is not for the faint at heart. Besides the other qualifications, there was the additional "how much he must suffer for my name." In his perseverance despite the suffering Paul was not a "quitter."

8. **Persuasive speaker.** In the trial before Governor Festus, Paul made his defense with this ending: "I appeal to Caesar," to which Festus replied, "To Caesar you will go!" (Acts 25:8-12). In his invitation to speak in his defense before King Agrippa and many others, Paul convinced the King of his innocence. (Acts 26:1-32)

9. **Paul was self-supporting as a tentmaker.** (Acts 18:3) Sending trained and well prepared Christian international students to their homelands where they can be self-supporting is by far the most economical form of ministry to their own people.

Conclusion: Like Paul, the Christian international students who return to their homelands today as well-trained missionaries, are better qualified and therefore more effective in carrying out the Great Commission to their own people than their non-citizen missionary counterparts. Also, being self-supporting is the most economical means for missionary work. It's just common sense for us to get behind and support ministries which reach out to international students and train those who are Christians in preparation for their return to their homelands. It is proving to be the most effective and efficient way to conduct global missions. **The fact that the following points are being repeated shows the importance of this information to the core purposes of this book.** We must:

- identify the Christian international students on our nation's campuses as soon after their arrival as possible.
- encourage and be supportive of them in their search for a church (it could be a church that serves their own language groups), campus Christian community group, and Christian friendship family.

- train and equip them with a good understanding of the scriptures and specialized training for re-entering their societies before returning to their homelands.
- Prepare them for their return to their homelands.
- Follow them up by doing whatever it takes to help them make the adjustment once again to their home environment and to locate groups of believers back home with whom they can fellowship. Stay in contact. Encourage them.
- Identify seekers - those who openly want to find out what Christianity and the Bible are all about. For those who make a commitment to be followers of Christ, help them in the same way we do those who arrive on campus as Christian international students. Befriend non-Christian international students and provide opportunities for them to attend Christian events and activities in which they would feel welcome, find of interest, and encouraged to continue the relationship.

5

Chapter

Missions in the Past were Inspiring; New Strategy Brings Even Brighter Missions Future

WE HAVE ALL BEEN inspired by stories of foreign missionaries of the past. To see their dedication and sacrifices made in traveling to distant lands caused many of us to make decisions to sign up to go. As a teen-ager viewing the movie "Stanley and Livingston" I marveled at the sacrifices of these courageous missionaries as they struggled through the jungles of Africa to reach dark skinned people with the Gospel. Both men and women - such as Raymond Lull, David Brainerd, Henry Martyn, William Carey, Hudson Taylor, John Paton, Lottie Moon and many others were trail blazers for the faith in the 18th, 19th and 20th centuries.

We couldn't help but shed a tear upon hearing the stories from the pulpit or reading about the lives of those who were willing to put it all on the line to get the gospel out to people in distant lands. Missionary stories of the past often told of a relatively young missionary and family with children who boarded a ship, leaving loved ones standing at the dock. With handkerchiefs in hand the parents, grandparents and all other loved ones waved their good-byes and wiped their tears away as the ship sailed off into the sunset for at least a month's journey to the "mission field" on another continent. There they stayed for seven years before being eligible to return for their furloughs. Phone usage and/or cablegrams, when available, were only for emergencies because of the expense and location of such services. Churches longed for missionary letters that could either be read from the pulpit or posted on the missionary bulletin board.

When furlough time arrived, the missionaries would then proceed on an itinerary that would take them to churches and individuals who formed their financial base of support and hopefully find new recruits. The children would spend the furlough time, often a year, attending school in America. Once the year was up, the families would again set sail on the long voyage back to the countries in which they resumed their missionary work.

Stories like those conjure up emotions of deep respect and adoration for those who sacrificed so much to take the gospel to the ends of the earth in obedience to the Great Commission. Stories like these also have those of us in church pews not wanting to tamper with the method in which foreign missions gets carried out. We want to keep the *status quo* when it comes to who the foreign missionaries should be. Our image is that foreign missionaries:

- are dedicated Christians in America (or another country mainly in the West) who are willing to go to other countries with the gospel.
- are willing to undergo foreign language and culture training for two years.
- do deputation work, raising their own support (financial and prayer).
- apply for the necessary passports and visas of the country to which the missionaries will be going (and will need to update these official documents).
- say "good-bye" with tear-filled eyes and warm embraces to loved ones, including supporters, not knowing for sure how many years it might be before they would see each other again.
- who have children, must find suitable education abroad to meet their educational needs.
- must find suitable housing abroad. It could be as simple as a shelter from the elements.
- experience culture shock with different food, unsafe drinking water, less than desirable accommodations and living circumstances

(where to shop, unsafe environment, noises, smells, lack of sanitary conditions and air pollution besides often being constantly faced with dangers.

- struggle with communicating (verbal, cross-culture nonverbal, and written) with the people to whom they are supposed to be ministering.
- must adjust to missions supervisory staff and other missionaries.
- must find medical doctors/specialists and dentists who can take care of their families' medical and dental needs.
- do their shopping with street vendors when modern stores and supermarkets are unavailable.
- are required to adjust to new modes of travel – such as crowded mass transportation, driving on the opposite side of the street in some countries, finding places for car repairs.
- cope with being the minority among people who are committed to vastly different religions, political ideologies, standards of ethics and integrity.
- are subject to security issues that Americans are faced with in traveling and living abroad. (Being an American in some parts of the world means you are not liked or wanted – ever read the book The Ugly American? The daily television news brings stories about robberies, murder, kidnapping, extortion, being imprisoned, and even killed).

Let's just stop a moment and evaluate the past practice of carrying the gospel to other nations through the traditional missionary approach. In reading the above, it should raise the question in everyone's mind, are there any methods in which we could achieve the same goals, but more effectively, more efficiently, and more economically? I have observed exponential changes in my lifetime in just about every aspect of life and I'm sure many of you have seen unimaginable changes over the decades yourself. Just go to a Hallmark store and look for a card that shows what was going on in the world in the year of your birth. It is shocking and quite amusing for some of us.

When it comes to global mission strategies, there is no question but that changes in methodology need to be made in order to keep up with this rapidly changing and mobile world. The immediate question is "considering the increasing mobility of the world's population, particularly among college students, who will become the future world leaders of their countries, shouldn't we be taking a closer look at where they end up attending college or a university as a foreign student?"

Answer: America is by far the number one choice for students from around the world who want to go overseas for their higher education. Therefore, there obviously needs to be a shift of missions' priorities and resources to keep up with these intercontinental population movements. This requires that we retool our global missions' strategy to include the more than one million international students who have come to America on temporary student visas or other visas for their higher education. There are tens of thousands of Christians among them who are on foreign passports and temporary student visas whom we should train and whom would be available to serve Christ in fulfilling the Great Commission. There are well-qualified people available who, with proper training, could become missionaries to their own people, and do the work more effectively, efficiently and at less expense. Read on . . . that's what this book is all about.

Here is an insightful observation from Neale Hightower, a leader of Westminster International Friends in Atlanta, Georgia,

"Somehow, the mystique of going to another part of the world captures attention among Christians everywhere. Mission work at home, somehow, seems less important.

The world has changed, 'the world has come to our doorstep'... particularly in large, well reputed US universities. And while the location has changed, the opportunity is still there. In fact it is a more 'efficient' way to meet that opportunity than we've had in the past.

When a missionary goes to a different culture, they have much to learn – and they are the person with needs – practical and spiritual. The needs for financial support are often high too.

Here it's the international student who has those needs. Since we are 'at home' it's less expensive to support a missionary here – and we have a built-in opportunity to minister to people by meeting many of their needs. So perhaps the idea of a 'new opportunity to become missionaries at home' would be a way to give visibility and validation to those who are laboring among internationals here in the US. Further, there are more people available to do 'at home' work on a full or part time basis than those who go overseas."

(Neale Hightower email to Dr. Jack Burke – March 6, 2014)

6

Chapter

PARADIGM SHIFT IN GLOBAL MISSIONS NEEDED TO KEEP PACE WITH INCREDIBLE OPPORTUNITIES PRESENTED BY INTERNATIONAL STUDENTS

IT IS INTERESTING TO note how strategies of making disciples of all nations have changed over the centuries. What about today? In today's world the best strategy is a return to the first century model of the Day of Pentecost when people from the known world came to Jerusalem and heard Peter's famous sermon.

As well-known Southern Baptist leader and author, Henry Blackaby[12] wrote on the topic "God Invites You to Join Him, the emphasis is on watching what God is doing and where He is working. Then join him." For example, Blackaby wrote, "God is a sovereign Ruler of the universe. He is the One who is at work, and He alone has the right to take the initiative to begin a work. He does not ask us to dream our dreams for Him and then ask Him to bless our plans. He is already at work when He comes to us. His desire is to get us from where we are to where He is working. When God reveals to you where He is working, that becomes His invitation to join Him. (Author's underlining) When God reveals His work to you, that is His timing for you to begin to respond to Him."[13]

He continues by saying, "When God reveals 'Where God is at Work,' God has tried, at times, to get our attention by revealing where He is at work. We see it, but we do not immediately identify it as God's work.

We say to ourselves, 'Well, I don't know if God wants me to get involved here, or not. I had better pray about it'. . . If you are going to join God in His work, you need to know where God is working. The Scriptures tell us of some things only God can do. You need to learn to identify these. Then, when something happens around you that only God can do, you can know it is God's activity . . ." [14]

A practical application is to discern God's direction in today's world in regard to missionary opportunities. For one thing, He has arranged for students from all countries, i.e. the future leaders of the world, to come to America in such large numbers it is beyond belief. As an added benefit practically all have studied English in their own countries. Following my Masters Degree at the University of Southern California, while doing my internship in the Foreign Student Office at USC, the official count of international students nationally was 64,705.[15]

When attending my first National Association of Foreign Student Advisers Conference (NAFSA's original title) at the Huntington Hotel in Pasadena, California, I wondered why the keynote speaker, Lucius Battle, was only an Assistant to the Secretary of State. I felt that foreign students should be so important to the U.S.'s developing strategic foreign policies that surely the Secretary of State himself would have been the keynote speaker. I still feel the same way today regarding the need for the leadership of every Christian global mission agency to make reaching international students a top priority in their missions' goals and objectives.

Through the years the international student enrollment count has continually increased. As has been pointed out previously, now the figure of international students enrolled exceeds an astronomical one million. I have also seen the growth of the annual NAFSA (National Association for Foreign Student Affairs) conferences. There were only 200-300 attending the first conference I attended. Now there are over 10,000. The secularists get it!

What better situation could we as mission-minded Christians have than to be in contact with the future leaders of the world enrolled in colleges near where we live and in proximity to where we attend church? Friends interested in missions, we no longer have to look for the global mission field as being across an ocean as if that was our only opportunity to share Christ's love with the world. Can't you see? God in his sovereignty has moved the mission field's future leadership to our very doorstep. This is what Henry Blackaby was talking about. **"Watch where God is at work and get with God's program."** Except for a relatively small percent who need to take intensive English courses after their arrival, most students pass the TOEFL, i.e. the Test of English as a Foreign Language, or IELTS, International English Language Testing System taken as part of their admission requirement, and are capable of pursuing full-time studies – **all in English!**

Wow! Aren't you awe-stricken by what God is at work doing? He has just moved the future decision-makers of practically every country on planet earth to our country, our states, our cities and towns, and to make it convenient they "just happen" to be enrolled at yours and my local campuses. And what has been our response, leaders of churches and denominations throughout America, brothers and sisters in Christ? From my vantage position as an author who is greatly concerned about this apathy, very little! If one of you were to say to me, "sounds like you are disappointed in us, Jack," to which I would reply, "Let me ask you." Have you heard this challenge before from your church missions leadership or from your Foreign Missions Board?" Here God has brought these future world leaders to us. He expects us to get right to work by placing this mission field emphasis into our church and denomination missions' goals and objectives, and most certainly our budgets. And what is our response? God is met with mute silence by all too many. Oh yes, those of us who have been open to seeing the vision God has put before us (I don't see how anyone could miss it), are doing our dead level best to stir up the masses of Christians to get with God's program and do something about this gargantuan opportunity. Although we find many churches still focused on missions, which is a good thing, we find far too little emphasis in discerning where God is at work and where He wants us to join Him. To be perfectly frank, we are still stuck in the past with our missions' methodology. The facts are that although there is growth in numbers there is still a relatively small number of those engaged in ministry to international students in churches and ISM organizations throughout America. Also, it has been my observation that on a national scale there are still not many believers in our churches who are talking about what God has been doing in bringing the mission field of international students to our very doorsteps.

By contrast, the university secularists are working overtime developing marketing strategies to expand the enrollment of international students into the thousands, even breaking the 10,000–15,000 range of international student enrollment in an expanding number of U.S. universities. Compared with those charged with global missions responsibilities in churches and mission agencies, it's quite evident that most have not yet felt the need to develop a ministry to international students. I think most churches would like to show some support for a campaign to put missionaries, either long-term or short-term, on the mission field. But when you look around, you find relatively few churches that have caught the vision for what their church could do if engaged in a full-blown missions challenge to become involved in a mission to the world through international students attending a nearby college or university.

God isn't simply rearranging the deck chairs. He's looking to Christians in America to take the lead. I cheer God on for His deluging our colleges and universities by the hundreds of thousands of those potentially capable of shaping the world's power structures and religious ideologies by placing Christ on center stage for all to welcome with open arms. Fellow committed believers in Jesus Christ, this challenge could not come at a better time. Let's not waste anymore time. We need to take the lead. We need to be at the center of action. We are the vessels God has chosen to present these potential world changers with the magnanimous offer of the life-changing advantages there are for those who too accept Christ's gracious invitation to "follow me." Doesn't that just send chills up and down your spine to know that our time has come?

We enthusiastically ask you, missions decision-makers in churches and denominations of this great land, to get on board. We whole-heartedly ask you to consider the vision of why He set the stage for international student numbers beyond belief to decide to come to America, known by students throughout the world as the "Christian country," for their higher education. (This isn't just hyperbole.) Having been involved with international student leadership for three decades in a university setting, I know how America is often referred to, it's a Christian country.

Without your support, to be quite frank, we may lose this God-given opportunity. There are other countries, some non-Christian, who would be only too glad to take over America's leadership in educating the world's future leaders. Yet, unless there is a positive change of missions' policies, involvement, and strategy with the decision-makers, not much is going to get done by those who name themselves as Jesus followers. Basically we send a relatively small number of Christian missionaries with the gospel message to foreign countries on long-term or short-term missions. What is mind-boggling is to realize the thousands coming from those same countries where our missionaries go and would love to make contact with, are either headed to our country or are already here. It makes us realize that we need to get back in the huddle and form a better strategy.

Another factor to consider is, who do missionaries have access to when they reach the other country? From what I have been told by missionaries themselves (including my own brother, Harry, a retired career missionary), it's the people who are available. "Available" meaning they are often the unemployed, workers with little influence, or young people, groups not known for their being in positions of power and influence.

Hanna, a former Pasadena City College student, and president of the International Relations Club from a Middle East country, told me that with a college education in the U.S. he could return to his homeland and be a person of influence. He went so far as to say that he could speak "nonsense and people would listen." Hanna was a particularly delightful student. After a Bible Study at InterVarsity's Lake Tahoe Christmas House Party during my seminary days, Hanna asked me what the expression "born again" in the Bible meant. After an explanation I had the joy of seeing him commit his life to Jesus.

God does care for each soul and so should we. What we are talking about here is a strategy to reach those who potentially will have the power of position, the purse and influence to carry out the Great Commission more effectively than many others in their own countries. It comes down to choices. It's like the story of what's the best strategy to show care for the hungry in a third world country – bring food to feed the poor or bring seeds, drill wells and train the poor how to grow crops, enough not only to feed oneself but many others.

The Most Effective Way to Share Christ with the World Requires a Paradigm Shift

When something has been done for so many years in a certain way, even if it has been proven that it is not the best way, we tend to stay with the *status quo*. Let's face it, it's tough to change. In many ways we all dislike change. We are creatures of habit. We go to the same stores. We buy the same kinds of food. We tend to stay with the same models in car purchases. When we go to church we usually sit in the same area. After church if we go out for dinner we usually go to the same restaurant. On and on it goes. We come up with answers like "If it's not broke, why fix it?" Even when the facts are placed in front of us that one product is better than another we still tend to stay with the one product we have used for many years. It's because it's an emotional thing to change. We often do not stop to think that it is actually loyalty to the product or team that drives us to stay with the same product or back the same team year after year.

There is always resistance to change especially when you are in the majority. These changes happen in the secular as well as Christian organizations and churches. Look at:

- Henry Ford and his horseless carriage. There were those who felt they should stay with the horse and buggy.
- Thomas Edison as he faced resistance when he tried to sell his idea of bringing light to homes and businesses after dark without the use of candles and lamps. He had to make doubters believe that it could be done by a newly invented light bulb, drawing power from generated electricity, then transmitted through a system of wires and plugs. For centuries people were accustomed to the use of candles and lanterns to light their homes and places of business after dark. Can't you imagine how the manufacturers of candles and lamps designed to hold a candle felt about this upstart Thomas Edison? Perhaps the same could be said about resistance encountered by:
- Alexander Graham Bell and his idea of developing a telephone to provide people with a way to talk to others across town or in different cities rather than depend on personal visits and the postal system to keep in touch.
- The Wright brothers when they took their solo flight. Do you think there was anyone around who could imagine what the future held for aviation? It took many years for the airplane to be an alternative to ground transportation. Some people to this day have a phobia about riding in transportation that goes high in the sky. Next there is:

- Jackie Robinson, the first African-American to gain entrance to big league baseball when he donned a New York Yankee uniform? It's well documented how it turned out. Jackie Robinson was not only the best batter on the New York Yankees roster but also the entire league.
- Steve Appleton and Bill Gates among others who revolutionized global communications by the introduction of computers and software. (I can recall how tough it was to change from using my IBM Selectric typewriter for typing an annual report to typing the annual report on my new office computer.)

How does this apply to the reverse role of Christian international students being the missionaries? Can you see that we then have access to new ways of increasing our effectiveness, efficiency, and at less cost by wrapping the message up in a person who looks the same as people in that country, talks the same way, that is, fluently in the same language and even without accent, thinks in the same way, so understanding the culture is not a problem? It even ends up being cheaper to do missions this way. Of course, missionaries to their own people are even self-supporting.

Once the new has been proven, and it has, what are we waiting for? Since it is a well established fact that well-trained Christian international students returning to their own homelands do such a great job in communicating the gospel to their own people, why hang on to the old ways of communicating the gospel overseas through foreigners, like ourselves? The foreigners we should be looking at to carry the message of hope are those who are citizens of their own countries, who right now are attending a college or university not far from where you live. It is time for an update. Times have changed. **Final reasons for the <u>urgent need for a paradigm shift</u>** in global missions.

- We have more than one million international students here in America now
- More students are traveling to other countries for an education than at any time in world history and the number one destination for these students right now is America.
- We have an unprecedented opportunity to share the "good news" about Jesus to these students. (Try being a missionary to these students back home where you are not wanted, not invited,

where they are surrounded by family and relatives who say "no to Christianity, we've got our own religion.") Therefore, we must act now. There is no time to waste. Realizing that the goal for many countries is to attract international students to universities in their own countries, more countries are going to the "full court press" to attract students to their countries. I saw it in my travels to China where university officials invited me to speak on services the university needed to be competitive in the market for attracting international students. They pointed out to me with great pride the newest, most modern dormitory on campus was for <u>foreign students</u>.

Remember when the <u>American</u> automobile was the world's most sought after automobile. Through fierce competition from other countries we lost that competitive edge. The same could happen to our nation's ability to be the number one leader in attracting international students to come under our country's umbrella of cultural (including Christian) influence through their coming here for an education. **We need to take advantage of this unprecedented opportunity to influence the world for Christ while we still have time. International students should become the church's highest priority for global missions' strategy.**

7

Chapter

STRUGGLE BETWEEN BEING A FOREIGN MISSIONARY CANDIDATE AND A CALL TO A MINISTRY TO INTERNATIONAL STUDENTS

The Suzanne Perry Story in Her Own Words
Baptist Chaplain/International Student
Minister, University of British Columbia

WHEN THE LORD CALLED me to cross-cultural missions, I assumed it would mean that I would be moving overseas, learning another language or two, and living amidst cultural differences. Raised in Southern Baptist churches in Oklahoma, California, Missouri, and Texas, the natural step was to approach the [Southern Baptist] International Mission Board [IMB] and begin the appointment process. Everything about my sense of calling and background lined up neatly with the IMB's priorities. However, when it came to being matched with an assignment, I didn't fall nicely into any of the job descriptions. Their question was "which people group (singular) has God called you to evangelize?" The answer to this question would determine location, language, cultural orientation, etc., which makes perfect sense from an organizational standpoint. But when I laid this question before God, His answer to me was always the same: "all of them." So the mission board was in a quandary: where do we send this person who is called to "all nations (*ta ethne**)?"

As we continued to pray about this and together wait for clarity and direction, they recommended I get some seminary training, which might be of benefit wherever in the world God was leading. As part of a class assignment at Southwestern Baptist Theological Seminary, I was one of a group of 10 students who accompanied a professor to Vancouver, BC to interview missionaries living and working in a large, world-class city. Our assignment that week was to ask, listen, and learn about urban realities as we interviewed 26 people serving in a kaleidoscope of ministry contexts. It was during that week that the Lord opened my eyes and said, "look around this city: *ta ethne* are here and this place is where I am sending you."

This posed an interesting dilemma if I was to obey this clear direction: the mission board would not send someone to an "all nations" type position. How would that fit into their "people group" (now "affinity group") strategy? And as Vancouver was still considered a "pioneer area" related to the Christian community, the majority of churches were too small to offer a paid position to someone other than the lead pastor. Many churches were particularly small, led mostly by "church planters" who were raising their support from American sources to start new congregations in the city. So I prayed and waited.

When Vancouver was chosen to host the 2010 Winter Olympics, Baptists in America and Canada responded by assembling a large financial grant to bring extra missionaries and church planters to the city as part of the pre-Olympic development in the area. One of the church planters mentioned the opportunity to my former seminary professor, who remembered me. It became obvious to all of us that God was opening a door for me to go to Vancouver. This grant provided most of the funding for my basic needs for two years, during which time the Lord had positioned me as a full-time university chaplain and international student minister at the University of British Columbia, and member of a church-planting team on the same campus.

At the end of those two years, the funding for the church planter in charge of our team became unstable and he was not able to continue in this role. Other members of the team were also in transition, and I was selected to become the lead church planter and to continue the vision for a church on campus. It was soon apparent that I was neither gifted nor capable to fulfill this role, and together we decided it was time for the fledgling congregation to close its doors. Thus began a season of joyous freedom to focus fully on the international student work, which grew more and more successful.

However, now that I was not officially part of a church planting team, there was no longer any funding available for the mission work I was doing and was convinced I was still called to do. The only option open to me was to begin to raise funds not only to support my personal needs, but also to fund any ministry initiatives. I was appointed by the North American Mission Board as a Mission Service Corps Missionary that year. Denominational priorities, including those of the North American Mission Board, directed all resources toward church planting efforts, and not toward student ministry—especially what was viewed as the sub-category of international student ministry, therefore no Cooperative Program funding was allocated for my salary, benefits, or ministry expenses.

At this time, after having graduated [from] seminary two years before, and having lived on the mission field in another country for two years already, I was suddenly in the position of reaching out to people "back home," wherever that was supposed to be. Local Baptist pastors in Vancouver were also raising support for their own salaries, and while they offered helpful advice there was to be little or no financial backing from church or association budgets. Thankfully, the Lord raised up a team of people from places I had lived before, and churches who understood my international student ministry as "missionary" work. The seminary professor who introduced me to Vancouver also worked tirelessly to advocate on my behalf with several missions committees and pastors, making appeals for funds, both short- and long-term.

Some of the very candid questions I fielded during the initial phase of my support-raising journey included, "Why didn't the IMB accept you?" "Are you having to raise your own funds because you're a woman and Baptists don't support women in ministry?" "Did you do something unorthodox to prevent you from Cooperative Program funding?" and "Do you hold some strange theology that disqualifies you from being sent as a 'real' missionary?" Having been raised in a Baptist pastor's home, I also had to deal with the very real and sometimes bitter disappointment of my parents that the Cooperative Program [which] we as a family had sacrificed for through the years was not available to someone from our family who was very obviously called to be a missionary. Although my mother as WMU [Women's Missionary Union] director had raised hundreds of thousands of dollars for missions work throughout her lifetime, Lottie Moon Christmas Offerings were not to be applied to anything I was doing, even though my full-time assignment was cross-cultural evangelism among people from other nations. The emotional toll of this reality was a significant barrier to my following the call to Vancouver to serve among "all nations" there. But the Lord lit the path one step at a time, and led me to stay and continue the work.

After I had been in Vancouver five years, I learned about ACMI for the first time, and was given a bursary to attend the annual conference. Walking into a room of 300 people who work in ISM fields was like water on parched soil. I wept at the opportunity to meet others and to be affirmed. It was a real lifeline to discover the veterans of this type of ministry and to realize the wealth of knowledge, experience, writings, resources, and network that was available. I spent most of that first conference weeping to know I was not alone. Meeting other Baptists in ISM was also a revelation. I had participated in BSU [Baptist Student Union] when I was in university myself, but was not aware of any outreach among international students on my campus, nor indeed that ISM was a viable concern in Baptist circles. Hearing about ISM work as vital missionary work might have meant a different career path for me much earlier on, and would certainly have encouraged me as I spent those first years carving out a new ministry in a pioneer area.

A couple of years ago now, the UBC [University of British Columbia] Baptist Student Ministry director and I were approached by a pastor in the area who was sensing God's calling to lead a fresh attempt to plant a church on or near UBC. As we prayed together, we affirmed that this was the Lord's leading, and welcomed a new church planting team to the campus. It was a great blessing to have been able to introduce this new team to many students and others on campus and to provide a ready-made situation for them to have an easy start. The question of church-based or campus-based international student ministry is not a simple one, and perhaps requires discernment and the leading of the Spirit in each case. In our context, I elected not to serve on the staff of that new congregation, but have continued to serve as a full-time missionary on campus, still raising my support through the Mission Service Corps structure which exists within the North American Mission Board of the Southern Baptist Convention in the U.S. American funding partners may send tax-deductible donations thru NAMB, while Canadian donors may send tax-deductible gifts through the local Westcoast Baptist Association in Vancouver.

As I spend my days hosting international students in my home, helping them navigate their culture shock, tutoring them in English, leading them in Bible study, distributing Bibles and discipleship materials, preparing them to return to their home country, <u>I am more deeply convinced that international student ministry is global missions</u>. [Author's underlining] My first point of contact with students is usually the English Corner I lead, which is held weekly in the Student Union Building on campus. Occasionally I connect with someone at a Chaplains booth at orientation. <u>From my vantage point, ISM appears even more strategic than some overseas mission work, since I have access to visiting scholars from levels of society and influence during their formative educational experience with whom missionaries residing in their country may never be able to connect.</u> [Author's underlining] As our campus is a highly scientific research-heavy university, UBC attracts the top scientists and policy-makers especially in the areas of engineering, physics, genetics, medicine, technology, and forestry.

The undergraduate students I connect with are most often here for two semesters, plus a summer for travelling. The graduate students I work with are often married. Some bring their spouse, which provides a unique ministry context, and others are separated from their spouse who may be in an important job back home. In addition to students (both undergraduate and graduate), there is a large number of researchers here in post-doctoral fellowships that typically carry a one-year contract. These realities create a very high-turnover environment. While some do come to faith in Jesus during their visit here, cross-cultural evangelism often takes time, trust-building, and repeated watering & seed-sowing. "Visible results" that typically appeal to funding partners are few and far between, making the challenge of raising ongoing support even more of a faith venture. Still-unbelieving or just-beginning-to-believe students who return home also means a meager alumni base which could potentially become part of a support base if there were more time for connections and growth to develop and deepen.

In the face of the funding obstacles, it has been my experience that the Lord is both faithful and trustworthy. In eight years now, I have never once missed a rent payment or gone without food, phone, or bus pass.

I have hosted an unending stream around my table and in the Student Union Building, and have always had something to serve them, Bibles to give them, and other resources to pass along. Students from dozens of countries have experienced Christian welcome and heard the good news of the kingdom of God. Many have received their first Bible, either in English or in their native language. Many, many seeds have been planted, and many lives touched.

Recently, my national supervisor in Canada, who is in charge of all student work and campus church plants, asked me to take a more visible role in casting the vision of international student ministry as an important and strategic missionary endeavour. When asked why he selected me for this role, he commented that I'm the only one in our denomination in Canada who is engaged in this work full time. The nature of the large Canadian cities is such that all student work includes at least some international students, but the current emphasis on planting and growing sustainable churches is presently overshadowing the idea of investing in short-term returnees. I am depending on the Spirit's leading to know how to spread my time between the pastoral care and relationships of student work and casting the vision for ISM work among others in the Kingdom.

On our campus, there are a few other parachurch student ministries that have full-time staff members who work with international students, including ISMC, InterVarsity, and OMF. It has been quite encouraging to be joined by others, and we have formed a prayer network that meets monthly to stay in touch and actively foster a non-competitive environment among our ministries. It is important to me that students see us as part of the same family of God, and not as individual organizations vying for their membership.

I am thankful for the opportunity to serve the Lord in this mission field, and am grateful for His direction and guidance. I hope that in the future, more and more people will also be given the vision to engage in this work, and that the field will be populated with gifted cross-cultural missionaries of all personalities and abilities. At this time, the harvest on the UBC campus, and on other campuses around the world, is still so white and the workers so few.

Blessings to you, Dr. Burke, as you share your lifetime of wisdom and experience with us and those coming after us. Thank you for capturing your stories in print and passing them along for edification, example, and to raise awareness of the needs among the field of International Student Ministry.

ta ethne – the evolution of Discernment into a worldwide discipleship training ministry
(Email from Suzanne Perry to Dr. Jack Burke, 3/11/14)

COMPARING SUPPORT FOR FOREIGN MISSIONS, HOME MISSIONS, AND STUDENT MISSIONS

1. (High priority) Foreign (global) missions
2. (Medium priority) Home missions – often means "church planting"
3. (Relatively low priority) Student missions

Foreign missions takes place in other countries and is often thought of as involving great personal sacrifice. It's a status symbol for the church's dedication and commitment to missions. Support for the mission comes from churches or denominations. Home missions, focuses on ministries that take place in our local communities, state or country, and so often it is church planting. Student ministries, often finds itself in yet a lower priority. Among the needs are for college students to be involved with missions' activities which take place anywhere from local to a city or state some distance from the church. If sponsored by a parachurch organization, the missionary has to raise his own support.

The idea of the Great Commission (Matthew 28:19-20) being carried out by foreign missionaries going to other countries is woven into the theological and social fabric of church life. It's basic church culture. The traditional theological interpretation of "go and make disciples of all nations" is for the missionary to travel to another country and make disciples there. The fact that one million plus international students from practically every country on the face of the earth have done the traveling in coming to America, the country which most American missionaries call home, it's almost impossible to understand how missions-minded Christians could overlook such a strategic mission field.

A statement was made from the pulpit during a missions-month' offering "Missions is all about praying and giving." There was no mention of need for church people also to be involved in missions. In following up with church staff who made that announcement, the staff member said, "Jack, that's just hype." It was driven by the need to reach the church's goal for raising "x" number of dollars for the annual missions campaign. On another occasion we heard a relative who was faithful in his church attendance and tithing, respond to our stated need of international student ministry support by saying, "that's what we pay our foreign missionaries to do."

Comparing degrees of support for missionary work done on Beijing's campuses with Chinese students and Boston's or New York City's campuses with Chinese students, also from China.

Let's take a closer look at the significant role of "foreign missions" on university campuses. If you are actively engaged in working with Chinese students at Peking University in Beijing, your church and missionary organization will classify you as a foreign missionary. But if you do exactly the same kind of work with the Chinese enrollment attending New York University, which has the highest international student enrollment in the U.S., with its 15,000+ international students, or another university like Boston's Harvard University where more heads of state in other countries attended while a student in the U.S., you most certainly will be classified by a church or denomination as doing home missions or student missions. Or even relegated to "raise your own support" with a parachurch organization and called a "student worker." Some might say, "Well, that is quibbling." However, when you stop to consider the much higher degree of support, in more ways than one, that is provided the missionary in Beijing over the one in New York City or Boston, who also works with Chinese students, you will find out there is a vast difference.

Whether you are classified as a missionary to Chinese students outside the U.S. or a home missionary or student worker with Chinese students at a U.S. university usually amounts to the difference between receiving strong support from the pulpit and church body or relatively weak support from the same sources. There is also a difference for those who have to raise their own support. Look at the comparison of priority for support of Missions to Chinese students cited above for the practical difference:

Notice this also. There are missionaries who return to America from the "mission field" to do foreign missionary work among international students from the same exact country where they had previously gone as missionaries. Though they feel their work is far more effective here with students from the same country where they had served, they soon found that their pay had been reduced or even stopped altogether. Reason: they were no longer classified as "missionaries" on the "mission field." They are now here in America. Therefore, they could no longer be classified as "<u>foreign</u> missionaries."

I personally know a married couple who were involved in international student ministry in Houston, TX before going to China and Hong Kong as missionaries. In Houston the couple carried out an effective ministry among international students but found it difficult to raise financial support. The husband told me that he had run up a $10,000 credit card debt. When this same couple went to China and later Hong Kong, they told me that raising money for support was no longer an issue that it had been for them when they lived in Houston. While in Houston they lived in the neighborhood just across the street from the University of Houston campus and therefore had easy access to Chinese students including those who returned to Hong Kong. However, like I just said it was difficult for them to raise funds to support their successful ministry. The students upon returning to Hong Kong were no longer easily accessible to this couple when they too moved to Hong Kong. These former international students were now busily engaged in the professional work world. However, the couple did find certain alumni helpful resources to them in many personal ways, including financial support.

Sad to say, church and denominations often want to list missions to international students under student missions mainly because they are students. They do not view them as strategic future leaders coming from the same exact countries where our foreign missionaries are sent. This points out how misguided this priority system is. Instead of focusing on international students in our country where access to them is relatively easy, the irony is that we send missionaries at great expense to their countries where it is more than just a challenge. There's a barrier to reaching people of this elite status with the gospel. I am concerned that the church does not realize that international students are often sons and daughters of the world's leaders and many are destined to become leaders of their own countries themselves after their arrival back home as you will see elsewhere in this book.

This ranking system makes it difficult for missions to international students to achieve its potential for outreach simply because of the lack of involvement and relatively low priority it is assigned by the church in terms of financial and prayer support. In my 60 years of studying the problem, this is my observation. International student missions has rarely had a fair and unbiased hearing in the court of those responsible for church mission budgets and the allocation of funds for missions personnel. The fact is that the church needs to recognize that returning Christian international students, armed with the gospel and good training, are almost without exception the most effective missionaries to their own countries.

Isn't it strange that missionaries to international students here in America, are not accorded the same level of priority by the church for support as is provided those classified as "foreign missionaries" by virtue of their ministering on real estate across the border or national boundary? Chief reason: missionaries to international students don't carry the "foreign missionary" label blessed by the church. Since missionaries to foreign students in Boston are doing essentially the same thing, though more effectively, than missionaries to students in Beijing, I raise the following question. Why should the church differentiate the following priorities between ministry in Beijing and for example, Boston by:

- providing greater support and recognition among the church body for work done by missionaries to foreign students in Beijing than those ministering to foreign students in Boston?
- providing support in more ways than just financial, such as greater "pounding of the pulpit" support from the pastor? (A minister of missions at a large mega-church once told our international student missions committee. "I can see the need for it [ministry to international students] but I just don't feel the passion for it.")
- providing more calls for prayer and financial support for those in Beijing, provide more information in Sunday church programs (bulletins) and church bulletin boards than those doing the exact same thing in Boston?
- spending more of the church budget for the foreign missionary's travel, sustenance, and logistics in Beijing than the one in Boston who is doing the exact same thing, but more effectively and at lower cost?
- providing greater exposure to the missionary in Beijing when he returns to his home church in America by allowing more church service platform time to tell about his mission to Chinese students in Beijing compared to time given the one serving in that exact same capacity of ministering to Chinese students in Boston instead of Beijing?

Answer: The missionary to Chinese students* in Beijing has the historic advantage over the missionary to Chinese students in Boston because the one in Beijing carries the time-honored tradition, respected sacrificial image, and status of being considered a "foreign missionary."

- with exactly the same constituents, Chinese students, as an example.
- easier to reach them here.
- commonly known that Chinese students quite often experience homesickness and have greater need for friendship with citizens of the host country (in our case Americans) as is also the case with foreign students coming from other nations.
- a time when Chinese are in a completely different environment, free to do and think for themselves as to ideological choices such as are found in religion and politics.
- Economically cheaper to reach them here.
- an advantage to having more Christian volunteers available to minister to them here.
- **more logical from any dimension conceivable to reach them here in America, a country still called by most a Christian nation** (From my research most would agree the U.S. has highest % of Christians)

*The use above of Chinese students is generic. One could insert just about any nationality/ethnic group's name.

Why returning Christian international students to homeland are more effective than the traditional foreign missionary?

Although this question will be answered in more depth in other chapters, simply put, they are returning to the country in which they were born and raised; therefore carrying citizenship of that country. They speak the same language fluently, without accent, and understand the complexities of the same culture (often baffling to Americans), which I understand is a BIG DEAL to many missionaries. For the foreign missionary such things as writing a letter, article, brochure or book without the skill of the foreign national's knowledge of correct grammar usage, sentence structure, more expanded vocabulary and choice of words, is a huge undertaking for the foreign missionary. After having studied five languages myself, I can easily feel empathy with foreign missionaries for the challenges they face, many of whom have to learn the language from "scratch."

The returning Christian international has the added advantage of having family and friends for support, and of course better and more widespread contacts to accomplish their objectives. They don't carry the stigma of being an American or from another western nation which is a growing concern on an almost daily basis in certain regions of the world.

Finally, once again it bears repeating, there is an urgent need for *a paradigm shift in global missions: With more than one million international students now enrolled in American colleges and universities, the highest international student enrollment of any country in the world, we need* to seize this unparalleled opportunity for global missions.

Conclusion

It is the author's heart-felt prayer that through the reading of this book those of you who have favored the traditional "business as usual" approach to foreign missions in the past will be awakened to this new reality. Christian international students who are well-trained for return to their homelands are far better equipped to be the most effective communicators of the gospel in this dangerous world. I am convinced that once Christian leadership in this country understands, accepts, and supports this paradigm shift in global mission strategy, reaching the world for Christ will spiral upward to one of the top levels, if not the top level, of effective global evangelism.

8

Chapter

SENDING GOD'S MESSAGE TO THE WORLD WRAPPED UP IN RETURNING CHRISTIAN INTERNATIONAL STUDENTS

THESE ARE STORIES OF international students who returned home to serve Christ in a church, ministry to homeland and beyond, or secular position. First three are former international students whom I knew at the University of Houston: Hong Kong's So Wing-chi (Patrick So) and Tin Hing Sin (Sam Tin), also Singapore's Suyin. ("Suyin" – as a writer it's a pseudonym) Another who had a significant impact for Christ was India's Bakht Singh (now deceased). Continuing to have an impact in Africa is South Africa's Rev. Michael Cassidy. Read other fascinating stories in Chapter 15.

Why stories? At a luncheon meeting with Dr. Jerry Johnson, former Nazarene denomination General Superintendent in charge of all Nazarene churches, seminaries, missionary organizations, property, and publications in the world, from 1980 -1998, I found out why. Although Dr. Johnson and his wife Alice had served as missionaries a number of years in Germany, when Dr. Johnson heard my stories about Patrick So and Sam Tin, he told me he had never heard stories like these before. He was so impressed.

"Jack, build your book around these two stories." Dr. Johnson went on to say that he had never heard of Christian international students returning home to make such a significant impact in ministry for our Lord. In fact, he admitted that he did not know of any American missionaries who did what these former international students were able to do for Christ in their homeland. Dr. Johnson is an example of why this book is so needed to build awareness of the presence of Christian potential world leaders who are on our nation's campuses and more than likely on a campus near where you live. You can begin reading the stories, all three being University of Houston international student alumni whom I know well. The first two are the former international students to whom Dr. Johnson was referring. The first former international student to be presented is Rev. Dr. Patrick So. He is pastor of the 19 story, 10,000 – member, Yan Fook Evangelical Free Church located in the Hong Kong area. Its 2,000 seat auditorium is put to good use each weekend while holding five services. Additionally, Yan Fook has two branch campuses and a seminary.

Next you will read the exciting story about Christian international student alumnus of the University of Houston, Sam Tin, an extraordinarily gifted businessman who walked in the footsteps of his highly successful manufacturing giant and philanthropic father. Upon his father's retirement in Hong Kong, Sam was asked to take over the reins of the company and the family's philanthropic foundation. As the CEO of the business Sam was able to use his business acumen and his financial empire for the glory of God.

The third story is about another University of Houston international student graduate, [pseudonym "Suyin:] She found the Lord as her Savior at an InterVarsity Christmas conference (called "House Party" held at Bear Trap Ranch in the mountains high above Colorado Springs. In returning to Singapore she found a ministry through a secular NGO (non-government organization) in which she has helped many whose lives were devastated through natural disasters.

Upon my retirement, as one of the top award recipients from NAFSA: Association of International Educators which now claims a membership of 10,000, I was asked who my most memorable student was during my 30 year career of directing an Office of International Student and Scholar Services at two major universities. Without hesitation I said "Sam Tin." You will find out why when you read my reflections on Sam Tin and his own personal testimony of how he came to commit his life to Christ, and what he did in his service for Christ as a highly successful Christian businessman in Hong Kong and China, as well as become CEO of what had been his family's philanthropic secular foundation.

Figure 1 University of Houston Alumni Dinner in Hong Kong. Seated (left to right) Wilson Chui, Dr. Jack Burke, D'Ann Burke, Rev. Patrick So, Penny So, Rear row: Anthony Ng, Larry Tam, William Tsui, Millar Tsoi, Lytton Lai, Sam Tin, Irene Tin, Mavis Poon (Featured in this chapter are Rev. Patrick So and Sam Tin.) Patrick So serves as Sr. Pastor of Yan Fook Church, one of the largest churches in Hong Kong (19 stories, 2,000 seat main auditorium with 5 services per weekend). Pastor So received degrees from University of Houston, Southwestern Baptist Theological Seminary (Masters and Doctorate) and Masters from Dallas Theological Seminary. Next to Patrick is his wife Penny, also a graduate of the University of Houston.

After returning to Hong Kong Sam Tin worked his way up the administrative ladder in his father's industrial empire to eventually become the CEO upon his father's retirement and also CEO of his father's Foundation. In 2012 Sam's father, Tin Ka Ping, received the highest award offered annually by the Hong Kong civil authorities for being the most highly respected citizen. He has clearly shown that through his generosity provided through his foundation. In 2013 Tin Ka Ping was baptized by Rev. Patrick So at a private ceremony attended by 300 at Yan Fook Church on a Monday evening. (D'Ann and I were there as Sam Tin's guests. I was invited to read the Scriptures. The family knew that I had shared my faith in Christ with Mr. Tin, Sr. a number of times and that D'Ann and I had prayed for years that he would turn his life over to Jesus.)

Yan Fook is an Evangelical Free denomination church which Rev. Patrick So developed from a starter church with only approximately 100 in attendance. Six church moves later, each larger than the one before, the leadership decided to build their own 19 story megachurch.

MEET SO WING-Chi (PATRICK SO), D.Min

Christian Former International Student
For many years now Sr. Pastor of the largest
Protestant Church in Hong Kong
A Recipe for Success in Global Missions
On-site Interview 5/24/13

Born in China – Move to Hong Kong - Patrick's conversion

Patrick So traces his roots to the China Mainland before moving to Hong Kong. "It took me almost 7 years to be emotionally and rationally convinced that Christ is the loving God and Savior. My booklet, "The Transformation of an Atheist" has my full detailed struggle before I became a Christian.

In short, the tense relationship between my father and me took me several years to realise that our real enemy was 'sin', our self-centred ego. After a serious conflict with my Dad, I went out of our house. But Matt.7:3-4 reminded me of my own sin. I prayed to confess my sin to the Lord and went home and apologised to my Dad. A miracle followed. My Dad didn't scold me, He even told me that the food for dinner was already cold and told me to eat. That was the first time he was so kind to me, not after my apology, but before. I was surprised to see the change of my Dad's attitude to me. I also began to feel the peace of mind inside. This experience drove me to a positive attitude to God. That also marked the beginning of me to seriously study the Bible. At the same time I surrendered my life to my Lord. Use me in whatever way you want, Lord was my prayer." (Patrick So's email to Dr. Jack Burke, 6/21/18)

In Hong Kong the Lord used Patrick's brother, who as a strong believer encouraged Patrick, an atheist in his teens, to attend church and eventually through much soul-searching, commit his life to Christ when he was a senior in high school. In his own words Patrick said, "From a staunch atheist, I was transformed into a believer willing to give my life to God's service. Looking back, I could see that the breakthrough had to be both intellectual and emotional."[16]

In my mind's eye I could just see Patrick So standing at the altar in a Hong Kong church saying "yes, to Jesus" and "good-by to atheism." His Chinese name is So Wing-chi (better known to most of us as Patrick So). His older brother had been God's messenger to his younger brother, Patrick. He was always encouraging Patrick in his youth to attend church with him. Then there came a day when Patrick agreed to attend church with his brother. It was there that he heard the minister talk about God, Jesus, the Holy Spirit, the Bible and Plan of Salvation.

Attending church, whet Patrick's appetite to hear more. So he gradually found himself attending church more often. Then came the exciting day when he accepted Jesus as His personal Savior and Lord of his life. Just as he had worked so intensely in his youth to spread atheism, he turned his focus to serving Christ and spreading the good news about Jesus to his family, relatives, friends, and neighbors.

While they were serving as school teachers God called Patrick and bride, Penny, to the ministry. While still in Hong Kong, Patrick taught high school for three years during which time Patrick said that he led "about 100 students to Christ." Patrick and his wife Penny resigned from teaching school in order to equip themselves for further service to Christ. To Patrick that meant, going to a university in the United States and upon graduation continuing for theological studies.

Patrick and Penny So applied and were accepted by the University of Houston. In 1977 Patrick's and Penny's families and friends were with them at the Hong Kong Airport as they were about to board the plane and fly to the United States. Can you just imagine the tears of sadness mixed with tears of joy that flowed from Patrick and Penny, as they boarded the flight to Houston, Texas.

Patrick and Penny were two weary travelers at the end of a 24 hour journey as they arrived in Houston and found their way to the University of Houston. After finding the apartment complex where they were to stay, they arrived at the University where they proceeded directly to the International Student and Scholar Services Office (ISSSO). It was there that the staff and D'Ann and I greeted them and helped them not only with their government documents but also to provide an orientation program for students lasting several days.

During his stay at the University Patrick wrote that he and Penny "began to know a group of devoted Christians from the International Student Office who later became good friends and partners in the ministry." He went on to say he was "deeply impressed by the love and all their thoughtful arrangements for the international students. The most memorable was the host family program." [This program was initiated and directed by my wife D'Ann as a volunteer.] D'Ann and other International Friendship Family program volunteers helped Patrick and Penny by assigning them to Gerald and Trevelyn Ray's family. [Gerald was the music department director at Houston's First Baptist Church.] One of Patrick's and Penny's fondest memories was spending Thanksgiving Day with the Ray family.

At the University Patrick's natural-born leadership qualities surfaced, coupled with his zeal for serving Christ when he became a leader in the Chinese Christian Fellowship. I am told that on occasion he even preached at a Chinese church in the city.

Patrick was very fond of the services our office provided international students by referring to our office staff in one place as a "team" and another place as "partners who love our kinsmen. I thank God for the dedication of these . . . partners who love our kinsmen so much that we can never forget [them]." (Patrick So: "Testimony for Dr. Burke." Email from Patrick So to Dr. Jack Burke, 4/7/12)

Busy schedule as a Christian international student in Houston

While at the University of Houston, Patrick indicated that he gave his testimony at Houston's First Baptist Church. He went on to say how terribly busy he was serving two city groups in their homes, in addition to the Chinese Baptist Church. At the University he worked in the university cafeteria like other students having to work and study. It was a struggle to pay tuition. He was self-supporting.

I hope you will be as thrilled in reading the Patrick So story as I was in seeing it unfold before my very own eyes and writing about it in this book. **This is a story about an international student who faced incredible odds against his succeeding in ministry, coming to America, receiving a university education, and completing theological education degrees at two evangelical seminaries (ending up with a doctorate). Then Patrick returned home to become the pastor of a flock of 100 and leveraging that with God's blessing to eventually become the largest Protestant Church in Hong Kong with an outreach to the world.**

It is stories like Patrick So's that make mission-minded Christians so excited about ministries to international students. It shows what can happen when an international student gets turned on to Jesus. Being an atheist in his youth and experiencing the tragedy of losing his mother to suicide while a child did not stop this young man from eventually becoming a pastor of one of the truly great churches in the Chinese world.

Committed to Christ, having a heart for missions and a vision for reaching his homeland for Jesus, all served as a catalyst toward a great future in missions. Combining his university education with a good, solid, in-depth theological training, that's all Patrick needed to prepare himself to return to his homeland as a missionary faced with the challenges of carrying out the Great Commission. For Patrick the possibilities were unlimited. [17]

Having a long-standing desire to enter the ministry, upon graduation from the University of Houston, Patrick entered the Southwestern Baptist Theological Seminary in Ft. Worth, Texas, where he received his Master of Divinity (M.Div.) degree. He continued his studies at Dallas Theological Seminary where he completed the requirements for a S.T.M. [Master of Sacred Theology] degree. He also finished the requirements for the doctorate of ministry, i.e. the D.Min degree at Southwestern Baptist Theological Seminary in 1985. ("Testimony of Rev. So," Notes from Interview with Patrick So, 4/23/2013)

Dilemma – Whether to stay in America or return home to Hong Kong. Faced with this dilemma Patrick decided to return to Hong Kong. Here are the reasons that led to his decision:

1. A review of the joint declaration between China and Great Britain showed that Hong Kong was to be returned to China in 1997.
2. Many people sought immigration to other countries.

3. A high percentage of church leaders also immigrated to USA, Canada and Australia.
4. Churches in Hong Kong cried out for mature pastors to nurture their flocks.
5. The need of the 1.2 billion Chinese souls also became the Macedonian call in Patrick's heart.

At the end of 1984 Patrick and Penny decided to leave and have their successors take their pastoral role [in Arlington, TX]. On March 31, 1986 Patrick and Penny were sent by their Arlington, Texas Church to Hong Kong.

Patrick was invited by his brother's church, the Evangelical Free Waterloo Church, to start a branch church in Kowloon Tong. ("Testimony of Rev. So," Email from Patrick So to Dr. Jack Burke" 4/17/13)

International Students Patrick and Penny So Return Home to Hong Kong

Upon returning to the Kowloon Tong area of Hong Kong Patrick So in his own words said, "we started with about 100 people from the mother church. She gradually grew." (Dr. Burke's interview with Patrick So in Hong Kong, 5/23/ 2013)

In fact from my talks with Patrick, their church grew so much that they moved six times before building their own church, the Yanfook Centre in 2004. They now have about 10,000 adults, 2000 youths and children.

Figure 2 Rev. Patrick So, former international student at University of Houston and two theological seminaries ending up with a doctorate from Southwestern Baptist Theological Seminary; Sr. Pastor of Hong Kong's Yan Fook Church, Hong Kong's largest Protestant Church affiliated with the Free Evangelical denomination; a Bible Institute, two other campuses and outreach to the world.

Patrick So stated his role is "to lead and empower my teammates to carry out the Great Commission of our Lord" by:

- Expository preaching
- Weekly Bible studies
- Sunday schools, with a thorough curriculum
- Holistic ministry: Children's ministry, couples' ministry, elders' ministry (a combination of physical, recreational, social and spiritual areas), medic-care ministry, youth ministry, worship and musical ministry, social care ministry, foreign missions (both China and world missions.)
- Evangelism Explosion integrated with our discipleship programs (Evangelistic Bible studies, Reconstructing our value system, New life and New living, etc)
- Bible and small group leaders' training

- Yan Fook Bible Seminary as a spiritual West Point: It was built by the church, in the church and for the church to produce pastors and church leaders for ministries all over the world. The seminary began in 2013. It now has more than 400 pastors enrolled as students of ConnectAll Bible Institute. (www.cbiglobal.net).
- Co-operation with a web-seminary to equip pastors and leaders for churches in China and overseas countries." ("Testimony of Patrick So," Email from Patrick So to Dr. Jack Burke 4/17/13)

Church Activities and Ministries

Number of <u>Worship Services</u> (according to language, age, or geographical location groups):

a. Cantonese – 8 worship services
b. Mandarin – 1
c. English – 1
d. Youth – 2
e. In Ma On Shan – 2
f. In Kowloon Tong – 2

1. Shelter house for the homeless – 1
2. Partnership with Evangel Hospital to start a clinic in Sham Shui Po
3. Indonesian maid ministry (with about 200 regularly attending the meetings)
4. Fellowships

a. Elderly – 2 groups
b. Adult – 10
c. Couples – 9
d. Career – 12
e. College – 1
f. Youth – 2
g. Mandarin groups – 1
h. English – 1

("Testimony of Patrick So," Email from Patrick So to Jack Burke 4/17/13)

Concluding Question

At the end of the 5/24/2013 interview with Patrick So in Hong Kong I asked him the question, "**If an American missionary were to come to Hong Kong, could he have accomplished for God's kingdom what you have done as a Christian international student returnee?**"
His answer in a humble but firm manner was "No."
(Dr. Burke's interview with Patrick So, 5/24/ 2013.)
I think Patrick's answer would have been the same if I had asked him the same question but changed "American missionary" to "any missionary from a western country" (not just America). Most likely it could be said of any missionary coming from any predominantly non-Chinese speaking country, trying to minister to an indigenous Chinese church.

Rev. So's comments on effectiveness of foreign missionaries in non-English speaking countries

"We have people who minister to those in China but progress is very slow. In 10 years maybe 10% are converted. They try but unless the Chinese people attending can master English they cannot catch the essence of the Gospel. **There are a number of barriers for people who try to minister in a different language. It's an uphill battle.** Even when I was in Arlington, TX, it was difficult. In ministering to those from China there are many differences in language, ideology, and life styles; it was more difficult to minister to them. When those from Mainland China and Taiwan came to church, they would talk politics, then problems would arise which would separate them into two groups. We emphasized to both groups, 'Don't talk politics. We belong to one kingdom, God's kingdom. When we become one family, talk about how this one kingdom changes our lives.' It's not easy to break down the barriers that divide them."
Author's On-Site Hong Kong Interview With Rev. Patrick Wing-chi So Details on His Student Experience in the USA; Impact His Life Has Had for Christ Since Returning Home (Interview, Hong Kong, 5/24/2013)

A close-up look at international student returnee, Patrick So

We have just looked at Christian international student, Patrick So's extraordinary successful career in returning to Hong Kong to pastor a church which eventually would become a mega-church, one of the largest Chinese churches in that part of the world. Rev. Patrick So, former international student, now senior pastor of the impressive megachurch, <u>Yan Fook Church, in Hong Kong</u>

Fast forward from 1979, Patrick's graduation date from the University of Houston, to 2017 when he is sr. pastor for the Yan Fook Church, Hong Kong's largest Protestant Church (associated with the Evangelical Free denomination.) There was a noticeable difference. For starters, it was difficult for me to get an appointment with him even starting far in advance because of his being the CEO of a church that has a membership of 10,000 adults and 2,000 children, with two branch campuses and a seminary. When we finally did receive a time for Patrick and his wife to meet us at the Renaissance Hotel on the harbor, we found out information about his church that should fascinate you too.

Yan Fook Church is in its seventh location, each move because of the need for additional meeting space. This time the Yan Fook Church was built from the ground up to its full stature of 19 stories with a 2,000 seat auditorium used for five services over the weekend. Other facilities hold another six services. When you look at it from either outside or the inside it meets all the standards for being considered a huge mega-church.

Church growth exceptional from its beginning

From the time Patrick So took over the small group of 100, the church began to grow. As the people kept coming there was continued need to move to a larger building. Programs such as Evangelistic Bible Study, The Practical and Relevant Gospel for Modern Man, Reconstructing Your Value System, New Life and New Living, and Evangelism Explosion, etc. account for some of the rapid growth, now adding up to 12,000 when you count the ministry to the children. There are also 1,500 in <u>small group programs</u>. Patrick said that the secret to growth with lots of ministries has been through the 8,000 involved in Discipleship Programs. There were more than 1,000 group leaders.

Yan Fook Church - one of Pacific Rim countries' mega-churches

I asked Rev. So to compare the size of his church with other churches in the region. In his reply, out of a sense of modesty I'm sure, he started out by saying "right now churches in China are growing rapidly. I spoke at the church in China started by Hudson Taylor. It's a new building that can hold 8,000. Now the congregation has more than 10,000." Singapore has an even larger church called the City Harvest Church with 20,000 in its congregation. There is a church in South Korea that has almost 800,000 in its congregation. **All of these churches have pastors who are indigenous to the region.**" Patrick So went on to say that "Yan Fook Church's distinction is that it emphasizes quality more than quantity, Bible studies and expository preaching more than activities."

Highest priority for Yan Fook Church – its discipleship and eventually, seminary

What really gets Pastor So excited is when he talks about the church's seminary, the Yan Fook Bible Institute, which started around year 2000. This came out of a vision he had while he was a student at Dallas Theological Seminary. He came to the conclusion that theological training should not be available for just the select few, but for all. He felt it was needed to mobilize all people for the growth of the church and for the people's Biblical and spiritual growth. The Bible studies were to train leaders. The seminary was started to train increasingly more people in Biblical doctrines. He felt the need to equip people and send them all over the world. Patrick So calls this the spiritual "West Point" which means that it has to be a spiritual training center. Many seminaries struggle financially, but Yan Fook doesn't have to engage in fund-raising. For Yan Fook Bible Institute was built in the church, by the church, and for the church. Some tuition is charged, but according to Rev. So it is only 1/5th the amount other seminaries charge. The balance is paid by the church. Yan Fook is considered an indigenous church. The church is entirely paid for. Patrick So sees his role as being pastor and teacher.

I asked Patrick about other former international students from the University of Houston who returned home to Hong Kong. Sam Tin returned home to eventually take over his father's business as CEO of a large and successful manufacturing company. In his reply he included Thomas Poon, another graduate of the University of Houston. Thomas is the Sunday School Superintendent at Patrick So's church. Patrick said that Thomas also holds a position in the Principal's Association. He is the Principal of a Christian school that is funded by Christians and sponsored by the Alliance Church. It is also government subsidized. Additionally, Patrick referred to Thomas Poon's wife, Mavis. Mavis serves as the Senior Inspector in the Education Department of the Hong Kong Government.

Generation gap in dealing with newly arrived Chinese students

In talking about the new students coming from China to the USA Patrick So said "they are quite different." (Patrick was referring to new students being younger students.) "But they are hungry for the Word of God, regardless of the generation."

Need for Chinese students in host family programs to be linked to Chinese churches

Patrick stated that the Host Family Program would be improved if there was a partnership between the Chinese churches and the universities' international student and scholar services offices. He went on to repeat his affection for the International Student and Scholar Services Office at the University of Houston by saying "Most students were greatly impressed by your brothers and sisters. They invited the students to have Thanksgiving dinner and to invite them to churches. Even for students who were not Christians, the favorable impressions drove them to ask themselves questions like 'Why do they do this? Why do they do that?' Once the students have experienced this, they are much more touched by the gospel message. The students could see that for those working in the office it was not just a job. There were lots of students seeking help. For students coming from English-speaking countries it was much easier. But for those coming from China, communicating in the English language is a barrier." The same principle would apply to missionaries going to countries that speak the same language as the sending country. It's much easier. However, **for missionaries going to countries with a totally different language and culture, in Patrick's words 'It's a barrier.'"** Therefore, I would hope that you, as you read this book, would agree with the author that <u>Christian international students returning to non-English speaking homelands have the added advantage of communicating the gospel because the language and culture barriers that missionaries face are removed.</u>

Expanding Patrick So's Ministry through his church's seminary and Web TV

We then discussed the possibility of sending Chinese Christian returnees for Biblical training at Yan Fook's seminary for three months to a year for Bible and seminary training. Patrick said his church had initiated such an idea. It would use television to transmit seminary courses. Patrick has Bible study through web TV. It's newly started and is called ConnectAll Bible Institute (CBI). There are 40 professors for Bible seminary to equip people for full-time ministry. It's designed for lay leaders in the church. Some programs are in English. There is a professor from Wheaton and another from Dallas Theological Seminary. Yan Fook is trying to do this because of the need in the entire world. In China, for example, 95% of the pastors do not have theological training in seminary.

(Email Patrick So to Dr. Jack Burke 6/21/18 Rev.)

Now Let Me Introduce my good friend and former international student, Tin, Hing-sin (SAM TIN)

Figure 3 Tin Hing-Sin (Sam Tin), Univ. of Houston alumnus, returned to Hong Kong to follow in his father's footsteps. Upon his father's retirement Sam Tin became CEO of a large manufacturing company and the family's foundation.

Introduction of Sam Tin by Dr. Jack Burke

Upon my retirement from the University of Houston, where I served 26 years as its Director of International Student and Scholar Services, I was honored by not only the President but also the Vice President for Student Affairs of the University who served as Co-Masters of Ceremony at a retirement banquet held in my honor. Honors also came from the leadership of the 10,000 member professional association, NAFSA: Association of International Education. The latter award was an honorary Award for Life Membership in recognition of "outstanding contributions to NAFSA and the field of international education and exchange." I said all this to introduce my special relationship with Sam Tin, an international student who came under my university administrative responsibility.

After receiving the award from NAFSA I was approached by NAFSA professional staff wanting to do an interview for publication purposes. I was asked who was my "most memorable student?" Without delay here was my response, "throughout my 30 year career of directing international student offices in which I dealt with tens of thousands of international students, Sam Tin was my most memorable student. He was an outstanding undergraduate student and also an outstanding alumnus of the University of Houston. He received the "Most Outstanding Alumnus of the Year Award" presented by the University of Houston's International Student and Scholar Services Office at a large university banquet honoring friendship families to international students in 1987. Sam and his wife Irene are featured among the outstanding alumni at the University of Houston's Alumni Foundation building.

Although you will read Sam's autobiographical material in "The Path of Faith of Sam Tin," I have introduced here my own brief biographical sketch of Sam Tin's life as an international student. A review of Sam's life would show that he was a committed Christian international student at the University of Houston. During his undergraduate years he attended Houston Chinese Baptist Church. I remember him attending free luncheons for international students at the University sponsored by the Church Women United. Also, Sam attended the luncheons sponsored by the Baptist Student Union [now Ministries] open to all students. Additionally I helped arrange for scholarships so that Sam and friends could attend the triennial national URBANA Conference which filled the gymnasium on the University of Illinois campus with a missions emphasis sponsored by InterVarsity Christian Fellowship. (Sam did not want to ask his father for the money because his father was not a Christian at that time.)

Upon graduating with a Bachelor of Science degree in Chemical Engineering in 1974, Sam returned to Hong Kong to work in his father's impressive large manufacturing business, the Tins Chemical Corporation. (On a tour D'Ann and I were impressed by the size of the factory and the hundreds of employees.) Sam became the managing director in charge of marketing and production of plastics in Hong Kong and Mainland China from 1974 to 2009, a career spanning 35 years. Sam eventually became CEO of the company and family Foundation upon his father's retirement.

With the governing board consisting of outside scholars and educators, "its work focuses on funding for enhancing quality education in schooling in greater China." (Email from Sam Tin to Dr. Jack Burke, 8/21/14).

Sam Tin's lovely wife, Irene, is also a former international student and graduate of the University of Houston. Irene received her Bachelor of Science degree in 1974. In returning to Hong Kong Irene worked as a medical technologist. Also, according to Sam, Irene led the choir of Chinese Opera-style gospel hymnals in the church and she was also a Children Program Supervisor in Bible Study Fellowship (BSF) in Hong Kong for many years. (Email from Sam Tin to Jack Burke, 5/23/14)

It was also D'Ann's and my privilege in 2010 to be included in the entourage that accompanied Sam on a tour of select Chinese university campuses. In behalf of his father who was not able to attend, Sam dedicated buildings on campuses in China at ceremonies organized by Chinese university officials. [I was honored by being invited to give speeches to Chinese university officials and students. At the Three Gorges University I was presented an "Honorary Professor" award.] Since Sam Tin was the honoree representing his father, it was interesting to observe how warmly he was greeted and treated by the leading Communist official for the Province. The same goes for the local university officials who were able to build campus buildings thanks to the generosity of the Tin Foundation.

In combining his faith as a believer with his business, Sam contributed to the support of Diane Lawrence, a missionary to Hong Kong from Houston. Diane is a friend of ours whose family home is in Houston, Texas, where she and her husband, Tom Lawrence (now deceased), were successfully involved in international student ministry. However, regretfully lack of financial support was a contributing factor which led to their decision to launch out as missionaries to China and Hong Kong.

Insights into Sam Tin's ministry in secular business.

After Diane Lawrence had spent an evening with Sam and Irene sharing about her continuation of the ministry since Tom had died, and Sam had moved the company operation to China, Diane wrote to D'Ann and me, "Sam was sharing that **he is seeing a lot of 'harvesting' in his business after so many years.** It started out in the maintenance department of the factory in China. There were usually a lot of complaints in that department but others began to see such a change in their countenance, attitude and work habits, that others have now believed." I also found out from Diane that **"Yesterday Sam organized a luncheon where he invited an evangelical speaker. It was held in a local restaurant [where] not only the employees but officials and police officers were among the guests."** (Email from Diane Lawrence to Dr. Jack Burke, 5/13/2007)

As a demonstration of the effectiveness of a Christian international student returnee, Sam Tin said: **"We Hong Kongers are in 'much better position than the foreigners' to work with the three-self churches."** (ACMI Conference Plenary Address by Sam Tin, Houston, TX, 6/1/12) Reason for Christian Hong Kongers influence: **"Chinese government is sensitive to foreign influence with respect to religious beliefs."** (Email from Sam Tin to Dr. Jack Burke, 8/28/14)

For his life time achievements, Sam Tin's father, Tin Ka Ping, "has won numerous awards of high distinction, the greatest being the Grand Bauhinia Medal (GBM) which is the highest award under the Hong Kong Honors and Awards System one can receive. It recognizes the selected person's life-long and highly significant contribution to the well-being of Hong Kong." You will read more about this later. (Email from Sam Tin to Dr. Jack Burke, 12/12/2013)

You can see all of these awards when visiting the family owned museum in Hong Kong. One picture shows Queen Elizabeth face-to-face placing an award around Mr. Tin, Sr.'s neck.

As grand as the awards are to the recipients, nothing compares with the highest point in Mr. Tin, Sr.'s life. That's when he committed his life to Christ and was baptized on May 27, 2013. It was D'Ann's and my distinct honor and privilege to be invited by Sam Tin to participate in this highly significant baptismal service.

Figure 4-A Baptism Service for Dr. Tin Ka Ping – (Left to right) CHAN Kin Hung (Tin Ka Ping Secondary School Principal), Dr. Jack Burke reading scriptures, Dr. Patrick So, Mrs. Tin, Dr. Tin Ka Ping, Tin Wingsin

Figure 4 – B Dr. Jack Burke reading the Scriptures at Mr. Tin Ka-Ping's baptismal service in Hong Kong, May 27, 2013. Photo left to right CHAN KIN Hung, TIN Ka Ping, TIN Wingsin, Dr. Jack Burke

Figure 5 Baptism of Mr. Tin Ka-Ping, May 27, 2013, in Hong Kong. Officiating was former international student, Rev. Patrick So, Sr. Pastor of Yan Fook Church, an Evangelical Free Church in Hong Kong.

Figure 6 Many photos were taken in group settings following the baptism, always with Mr. Tin Ka Ping and Mrs. Tin at the center. Pictured left to right: Front row: Dr. CHOI Yuen Wan Philemon (Chairman of Commission on Youth); Rev. Patrick So (Sr. Pastor of Yan Fook Church), Mr. TIN Ka-Ping, Mrs. Tin, Mrs. Burke, Dr. Jack Burke; Rear row left to right: CHAN KIN Hung (Tin Ka Ping Secondary School Principal) Rev. Dr. LEUNG Ka Lun (President of Alliance Bible Seminary)

The Path of Faith of Sam Tin

Upbringing in Secular Family but in Christian Schools

In the first ten years of my life in the 50's, I was living in Indonesia without any knowledge about salvation but surrounded by the local belief of superstition and spirits. The family moved to Hong Kong in 1959. My family had no particular interest in religion except observing the traditional ritual of ancestor worshiping during some important occasions in the year. We never had to go to the temple to offer or to ask for fortune. Worshiping and paying respect to the ancestors is an important tradition and belief of the family.

When we came to Hong Kong, my siblings and I went to the schools from primary to tertiary that were run by Christian organizations. We therefore naturally learned about the Bible and the stories of Jesus in class. Nevertheless, I was not serious about the Bible class but treated it as a religion subject. I remembered on some occasions when the other young students and I were invited to attend the student Christian fellowship events on campus. However, the tea treat and the music performance were the things I was attracted to.

Figure 7 Tin Family with 2 American exchange students (on left) pictured with the family in late 1960's.

God however never gave up calling me to come to Him. When I just entered the pre-university studies in Hong Kong Baptist College, I was invited by a senior of the Baptist Student Union to join the retreat of a local Baptist church for the young people. I was overwhelmed by the warm welcome and friendly fellowship during the 3-day retreat. The message about the sacrifice of Jesus Christ given by the pastor hit my heart and led me to think more seriously about faith. Shortly, my family encouraged me to study in the U.S. for the purpose of widening exposure to the world and better education opportunity. Then I chose University of Houston for its reputation in Chemical Engineering and lower tuition fee of Texas.

The family hosted two American exchange students (on left) pictured with the family in late 60's.

College Life in US

I didn't have any connection in Houston but was fortunate to be taken care by the friendly staff of the International Student Office in orientation as well as in settling down. There were not many students on campus from

Hong Kong at that time. Very soon, I was approached by some Hong Kong Christians who were studying in graduate schools. They invited me to join the weekly Bible study fellowship in their apartment on MacGregor near the campus. This was the first time to learn the Bible in detail. Sharing of life application of Bible messages and hymnal songs was particularly helpful to my understanding of God's love. The experience of love, support and care among the members in the Bible Study Fellowship was what I had never had before. On the campus, there were Christian activities testifying about the love of God. Particularly, the "Free Luncheon" for the international students every Wednesday in the University Center was the most unforgettable event on campus because we were offered not only sandwiches and coffee but were received with smiles and care by the friendly American ladies. I later learned that these ladies were the volunteers from the churches in town showing friendship and Jesus' love to the internationals. The Baptist Student Union on the campus was already familiar to me, remembering the past connection in Hong Kong Baptist College. They were so friendly to share the good news to the internationals.

In the start of the fall 1970, I came to know Dr. Jack Burke who was the Director of the Office of International Student and Scholar Services (ISSS) at the University of Houston when he recognized my involvement in Bible Study. He offered scholarships [from an outside source] to attend InterVarsity's Urbana Christian Convention at the University of Illinois to me and the other Chinese students. We ended up joining as a group of 8. We took advantage of enjoying a free travel trip.

Figure 8 Sam Tin and friends after arrival at Univ. of Illinois for InterVarsity's Urbana December'70 conference.

It was an eye opening and astonishing experience for me to see the size of tens of thousands of Christians gathering to share their faith in one occasion for the common cause for God's world mission. I was deeply touched by this Christian movement in the U.S. and thought that Christian faith could have a great impact in transforming the hearts of Chinese people back in the home country who were greatly in need of salvation.

After the trip, Dr. Burke was eager to know what our impression was about the convention and he asked us to share our experience before the church members in a banquet. I then realized that the scholarship was sponsored by an American Church who had been involved in ministering to internationals.

As a matter of fact, the convention did sow seeds of faith within many of us. Within a year of arriving in the U.S., God made me experience Him which has been a strong impact on my path of faith.

In the five year time of my college studies, I regularly attended Houston Chinese Baptist Church in downtown Houston. I worked with the other students to register Chinese Student Christian Fellowship Group as a campus organization with the great help from the Office of ISSS so that we were able to use the facilities of the Student Center. The Group has grown in size covering the students from Mainland China, Taiwan, Hong Kong and other Asian countries and has become famous in the region. We attracted quite a number of famous pastors to come to speak and give Bible training.

I met my wife who was studying Biology at U. of Houston. She was a believer and happened to be going to the same church that I first attended in Hong Kong. We were buddies in the choir and the Bible studies. We were baptized and got married in 1975, the second year after our return to Hong Kong.

Some of my siblings received Jesus during their study in the U.S. Our parents said that they were happy with us and gave the credit for our having good character with our being Christians. I was assigned a friendship family together with the other students. The American families were all Christians willing to welcome the internationals. We were invited to special events such as the Rodeo Show, football games in the Astrodome, and to celebrate Thanksgiving and Christmas with the families. I was impressed by their hospitality and the sharing of American culture and Christian values. The friendship program was particularly helpful for the international students during the first 2 years of adapting to the new culture.

Figure 9 The international roommates from Egypt, Pakistan, and Argentina (left, middle and right) 1971

Figure 10 Celebration in the home of Host Family, Christmas 1970

Career and Faith Back in Hong Kong and China

Upon return to Hong Kong in 1974, I joined the family owned business of plastics processing where I spent 3 years of training in different functions. Then I soon started the managerial position responsible for the manufacturing and technical development. In the 90's, I assumed the full responsibility of the company. The operations were moved to the mainland China across the Hong Kong border in 1992. The experience of running the business with two factories, one in Dongguan, a distance of 70Km from Hong Kong and another in Guangzhou. Spending most of my business time in China for the past 18 years was tough but rewarding. The "China knowledge" that I attained helped learn the mind-set and working culture of the people who had been isolated from the modern world for decades due to the culture revolution. There are business and social practices that are in conflict with Christian faith. However, I managed to get along with the people very well and developed a heart of love for the country in spite of the differences.

During the 90's, **I was able to organize delicately a factory fellowship group which was a voluntary function in Bible studies and life sharing. Over four years, there were 26 workers who accepted Christ and were baptized. Together with a Hong Kong Christian expatriate, we also started a Business Owner Christian Fellowship for the local businessmen meeting every Tuesday. It has enlarged in number and now becomes influential in the community today.**

Irene and I are active members in the house church in Hong Kong serving the elders, Bible teaching, leading the classical Chinese song Gospel Choir group and the fellowship group. [Bold type added for emphasis by author]

Involvement in Education work

In the late 70's, I was serving the chairmanship in the School Management Committee of a government subsided secondary school and the directorship of another which still continues. I developed the passion for education work and recognize the importance of quality education in schools.

On my retirement in 2009, I joined the Board of Directors of Tin Ka Ping Foundation which is a charitable non-profit organization. The Foundation had been established in 1982 by my father to which he donated most of his wealth for the education purpose by funding and organizing educational programs for quality education and school improvements in mainland China, Taiwan, Hong Kong and Macau. The Foundation emphasizes teachers' professional development and disseminating successful programs to the schools in China. This is another opportunity for me to continue my involvement in education. The education programs are secular, nothing related to Gospel teachings but are in line with the principles of Bible teachings with respect to Christian values and characters.

Commitment to His service

God has been gracious to our family. It is a miracle that my parents came to accept Jesus Christ as their personal savior during their old age. I see that God has purpose for my family and me to be His people and to serve Him. He brought us to Hong Kong, a place where we first came to know Him. I was given the environment of Christian love and training during the time at the U. of Houston where Dr. Burke, and his Christian staff members ministered in a very different way that won the hearts of the internationals. It has been God's work to bring all these blessings to me . . . as inspired by the good example Dr. Burke implemented in the States.

MEET SUYIN* (Pseudonym)

Attended University of Houston and Cal State-Fullerton Became a Christian, Did Missions Work Upon Return to Singapore & SE Asia

Another student I (the author) came to know at the University of Houston was Suyin, from Singapore. It did not take long after Suyin's arrival at the University of Houston from Singapore that those in leadership of the ISSS Office's Friendship Family Program and I recognized her to be an attractive, bright, articulate student, with the poise of having come from a distinguished family in Singapore. This turned out to be true. Desiring to be placed into a relationship with a friendship family, D'Ann assigned her to Peter and Evelyn Kemery. Peter was a Shell Oil Company executive who at one time had worked in Singapore. In Houston he also served as the volunteer leader of the Men's Bible Study Fellowship.

Having a good friendship family experience in Houston and being a good public speaker I invited Suyin to accompany me on speaking engagements to the Rotary Clubs in Houston. Her part was to share her experience of having a friendship family and to encourage the Rotarians attending to sign up for the University of Houston's Friendship Family program. After her speeches it was always interesting to observe the number of men who would line up to receive the brochure explaining the friendship program and to sign up to be a friendship family.

As you will read, Suyin became a Christian at InterVarsity's Bear Trap Ranch International House Party during a Christmas break. Upon returning to Singapore she became involved in hosting missionaries, organizing missionary organizations, going on short term mission trips to countries in South and Southeast Asia. Much of her work was done through a secular NGO that provided emergency aid to countries suffering losses from natural disasters. Some areas of travel into Taliban controlled areas were at high risk.

Suyin has given her permission to share her heart-warming story as to how she became a follower of Jesus: "I made my decision for Christ at Bear Trap Ranch during an Inter-Varsity [Christian Fellowship] House Party for International students in Colorado Springs, CO, on Christmas morning 1972. The night before, students were assigned to visit Christian homes and I visited the Hollingsworth family. Mr. Hollingsworth was the principal of a small Christian school in town. Their family had a birthday cake with 3 candles - Jesus' birthday, one candle for the past, the present and the future. I can still remember the name of the kids!

I made the decision in an activity hall at Bear Trap Ranch, thick snow outside and after I had made the decision, there was a beautiful deer looking in the big picture window. The deer scampered away after a few minutes.

The people that were influential were you, Dr. Burke and Mrs Burke, Tom and Diane [Lawrence] and Diane's family, the Kemerys, the Naylors and the many lovely believers that formed part of your ministry." (Email to Jack Burke, 12/16/2013)

Some years after Suyin's graduations from U. of Houston and California State U. at Fullerton, and her return to Singapore I received an exciting email from a Hong Kong missionary, Diane Lawrence, who had previously offered hospitality and friendship to Suyin during her student days in Houston. Here is what Diane wrote, "Recently I was in Singapore and stayed with **Suyin** and had a wonderful visit with her. **She has almost singlehandedly set up the Pioneer [missionary organization]-Singapore base there, which will be a sending base for Singaporean candidates and others in the area.**" (Email from Diane Lawrence to Dr. Jack Burke, Nov. 8, 2001)

At the turn of the century (2000) we received a Christmas card from Suyin in which she thanked us for the University of Houston's ISSS Office friendship family program. Using it as a model she said that **she had hosted 25 missionaries that year in her home there in Singapore.**

I asked Suyin to share her experiences which led her to do missionary work back home in Singapore following her college days as an international student who had come to Christ in America. Much of her service to Christ was done through secular non-government organizations (NGOs).

In Suyin's own words she describes her "calling."

My "basic call" is to pray in nations and somehow, God uses disasters to draw people to himself especially in closed areas like Aceh. [code name for security reasons] We can think of Haiti and the voodoo, and the large numbers who have become Christians since the hurricane to understand that. While some may say that we should not take advantage while people are down and out to force changes in religion (something we definitely don't do), **we find that using opportunities to provide relief and restoring livelihood in community development programs plus praying quietly can bring about changes.** I can tell you story after story how people especially of Muslim background are coming to Christ because He has appeared to them in dreams or visions.

Since late October, I've been to Malaysia for a consultation on a refugee Myanmar people group, Pakistan to do some food distribution, Aceh to provide technical assistance to 3 village community centres. Then I joined Dave [Pat's husband] on his business trips to Laos and Borneo." (Email to Dr. Jack Burke, 12/21/2010).

After graduation (from the University of Houston), in answer to prayer, I received a Scholarship from Lee Foundation in Singapore, along with a part time position in the Office of International Students at California State University Fullerton and a graduate fellowship. This "package of provisions" enabled me to propel completion of my Masters in Public Administration within a year.

With all the youthful idealism, I set off to a job in one of the world's richest oil countries, with a culture dating back more than a thousand years, in West Asia. I wanted to start a career in (Third World) Development with a foremost global non-government agency in literacy. But having grown up in multi-religious, multi-racial Singapore, overt discrimination from Muslims in West Asia was something alien to me.

The low point was an "outrageous visit" by the Patron of the rural literacy program where I worked. The Patron was a princess, twin to the King in the royal family and the visit hardened me to new realities. This princess never actually touched the desert ground. Her entourage of helicopters hovered just above us to where we could see her eyes, while the rotors churned up enough desert sand to create a dust storm. The princess smiled and waved from the co-pilots seat and then sped on to the Gulf. The villagers had taken days to prepare for this "visit" which took less than 10 minutes. The dust took an hour to settle and the NGO had to settle the bill from the Palace for this Patron's visit – which cost approximately three months of our operations budget!

Disillusioned at my first foray into the world of development, I returned to California and tried different roles in the non-profit sector. I volunteered on a few political campaigns, going as far as Maine with a presidential campaign. I settled with an agency that developed programs to help new immigrants (the "boat people from Vietnam"). No English classes here, but helping them apply for small business loans, financing for housing and renovation loans. The organization bought up tenements and renovated them into low income condos for the refugees. When ordinary credit was not available to newcomers, we set up a credit union that is still doing reasonably well today. These types of programs helped turn refugees into new immigrants who settled rapidly and successfully in America. (The average time these refugees stayed on public dole was approximately 4 months). Plus, these programs helped turn urban slums and red light districts into respectable and safe ethnic neighborhoods in a few short years.

Then I received an urgent call from my father in Singapore informing us that mother was in hospital due to kidney failure. I took a week's leave from work to go to Singapore and spent all daylight hours at the hospital, taking care of mum. In between her naps, I decided to take 6 months no-pay leave just as soon as I could to spend more time with my parents. In all, I had been away for more than 11 years.

Shortly after I returned to Singapore, my dad fell and fractured his arm, was further diagnosed with multiple myeloma and died 6 weeks later! About the only ray of sunshine, which his insurance company investigated, was that he was certified dead close to midnight, on the last day of his medical insurance coverage!

In the following decade, life moved on, I married a businessman and had a lovely daughter, balancing a flexi-hour career with family. For a while I traded on global monetary exchanges and worked split shifts, 6-7 hours "in the trading pit" of the exchange in Singapore, and a few hours in the middle of the night monitoring Chicago exchanges.

However every year, around November, wherever I am, I drift into an internal review of my *life so far that year*. This practice had started shortly after I became a Christian and attended Inter-Varsity's Urbana Missions Conference two decades before. I had made a pledge at the conference, "if called, I will serve in missions." And this I dutifully revisited each year.

I was sitting in a class at church one day, when there was a different stirring. A new voice said to me, "The speaker will not cover today's lesson plan but instead will talk about a training program. This is where you start your Missions prep."

Sure enough, the pastor shared excitedly about the launch of a one-year training program for pastors and missionaries. And yes, he did wonder why I was dabbing quiet tears for over an hour. I had started hearing God's stronger voice.

There was a minor hitch as I did not have the prerequisites for the training program. However when the Director for this training program interviewed me, he said: "Suyin, I only wanted to hear from you why you want to join the program, God has already told me to admit you, not to become pastor or missionary here, but for what you will do for Him."

"Great," I remarked, "what does God want me to do for Him after the year?" The Director smiled paternally and said, "He'll let you know"!

Our family lives close to the Orchard Road shopping belt and enjoys having houseguests. Both my husband and I had lived and worked abroad and had received warm hospitality from friends as well as strangers. Our daughter, who is our only child enjoyed having little playmates her age as well. Through hospitality, we met many friends from an American outreach group and along the way, we were invited to visit their HQ in Florida. In Florida, the leader of the group mentioned that the vision was to go global, as they did not want to remain as merely an American outreach group. People who joined are Christians called to be catalysts for church planting movements, to people groups or areas where the gospel had not been heard. To us, what was intriguing about this group was that it was not about geography but about *ethne-* or people groups. Perhaps the better way to explain the concept is "pockets of people sharing language or ethnic background". In any country, region or urban areas, somehow there are **always small pockets of people, usually not the majority and who have never heard the name Jesus.** It could be Vietnamese refugees in Maine, or Afghani taxi drivers in the San Francisco Bay area, or Thai construction workers in Singapore, or **even foreign students on college campuses.** (bold type and underlining added by author)

And then there are **some who may have heard the name Jesus but are unclear about his identity.** To the Muslims, Jesus is prophet, Isa – a figure in the Koran, born of Mariam and Yusuf. To the Hindus, he's a name among 300 *million* other names of various deities, some with clear descriptions or prescriptions yet "Jesus" remains rather vague to many Hindus. To Buddhists, he may have been another enlightened one. And in most of South (Indian subcontinent) and East Asia, Jesus is god of the Westerners, who came with the thievery and violence of Colonialism!

The process to establish outreach work or a base in Singapore took seven years, a long time when compared to today when it can be done online in two minutes! The time was not ripe since in multi-religious Singapore there are sensitivities about proselytizing among religious groups. However, I persisted as the call to me was clear, and had been affirmed by the Director of the Training Program at church and others along the way. This start-up group was a well-knit group of 8 believers of different backgrounds (gender, church, ethnicity), each convinced by God that this was His plan. It certainly was not my idea.

During the long years, I had a "few discussions" with God. I wanted to know why Singapore needed another missions sending group when so many other well known groups were already established here. Plus I had no qualifications, prior missions experience - field or office.

The last two pieces came with a clarity that still takes my breath away. **I was at a prayer meeting in another country, when an absolute stranger came up to me and said: "God has a word for you.** You are like an eagle waiting, perched high up and when the right wind current comes along, you'll step off and soar. Something you've been waiting for will come to pass. God knows you will do what he tells you to do." Within two weeks of receiving that word of knowledge, yet another stranger called me from another country one morning at 7 a.m. and said – "I understand that you want to register a sending base in Singapore. I have one to give to you!"

And that is how we received a registered non-profit company.

He (God) did let me know through words of knowledge from strangers. And what has been the impact of this group?

This agency has been used by God to send out more than 40 cross-cultural workers from around Asia to other parts of Asia, to share good news with those who have never heard!

I began to visit some of these cross cultural workers and one day while I was stretching my legs after a long taxi drive to the Pamir knot, **again I heard *that* audible voice saying to me: "For the next ten years, you'll go on the road praying".**

My two traveling companions for the day heard nothing. However, they did share that when we had met casually the afternoon before, and they had declined my invitation to share a cab from the silk route capital to the Pamir knot, both of them had separately heard from God: "Go with this woman to pray wherever she is going to pray." They showed up at 7 am at the city gate where we were to start our taxi ride.

At the Pamir knot there is an old stone fortification that has lain for centuries on this plain between the "~stans" (Pakistan, Afghanistan, Kyrygyztan and Kazakhstan) on the west, and a glaciated Himalayan mountain to the east. It is a wide sweeping area with China to the east and India to the southeast. The taxi driver pointed to a gap in the western mountains and told us that there was a small border station (now closed) from China to Afghanistan (through the Wakan corridor) where the infamous terrorist Osama bin Laden was thought to be hiding. **The 3 of us prayed at the stone fort that God would allow His good news to flow from East to Western China, and that this knot would be "untied" so that the good news could go flow further west through Central Asia and ultimately to West Asia.** This corresponds to the vision that China's Chinese will take the gospel "back to Jerusalem."

It has been ten years since that trip and I have never seen those two gentlemen again, yet God's word has come to pass as I have travelled to the 10 ASEAN nations, five countries around India and a few more in East Asia. The door to these places has often been opened by major natural disasters like massive earthquakes and tsunamis, cyclones and typhoons, epic floods.

I've been to villages with no known local believers, and countries where there is strong opposition or persecution against the gospel. In some of these places where I've prayed with teams of local believers, I have now met new followers of Jesus, individuals who have told me that they have had recurrent dreams or repeated visits from a man in white who has spoken to them and told them that his name is Isa or Jesus, and to follow him. Among these are *imams* (leaders in mosques), housewives, maids, farmers and fishermen.

As I look back on this 40 year journey, I realize that perhaps my understanding of what God is up to in this day and age is too limiting of who He is. Just two months ago, I realized that 65 out of 66 books in the Bible record actual events that took place a long time ago, close to maybe 2,000 years ago. And I thought perhaps I should pay more attention to the one book that still lies ahead, Revelation. So that is a "work in progress." **By being involved in community development and relief work, I've had opportunity to pray in and through these places and see greater numbers coming to know and follow Jesus.**

I long to understand how I can harness or harvest even more resources for relief and perhaps "re-formatting logistics and transporting" of subsidized food surpluses to the people in the other corner of the world that are starving. Or how to harness inexpensive technology to improve yields, re-capture water run-off to irrigate parched land and tap on God's organic know-how to reduce toxicity in our food and environment. **One area where I have seen a remarkable shift in my belief system has been in the area of understanding the authority God has given to us, and the power that resides in us to use memorized scripture to proclaim good things and bind up evil, to speak in prayer and expect miracles,** like cancerous tumors disappear. Rather than discuss whether gift of tongues and prophesies exist today, I prefer to hear those who are so gifted in unknown tongues and the interpretation to see those things come to pass that are not in realm of logic, natural or normal. Well, that is my God!

God's package deal of forgiveness, grace, His gift of the Holy Spirit to me, to everyone is unlimited, even knowable although some [gifts] may be beyond our imagination and thoughts . . . (beginning with rest—He's a strong advocate.) He promises safe and comfortable places to rest; he tells us not to be anxious or worried about food, clothes.

I am constantly provoked to consider the next and perhaps last chapter of my life – what did He create me to do, apart from worshipping Him?

(Email from Suyin to Dr. Jack Burke, 10/8/2013)

MEET INDIA'S BAKHT SINGH

INTERNATIONAL STUDENT IN ENGLAND & CANADA, BECAME FOREMOST EVANGELIST, REVIVALIST, AND WORLD-RENOWNED N. T. CHURCH PLANTER OF 20th CENTURY INDIA

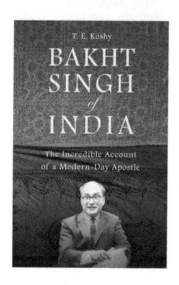

Figure 11 Brother Bakht Singh of India: The Incredible Account of a Modern Day Apostle*

The book titled <u>Brother Bakht Singh of India</u> written by Dr. T.E. Koshy, a beloved friend of mine from the past, focused on the life of **an outstanding international student returnee to India. Bakht Singh became a most dynamic force for Christ in India.** *The book was written by a close associate of Brother Bakht Singh and founding elder of the International Assembly Church based in Syracuse, NY, T.E. Khosy. D'Ann and I were privileged to have met and heard Bakht Singh speak to a group in Pasadena, CA, in the late 1950's. Bakht Singh was actively engaged in ministry throughout most of his life. September 17, 2000 was the day when the Lord welcomed him "home" to his heavenly reward.

I enjoyed working alongside the book's author, T.E. Khosy, while he too was in ACMI's Board leadership in the 1980's and early 1990's.

In the book's outer jacket, the writer stated, "This is an amazing account of a marvelous movement of God through a man who in his youth-growing up in colonial India as a Sikh, hated Christ, the Bible and Christians. While studying engineering in England, he became an atheist, renouncing his Sikh religion and any other form of religious faith; yet while on his way to Canada for his summer holidays on board a ship, God's irresistible and amazing grace reached out to him. After his miraculous conversion to Christ, he became a true disciple of the Lord Jesus, seeking and doing the will of God at any cost . . . **This book narrates how the Lord led him to establish indigenous local churches, patterned after New Testament principles which helped to dispel the misconception of those who think that Christianity is 'foreign' and not relevant to the people of India.**"[18] Dr. Khosy started his book by describing Brother Bakht Singh as "God's man with God's message calling people to God and to His Word. In the early thirties, **Bakht Singh, a Sikh convert to Christ, returned to Bombay, India from Canada having had his education in the West. Little did he realize then that the God of love was going to use him mightily as His vessel to do a new thing in India, to bring about an unprecedented spiritual reformation and revolution of love based on the Word of God.**"[19]

Then Dr. Khosy quoted Dave Hunt who wrote, "The arrival of Bakht Singh turned the churches of Madras upside down. Upset because their members, who were nearly all **nominal Christians, were being converted by thousands through his preaching, crowds gathered in the open air, as many as twelve thousand, on one occasion, to hear this man of God preach.** Many seriously ill were healed when Bakht Singh prayed for them, even deaf and dumb began to hear and speak.[20] "Bakht Singh was equally at home with the poor and down-trodden of rural India as well as with the sophisticated urban India."[21] [He could do this through his upbringing, his education and during his days as an international student in England and Canada.] Among the examples Dr. Khoshy cited was **Bakht Singh "made Christianity relevant to the people of India.** The majority of Indians still believe that Christianity is essentially a religion of the West, and one could not be a Christian and an Indian at the same time."[22] [Helped tremendously that Bakht Singh was also a fellow-citizen of India for it illustrates how indigenous Christians have a distinct advantage in ministering to their fellow citizens.] Note what T.E. Khosy said next about Brother Bakht Singh: "People regardless of their religion, cast or class followed the Christ of the New Testament without having to follow Western culture. He applied the New Testament principles of the Church within the cultural background of the people of India without contradicting the Word of God." [23]

MEET REV. MICHAEL CASSIDY[24]

Amazing Story of a Christian Former International Student; Returned Home with the Vision of Reaching not only South Africa but also the Continent of Africa for Christ

Introduction

Source of Information on Michael Cassidy

Though I am familiar with much of the following information because of its coming through the Fuller Seminary alumni news, the source of all other information for this article came from the internet under the website address (https://africanenterprise.org/michael-cassidy/)

- **Born and Raised in South Africa**
- **Former International Student in England & USA**
- **Christian Leader in South Africa & African Continent**
- **Founder of African Enterprise (AE)**
- **Michael Cassidy's vision in his own words:**

To become the most faithful and effective evangelistic catalyst for holistic evangelism in Africa.

Michael Cassidy's Mission

- To evangelize the cities of Africa through word and deed in partnership with the church.

Michael Cassidy is the Founder of African Enterprise (AE), and has been involved in evangelism, teaching and leadership ministries since 1962, the year he launched AE with a mission to Pietermaritzburg, South Africa. Since then, he has led numerous missions to cities throughout Africa, as well as in other parts of the world, including Australia, Belgium, Costa Rica, Israel, Nicaragua and Panama.

Michael was born in Johannesburg, and grew up in Lesotho but what made him an international student was receiving a Master in Modern and Medieval Languages from Cambridge University in England and a Bachelor of Divinity from Fuller Theological Seminary in California. Cassidy launched African Enterprise in 1962 with the assistance of four seminary friends via an evangelistic mission to Pietermaritzburg.

Out to make the impossible dream possible

Michael Cassidy has become a significant Christian leader in South Africa and across the African continent leading hundreds of evangelistic mission[s] and calling Christians together via the South African Congress on Mission and Evangelism in 1972, the Pan African Christian Leadership Assembly in 1976 and 1994, the South African Christian Leadership Assembly in 1979 and 2003, the National Initiative for Reconciliation in 1985 and the National Initiative for the Reformation of South Africa in 2008.

Cassidy's achievements in ministry would include:

- Led numerous missions to cities throughout Africa . . . Evangelizing cities of Africa . . . led numerous missions in other parts of the world . . .To further the accomplishment of AE's mission – Cassidy's team evangelized Cities of Africa through Word and Deed in Partnership with the Church – he has established evangelistic teams in Congo (DRC), Ethiopia, Ghana, Kenya, Malawi, Rwanda, South Africa, Tanzania, Uganda and Zimbabwe . . . Instrumental in calling several major gatherings of African church leaders,

"These included 'the South African Congress on Mission and Evangelism in Durban in 1973, the Pan African Christian Leadership Assembly (PACLA) in Nairobi in 1976 and 1994 and the South African Christian Leadership Assembly (SACLA) in Pretoria in 1979 and 2003. In 1985, in the deepening polarisation of South African society."

- Launched the National Initiative for Reconciliation.

"This attracted church leaders of widely disparate denominations and races for the purpose of reconciling with one another and implementing this practice in their respective churches and communities. He was one of the leaders of the historic National Conference of Church Leaders at Rustenburg in 1990, and in 1993 chaired a Consultation on Human Rights and Religious Freedom in Pietermaritzburg. In 2009, he spearheaded the National Initiative for the Reformation of South Africa."

- "Involved in South Africa in behind-the-scenes facilitation of initiatives which have brought together a wide spectrum of political leadership in dialogue."
- "Widely acknowledged miraculously peaceful South African election in April 1994. In 1996, at the request of President Nelson Mandela, he and other church leaders were deeply involved in spearheading Project Ukuthula, an extensive and successful peace initiative in KwaZulu-Natal in the run-up to the province's local government elections. Most recently, he has been involved with the Marriage Alliance of South Africa, an interdenominational Christian concern seeking to keep marriage in South Africa heterosexual and monogamous."
- Author of numerous books, including "A Witness For Ever – The Dawning of Democracy in South Africa, which recounts much of the work of some of the backstage players in the run-up to South Africa's 1994 election, as well as a two-month devotional called Michael Cassidy's Window on the Word. Some of his other books are: The Politics of Love, The Passing Summer, Chasing the Wind, Bursting the Wineskins, The Relationship Tangle and

Where Are You Taking the World Anyway? African Harvest by Anne Coomes tells the story of both Michael Cassidy and of the African Enterprise ministry. He has most recently written *Getting to the Heart of Things – Reflections on Christian Basics* and *"What On Earth Are You Thinking for Heaven's Sake?"*

Honors

"In 2012 he was made the Honorary Chairman of the Lausanne Movement for World Evangelization, succeeding the late John Stott, and was also made the Distinguished Alumnus of the year at Fuller Theological Seminary in California.

"Received an honorary Doctor of Humane Letters from Azusa Pacific University (1993), in 1983 he was admitted to the Order of Simon of Cyrene, the highest honor accorded a layman by the Anglican Church of Southern Africa. The Rotary Foundation of Rotary International made him a Paul Harris Fellow and he received the St. Michael's Award from Michaelhouse School in 1997."[25]

AUTHOR'S PERSONAL WORD

I have heard nothing but praise from Fuller Seminary about Michael Cassidy, one of Fuller's most distinguished graduates. Concluding his years as an international student Cassidy returned to his country, South Africa, and has had a significant influence for Christ not only in South Africa but also Africa as a continent. In asking the ACMI network of those engaged in international student ministry for recommendations of alumni who returned to their homelands and made an impact for Christ, Bruce McDowell, Missions Minister at Philadelphia's Tenth Presbyterian Church (a church made famous by former minister Donald Gray Barnhouse), provided an enthusiastic endorsement for Michael Cassidy. McDowell informed me his church has supported Michael Cassidy since African Enterprise's beginning.

(African Enterprise now has a staff of 600.)

You can't help but find the additional stories found in chapter 15 also fascinating. They are about other Christian international students who upon returning to their home countries entered ministries of service to our Lord and Savior Jesus Christ. They are truly missionaries, more effective than most, to their own people.

Chapter

MY EXPERIENCES WITH FAMOUS FAMILIES FROM WHOM SOME INTERNATIONAL STUDENTS CAME

- BRITISH PRIME MINISTER
- HONG KONG MANUFACTURER, BILLIONAIRE, PHILAN THROPIST
- MAYOR OF TAIPEI, TAIWAN
- INDIA ARMY GENERAL

British Prime Minister Harold Wilson

WHILE SERVING AS DIRECTOR of the International Services Office at the University of Pennsylvania in Philadelphia I received a call from the British Consul General whose office was located in Philadelphia. He informed me that British Prime Minister Harold Wilson was making a "secret visit" to Philadelphia after having addressed the United Nations and a meeting with President Johnson in the White House. Before returning to London he and Mrs. Wilson wanted to visit their son, Robin, a graduate student at Penn. D'Ann's and my name had been submitted by Robin to the British Consul General as friends to be invited to join the small gathering to meet his mother and famous father at a dinner and reception which followed at the Consul General's home on the outskirts of Philadelphia.

That invitation led to a scurry of activity in preparation for the evening with the PM. It was to be a formal event. Our next door neighbors on both sides reported to us that they had been visited by FBI agents to check us out. An FBI agent visited me at my office to discuss the security that had gone into the preparation for the evening event.

In approaching the British Consul General's home, we were stopped by FBI agents soon after entering the long driveway. We were instructed to leave any purses or bags in the screened entry way to the house. Soon after entering the home we were introduced to Prime Minister Harold Wilson. Later I noticed him leaving the people he had been talking with and walked across the rather large living room to greet us. The Prime Minister said that Robin had asked him if he knew Mr. and Mrs. Burke, to which he reported that he replied, "Of course I do." As an aside we learned a lesson from the Prime Minister about an application for the word "perseverance." Following a compliment which I had paid him regarding the way he had handled a tough Zimbabwe situation, he said that he had learned early on that if you do not succeed in your first effort at something important, keep trying even if you fail repeatedly. He continued by tapping me on the shoulder with pipe in hand as he made his salient point, there is always the "fourteenth time" which brings success.

In meeting with the "First Lady," the British Press Secretary, and others in the entourage who at times are in the news themselves, makes a statement about the distinguished family backgrounds and executive positions held by the parents of many of our international students.

In December D'Ann and I were pleasantly surprised to receive a Christmas card from Number 10 Downing Street in London, signed by the British Prime Minister.

HONG KONG MANUFACTURER, BILLIONAIRE, PHILANTHROPIST

Dr. Tin Ka Ping, after having been presented with Hong Kong's highest award, the Grand Bauhinia Award Sam Tin sent me the following information about the presentation of the award. "The Hong Kong Chief Executive presented honours and awards to 286 recipients at the 2010 Honours & Awards Ceremony at Government House, on 23 Nov. My father (Dr Tin Ka Ping) was the one awarded the Grand Bauhinia Medal along with 6 other people. (The Grand Bauhinia Medal [GBM], the highest award under the HKSAR* honours and awards system, is to recognize the selected person's life-long and highly significant contribution to the well-being of Hong Kong.) My brother Wingsin and I took the photo after ceremony." (Sam Tin's email to Dr. Jack Burke, December 16, 2013.)

Considering Hong Kong's population this year reached 7,405,685* that indeed is a great honor to be singled out by Hong Kong's honours and awards system to win such a highly distinguished award.

*According to http://worldpopulationreview.com/countries/hong-kong -population

On March 22, 2011 Tin Ka-ping was awarded the "Doctor of Social Sciences honoris causa" confirmed by Hong Kong's elite Hong Kong University. (Sam Tin's email to Dr. Burke, dated December 11, 2013.) According to Sam Tin, "my father has received more than a dozen Honorary Doctoral Degrees from universities in Hong Kong and China." (author underlined) (Sam Tin's email to Dr. Burke, dated April 30, 2011)

I found my jaw dropping in awe upon seeing all the awards and honors received by Dr. Tin displayed in the Tin family museum. One was Queen Elizabeth placing a ribbon with award medal around Dr. Tin's neck in a face to face pose.

Upon arrival at the Hong Kong Airport in May 2013 while making an inquiry at the Information Booth I mentioned Tin Ka Ping's name. The receptionist's enthusiastic response was "I know who he is." We found out from another airport employee that Sam Tin had sent a Mercedes and driver to the airport to pick us up on arrival. Sam was delayed because of an important meeting.

A University of Houston alumnus who lives in Hong Kong, Millar Tsoi, contacted me some years back telling me that he had seen Dr. Tin on a television series featuring Hong Kong's billionaires.

There is much more material that shows the fame of Dr. Tin, Sr. through his philanthropic giving to educational institutions, hospitals and the building of bridges. You can understand his top priority to educate the masses in China, but why bridges? It was as a memorial to the many people in China who had drowned during his youth who were trying to cross the town's swollen river. A bridge provided the protection for the community where he grew up but also other Chinese communities as well.

However, in deference to Sam Tin's request to "maintain a low profile for my father regarding his reputation and fame . . . [but] rather **emphasize the reflection of grace and glory of the Lord on him,**" I will not go further than to make Dr. Tin, Sr.'s testimony available to you. **Here is what Dr. Tin, a 95 year old convert to Christ said during the baptism ceremony on May 27, 2013 at Hong Kong's Yan Fook Church.** (That you will recall is where University of Houston graduate, **Rev. Patrick So, serves as Sr. Pastor and was the one who led Dr. Tin, Sr. to commit his life to Christ, as well as to perform the baptism.) Rarely does one meet anyone of Dr. Tin, Sr's fame and fortune in one's lifetime. I found the following testimony of Dr. Tin Ka Ping priceless.**

Dear brothers and sisters, relatives and friends,

Standing here in front of you today feels different and funny. There have been many occasions when I am asked to give speeches; often, I am indulged with undeserving honors from the generosity of friends. Similarly, friends from different corners of the world are here today, but not for my honor — **we've gathered here to honor the name of God.**

A lot of people don't understand why I believe in Jesus. Quite frankly, I have lived by good conscience throughout my life; I am unashamed to call myself a good man even before I've come to know Jesus. Yet, a "good man" in the definition of a "good man" is not perfect. I may be flawless in the eyes of men; but in front of God, I am a sinner. Pastor So once likened it to our visiting a patient in the isolation ward of a hospital: no matter how many times we have washed ourselves, there would still be germs and bacteria on us. We cannot just walk into the isolation ward even though we are considered "clean" in the eyes of men. The seeming dilemma is that, there's no righteous man in the eyes of God but, on the other hand, everyone can become righteous — as long as he is willing to accept Jesus Christ as his savior.

My contact with Christianity began in the days of my youth back in my hometown in Dabu, Guangdong. Many missionaries were around back then, preaching Gospel and teaching children to sing. I did not pay much attention to what they were preaching but greatly respect their willingness to serve. Even though **I am accepting Christ only at this old age of 95,**

I must say, however, that I have always admired the selflessness of Jesus and the Christian teaching of loving one another. Accordingly, I have always taken Jesus as an example to follow even before accepting Christ. I have always told the Chinese officials not to prohibit Christianity in the Mainland China. If we want to improve the quality of our people, to change the life of each person, we need the Gospel.

It is by God's grace that I have come to Him; but there are also a lot of people that I wish to thank. First of all, my wife and many of my children are Christians; they have been praying for me for many years. My four daughters are here from Australia, the United States of America, and Canada for my baptism today. Many of my friends have also showed their love and care by constantly remembering me in prayers — I wish to thank each of you. Last but not least, **I must give special thanks to Pastor So. Pastor So has been a friend with my son for almost 40 years and has been perseveringly waiting for this day. Regardless of how busy he is with church work, he regularly visits me at home to read the Bible, to share the Gospel, and to pray for my need.** I'm going to be honest: there have been times when I feel really tired and uninterested, but his passion and persistence have touched me deeply.

I pray to God every day for a closer relationship with Him. There are teachings in the Bible that I still find hard to understand. Indeed, I may not be a "qualified" Christian to many people's standards. However, as it is written, "For with the heart a person believes, resulting in righteousness, and with the mouth he confesses, resulting in salvation." (Romans 10:10). By faith, I am willing to take this step forward to accept Jesus as my personal savior. I believe that God, as real as He is, would open my heart and let me get closer to Him and get to know Him more dearly.

Finally, I wish to thank all my friends for coming to my baptism today. There are so many of you that I apologize for not being able to mention names one by one. Some officials from the Mainland [China] are here today; I thank you for your coming, and I urge you to try **exploring the Gospel** to see if Jesus is worth the faith. I must extend special appreciation to **Dr. and Mrs. Burke** for coming all the way from Houston, Texas to witness my baptism. The Burkes have been my friends for over 40 years. I know what it is like to take such a long-haul trip at this age — I'm so grateful and feel undeserving of this kindness. My children tell me that nothing — not any honorary degrees or medals — compares to my acceptance of

Christ. This is why everyone is so excited and enthusiastic to be here to share the joy. I humbly accept all your loving kindness.

Glory to God in the Highest.

TAIPEI, TAIWAN'S MAYOR GAO

I had heard about the admission of Chen Yuan Gao, the Mayor of Taiwan's son prior to his arrival at the University of Houston in 1979. Therefore, I was looking forward to meeting him. During the days of orientation for the new international students somehow I missed meeting him. In attending the soccer game the last day of orientation I was told that there was a sick student among the group. Realizing the Student Health Center at the University was closed, my wife and I decided to take him home and help see him through the weekend until the Student Health Center would be open for business on Monday morning. We felt that it would be quite expensive to take this student, not yet having medical insurance, to a hospital emergency room.

At home I put a call in to Dr. James Whitehurst, the director of the Student Health Center, to report that we had a sick international student at our house. He told me to take his temperature every 3 hours and to give him a call if it increased over 104 degrees. He said also to keep him hydrated and give him an aspirin at regulated times throughout the weekend. Also I called Dr. Ernest Schwaiger whose wife Mary was a key volunteer in administering our office's International Friendship Program. He added his advice to that received from Dr. Whitehurst.

Although "Cheyenne" (Chen Yaun's nickname) did not feel like talking or eating anything of substance, he seemed content just to lie in bed and sleep. Either D'Ann or I would monitor his temperature and give him an aspirin at the appointed times throughout the night.

On Sunday morning, we received a call from a professor at the University who had originally come to the states himself from Taiwan. Through the grapevine the professor had heard about Cheyenne Gao being sick and that we were taking care of him in our house. The professor asked, "Do you know who you have in your house is the Mayor of Taipei's son?" I was greatly surprised that the student we had been looking for during orientation was in our house. The professor went on to say, "You should take him to the hospital." I told him that I was in contact with the university's director of the Student Health Center and he did not feel that such a move was currently necessary. Following that conversation I told Cheyenne that I had been looking for the Mayor of Taipei's son during orientation but did not find him. Cheyenne's reply was classic. "Here you took him home and had him in your hip pocket all the time." (Right there I could see Cheyenne had a sense of humor.)

Needless to say, we took Cheyenne to the Student Health Center when the Center opened for business on Monday morning.

Although that is less than the ideal way to become acquainted with a student, that relationship blossomed. The following summer D'Ann and I were invited by the Taiwan Consulate's leadership in Houston to be among a dozen counterparts from U.S. universities across the country to visit Taiwan. While in Taipei an appointment was set up for us to visit Cheyenne Gao's locally famous father, the Mayor of Taipei, in his office. When we arrived at the Mayor's office there was a camera crew awaiting our arrival from a local television station ready to televise the meeting between Mayor Gao and ourselves. Although we were able to watch the interview on the evening news we could not understand a word of what the station news person was saying because of course it was all in Chinese. One evening before our group's tour of Taiwan educational institutions had ended, D'Ann and I were invited to the Mayor's home on Green Mountain for dinner. Cheyenne was with us. It turned out to be such a delightful evening visiting with the Mayor and his family.

I might add that wherever we traveled D'Ann and I looked for opportunities to be witnesses for Christ. Back at the University there were "opportunities" with Cheyenne because I was able to spend quite a bit of time with Cheyenne during sessions in which he was teaching me key phrases in the Chinese Mandarin dialect I would need for traveling in Taiwan and China.

As an aside, D'Ann arranged for Ralph Lee, a Christian bank president in Houston, and his wife to be Cheyenne's friendship family. During a trip to Taiwan, Ralph spent time on the golf course with Mayor Gao. Knowing Ralph I'm sure he found opportunities to converse with Mayor Gao about faith-related matters.

SANJAY'S (fictitious name) FATHER – INDIA ARMY GENERAL

At the University of Houston, another example would be Sanjay (last name not listed) from India. When it became known that the immediate past president of India was coming to Houston to have open heart surgery at the St. Luke's Hospital in the Texas Medical Center, Sanjay came to my office and asked if I would like to meet the immediate past president, Zail Singh. Of course I assured him that I would be honored to meet India's former president. So Sanjay contacted his prestigious father, a top general in the India army, who then made the necessary arrangements through the Embassy of India in Washington, DC, for me to meet the President of India. When the appointment time came I had secured permission also for my office associate director, Anita Gaines, to accompany me for the meeting. After passing through security we were escorted to the hospital suite of the President. (In walking to the room we noted the entire floor was closed to the public.) There we met the President and his accompanying family members. During the visit I told the President that we were Christians and would be praying for him, knowing that he was scheduled for open-heart surgery the next day. Past President Zail Singh's reply was a warm thank you and added, "Prayer is the best medicine."

10

Chapter

WHY INTERNATIONAL STUDENTS ARE SO STRATEGICALLY IMPORTANT

INTERNATIONAL STUDENTS HAVE THE potential of being the very people who can best fulfill the Great Commission, especially when it comes to "making disciples of all nations." (Matt. 28:19) Simply put, they come from those nations which Christ was talking about. They are much more effective in communicating the gospel to their people than strangers from other nations. The point has been made before, they should be. They know the language, culture and customs of their people. They are citizens of those countries. This is home to them. The same was true on the Day of Pentecost spoken of in Acts 2 when people were gathered in Jerusalem from 17 nations. Peter preached. They received Christ as Savior. They went home to share the "good news" that they had heard when they were involved in the Day of Pentecost in Jerusalem. Now, who could have done a better job of communicating the Gospel to people of these countries than returning fellow citizens?

Through my contact with international students over the past 60 year career of working with international students professionally and as a volunteer, I have been impressed by the number who are the sons and daughters of world leaders in government, business, the military and education. Their families are truly the "movers and shakers" in their countries. Most of the Christians, whom it has been my privilege to know personally, or have heard about, have made an impact for Christ upon their return home and have been most influential in their own cultures.

By contrast, while visiting a church in Hong Kong in 2001, whose pastors were English speaking American and Australian missionaries, I noted that there were only16 in attendance, mostly Filipino maids. I am sure there must be larger churches in Hong Kong with pastors from Western countries. But according to Patrick So, they are mostly effective when they serve in English speaking churches. The next Sunday D'Ann and I visited Yan Fook Church, the mega-church whose pastor is Dr. Patrick So whom you have already read about. This large mega-church was packed with well over a thousand people. He spoke in the Cantonese dialect of Chinese. (I would assume in perfect Cantonese dialect and with no accent either.)

Upon graduation from Fuller Seminary, as mentioned earlier D'Ann and I traveled to a home in Damascus, Syria, with two brothers who were Syrian students who had become Christians while studying at Pasadena City College, a prestigious community college in Southern California. It was interesting to observe the two brothers' relationship with other family members, especially their father who was head of the General Motors car agency in Damascus. We were able to capture their visits on film at the home of relatives, also with their close friends on a trip to a mountain resort, a Syrian Orthodox Church, and to those at a missionary compound in Damascus. This point bears repeating, <u>the missionaries said "they would never have had the opportunity to visit with people at this high level of society had we not brought them to their mission's headquarters in Damascus.</u>" (author underlined)

The logic of international student ministry made simple

Imagine North American missionaries sponsored by various churches in a fictitious city we will name, Longhorn, Texas (could be any other American city). The missionaries need at least two-years of language and culture training (and lots of money) to go to the countries "China, South Korea, and Saudi Arabia." Meanwhile international students from those same countries came to Longhorn, TX, where the missionaries' sponsoring churches are located. The students from China, South Korea, and Saudi

Arabia went to the trouble of studying the English language and culture for at least two years before coming to America. The missionaries from Longhorn struggle to make contact with people in China, South Korea, and as "closet Christians" try to make contacts with Saudi Arabians, a country tightly closed to missionaries. The international students from China, South Korea and Saudi Arabia would like to make contact with friendship families in Longhorn's churches, the sponsoring churches of the missionaries. However, the tragedy is that churches who were enthusiastic about sponsoring the American missionaries going to China, South Korea, and Saudi Arabia lack that same degree of enthusiasm in welcoming students, the future leadership of those same countries who are attending local universities from China, South Korea, and Saudi Arabia, into their homes. Does that make sense? The problem just described is not fictional other than the use of the city's name Longhorn, Texas. It is reality. In my travels throughout the 50 states and discussions with Christian leaders across denominational lines and independents I have found that this problem exists throughout America. Christian leaders, we can no longer afford to ignore this golden opportunity to introduce these students to Christ who are in colleges nearby. What would you do to fix the problem? This book is committed to addressing this problem.

11

Chapter

WORLD LEADERS CURRENT AND FORMER WHO CHOSE U.S. CAMPUSES

THE TRADITION OF SENDING American missionaries abroad worked well for us during the 19th and 20th centuries. It still does to some degree. However, for us not to acknowledge the fact that more than one million of the future world leaders are on our nation's campuses today is a miscalculation of our potential missionary resource. We have to understand that many international students are the sons and daughters of the world's most influential citizens. When they complete their studies and return to their homelands they become budding leaders of their respective countries' governments, businesses, education, military and religious institutions. Just take a look at the following impressive list of world leaders who received training in America before returning to their respective countries of origin. Think of it this way. International students present us with the unique opportunity to share with a nation's citizens the "good news" by reaching their future leaders who are on our campuses today.

The list of world leaders who studied on U.S. campuses was compiled by the U.S. Department of State, Bureau of Educational and Cultural Affairs. To find it, google "International Students as World Leaders" or related title knowing these titles are subject to change. Then click on "**FOREIGN STUDENTS YESTERDAY, WORLD LEADERS TODAY.**"

In going to the internet you can find different lists of international students who came to the U.S. and returned to their countries to eventually become the leaders. The University of Southern California where I received one of my masters degrees and Ph.D. even has their own list of former international students who as alumni eventually rose to the top of their respective country's leadership. The following is another example provided by the internet: List of world leaders who attended school in the USA, **according to USA Study Guide** [26].

Austria	Georg Reisch, Executive Secretary, European Free Trade Association
Argentina	Raul Ricardo Alfonsin, President Guido Di Tella, Minister of Foreign Affairs
Bangladesh	Salma Khan, Divisional Chief, Women's Affairs, Ministry of Planning
Bolivia	Sanchez de Lozada Bustamante, President Jorge Quiroga Ramirez, Vice President
Belgium	Francois-Xavier De Donnea, Mayor of Brussels
Canada	Pierre Elliott Trudeau, Prime Minister
Egypt	Boutros Boutros-Ghali, UN Secretary-General
El Salvador	Francisco Flores, President
Germany	Ernst Carl Julius Albrecht, Prime Minister
Ghana	Kofi Annan, UN Secretary-General
Greece	Adamantios Androutsopoulos, Prime Minister
Indonesia	Juwono Sudarsono, Minister of Defense Yahya Muhaimin, Minister of National Education
Israel	Ehud Barak, Prime Minister
Jordan	Abdullah Bin Al-Hussein, King
Korea	Kang Young Hoon, Prime Minister
Malaysia	Mahathir bin Mohammed, Prime Minister
Mexico	Vicente Fox, President Carlos Salinas de Gortari, President Herminio Blanco Mendoza, Secretary of Commerce/ Industrial Dev.

Monaco	Prince Albert
Nepal	Birendra Bir Birkram Shah Dev, King
Nicaragua	Antonio Lacayo Oyanguren, Minister of Presidency
Pakistan	Benazir Bhutto, President
Peru	Alejandro Toledo, President Alberto Fujimori, President
Philippines	Gloria Macapagal-Arroyo, President Fidel Ramos, President Corazon Cojuangco Aquino, President
Singapore	Goh Chok Tong, Prime Minister
Spain	Javier Solana, NATO Secretary-General
Taiwan	John Chang, Vice Premier Lee Teng-hui, President Chen Li-An, Minister of National Defense Lien Chan, Vice President
Turkey	Suleyman Demirel, President
Zimbabwe	Canaan Sodindo Banana, President

Nobel laureates

The University of Chicago claims 73 recipients of the Nobel Prize amongst its past and present faculty members, students, and researchers. Harvard University has had 38 Nobel laureates as members of its faculty and can also claim three graduates who have received Nobel prizes. The University of California at Berkeley has had 17 Nobel laureates serve as researchers or professors. Numerous other American schools can also boast Nobel prize winners who have either taught or studied at their institutions. If you know of other famous international students from any field or profession who are not on the list, the following editor would like to hear from you. TheEditor@USAStudyGuide.com.[27]

Another article you will find quite informative is **"ARMED WITH US EDUCATION, MANY LEADERS TAKE ON WORLD"** by Ben Wolfgang, The Washington Times, Sunday, August 19, 2012. Of interest the author quotes the State Department as listing "nearly **300 world leaders, current and former, who chose U.S. institutions.**"

In reading the above article, as a strategically minded Christian, one cannot help but think of it in this way. International students present you and the book's author with the unique opportunity to share with a nation's citizens the "good news" <u>by reaching their future leaders who are on our campuses today</u>. As an example a leader from the past is: . . .

Muhammad Zia ul-Haq, General/President of Pakistan
U.S. College Alumnus - Pakistan's General Muhammad Zia-ul-Haq, Pakistan's 6th President, 1977 – 1988

D'Ann and I were eager to meet President Muhammad Zia-ul-Haq at a reception hosted by Houston's Mayor. I have long since lost contact with Muhammad Zia-ul-Haq's host "mother" back in the 1960's. She and her husband's home in Ft. Leavenworth, KS had become Zia-ul-Haq's "home away from home." The Pakistani had become like a son to this couple and they were like parents to him. Years later Muhammad Zia-ul-Haq became a top executive leader of Pakistan. When he was about to become Pakistan's President he invited this American Christian couple to spend some time with him in Washington, DC. While with the one whom they had established such a deep friendship, he invited them to Pakistan as his guests to witness his being sworn into office. He told them that when the ceremony and festivities were over he would take them on a personal tour of Pakistan, which according to the couple he did.

To find more information about General Zia-ul-Haq, Alumnus of U.S. Army Command and General Staff College, Ft. Leavenworth, KS, 1962-64, there are a number of sources found under *Muhammad_*Zia-ul-Haq, 9/23/2014) (also spelled Mohammad Zia-ul-Haq according to Encyclopaedia Britannica, last updated 7-20-1998)

It goes to show once again the many opportunities available for us to share Christ's love with the nations' international students who might just one day become top executives like Muhammad Zia-ul-Haq or manufacturing giants like my Christian former student and good friend, Sam Tin, or senior pastor of a 19 story church in Hong Kong, Patrick So. It is exciting to see how God brings students from non-Christian countries to Christian countries like America to study in fields which will make them highly influential upon their return home. Yet, sad to say, what continues to disappoint me is so relatively few Christians take advantage of this marvelous opportunity to befriend any of these students. I say "marvelous" because of what we miss out on when we don't befriend the future Mohammad Zia-ul-Haqs of this world. The couple referred to from Ft. Leavenworth, KS, whom I spoke with by telephone, would not trade anything for the wonderful experiences she and her husband had through taking some time out to befriend one lonely Pakistani student in Ft. Leavenworth, KS, who "just happened" to turn out eventually to become the country's president.

Many of these students are destined to become the most influential people for Christ or at least "Christian-friendly" in their own countries, yet many church people ignore the opportunity to befriend the Muhammad Zia-ul-Haq's at the closest college. Yet, they still feel, to put it bluntly, they have "bragging rights" to being members of such a mission-minded church. May God forgive our indifference as churches and mission boards for such sins of omission. During missions emphasis month when we sing the missions rallying song with *gusto*, "We've a story to tell to the nations" yet don't bother checking out the closest college to tell that story to a single non-Christian international student. Does that make sense? Raises questions about misplaced priorities, doesn't it? I know someone who is a leader of a church organization that administers two short-term mission trips a year to Beijing. That's commendable. Yet, when urging him to be involved in ministry to the Chinese students at one of the local colleges, his reply was "I have a job. I'm too busy." Could it be that the foreign mission field in most people's eyes is still defined as being <u>overseas</u>? Even when God has brought the mission field to our very own campuses we are slow to recognize that these people are here, for the most part, on a temporary student visa status.

FOREIGN ALUMNI

Have you ever stopped to realize that members of the highest levels of the military from many countries come to the U.S. Army Command and General Staff College (CGSC) in Ft. Leavenworth, KS for training? When you google the CGSC you will find their mission statement. There is a claim that since 1894 more than 50 percent of CGSC International Military Student (IMS) graduates attain the rank of general. Here is a list of some of them:

- Major General <u>Edmund E. Dillon</u> of <u>Trinidad and Tobago Defence Force</u>

- General Rodolfo G. Alvarado of the Philippines
- Prime Minister and General <u>Tran Thien Khiem</u> of <u>South Vietnam</u>
- General <u>DoCaoTri</u> of <u>SouthVietnam</u>
- Major General <u>Edmund E. Dillon</u> of <u>Trinidad and Tobago Defence Force</u>
- General Rodolfo G. Alvarado of the Philippines
- Prime Minister and General <u>Tran Thien Khiem</u> of <u>South Vietnam</u>
- General <u>Do Cao Tri</u> of <u>South Vietnam</u>
- Colonel <u>Le Huy Luyen</u> of <u>South Vietnam</u>
- General <u>Hau Pei-tsun</u> of the Republic of China (Taiwan)
- President <u>Paul Kagame</u> of Rwanda
- Brig Gen <u>Muhoozi Kainerugaba</u> son of Ugandan president, 2007–2008.
- General <u>Muhammad Zia-ul-Haq</u> of Pakistan*
- General <u>Rahimuddin Khan</u> of Pakistan
- General <u>Jehangir Karamat</u> of Pakistan
- General <u>Ashfaq Parvez Kayani</u> of Pakistan
- Brigadier <u>Abdul Shakur Malik</u>Force Commander for the Northern Areas, Acting Director-General Military Training, of Pakistan
- General <u>Eiji Kimizuka</u> of Japan
- General <u>Hisham Jaber</u> of Lebanon
- General <u>Krishnaswamy Sundarji</u> of <u>Indian Army</u>
- Prime Minister and Brigadier-General <u>Lee Hsien Loong</u> of Singapore
- General <u>Dieudonné Kayembe Mbandakulu</u> of the Democratic Republic of the Congo
- President <u>Gaafar Nimeiry</u> of Sudan
- Lt.Col <u>Anastasio Somoza Portocarrero</u> of the Guardia Nacional de Nicaragua
- General <u>Nguyễn Hợp Đoàn</u> of <u>South Vietnam</u>
- General <u>Nguyễn Khánh</u> of <u>South Vietnam</u>
- General <u>Phạm Văn Đồng</u> of <u>South Vietnam</u>
- President and General <u>Susilo Bambang Yudhoyono</u> of Indonesia
- General <u>Veljko Kadijević</u> of <u>Yugoslavia</u>
- General <u>Antonio Domingo Bussi</u> of Argentina
- General <u>Alfredo M. Santos</u> of the Philippines
- General <u>Moeen U Ahmed</u> of Bangladesh
- General Amer Khammash of Jordan

- General <u>Arne Dagfin Dahl</u> of Norway
- General <u>Gustav Hägglund</u> of Finland
- General <u>Avigdor Kahalani</u> of Israel
- General <u>David Tevzadze</u> of Georgia
- Lt. Gen. <u>Rafael Ileto</u>, Secretary of <u>Department of National Defense</u>, Philippines
- General <u>Moeen U Ahmed</u> of <u>Bangladesh</u>
- Minister of War and Chief of Intelligence Amin Howeidy of <u>Egypt</u>
- Général d'armée <u>René Imbot</u>, (<u>fr:René Imbot#États-majors et commandements</u>) Chief of Staff of the French Army, General Director of <u>DGSE</u>, France.
- <u>King Hamad bin Isa Al Khalifa</u> of <u>Bahrain</u>[11]
- General <u>Abdulkadir Sheikh Dini</u> of Somalia
- Colonel <u>Ahmed Mohammed Ali</u> of Egypt
- Lt. Gen <u>Sean McCann</u> of Ireland

6th **President of Pakistan**, 5 July 1977 – 17 August 1988 (**en.wikipedia.org**/wiki/Muhammad_**Zia-ul-Haq**, 9/23/2014)

Cannot emphasize this enough: International Students Today- World Leaders Tomorrow

A central purpose for writing this book is to increase the awareness in the Christian community of the exciting opportunity God has given each one of us to reach the future world leaders for Christ right here in America. They are the international students who are members of the student body at the local college or university right near where you live. I know from personal experience and from a review of US State Department publications that many become world leaders.

Another purpose: since many international students are Christians, we the Christian leadership of our own countries need to grasp the vision for the need to train Christian international students for returning to their own homelands as effective witnesses for Jesus Christ. My prayer is that those responsible for missions goal setting, budgets, and personnel selection will see the need to support missionaries who carry out the Great Commission by reaching international students for Christ and training those who are Christians located right here on our nation's campuses. This most strategic missions' opportunity is grossly overlooked. The one million plus international students from nations around the world attending colleges and universities on our nation's campuses is ample evidence that this constitutes the greatest "blind spot" for foreign missions. The way to fix the problem is for everyone who has an official church or denominational responsibility for carrying out the Great Commission, to realize the potential of international students for being "world changers."

The mindset of the typical Christian traditionally is that the foreign missionary is on the top rung of the ladder in fulfilling Jesus' Great Commission as found in Matthew 28:19-20. That normally translates itself into being an American citizen (or other country in the West) who is selected to be a foreigner himself by becoming a missionary to another country. But there is a more effective way as is described in this book.

Reaching out to international students with potential to become their nations' leaders is at the heart of our missions challenge.

The first international student who comes to mind is Fouad, a Muslim and friendly, outgoing graduate student from Egypt at the University of Pennsylvania. As the newly elected President of the International Student Organization (ISO) Fouad used to come to the International Services Office every day around 4:50 pm, just before closing time, to talk over his ISO plans with me. I soon found that Fouad expected me to help him and the ISO carry out these plans. He invited D'Ann and me over to his apartment to experience an Arab dinner. Wedad, his wife, always served the Arab delicacies with such grace and humility. It wasn't long before Fouad had me working alongside him to carry out plans for an International Week on campus.

Fouad found someone who would help international students form a soccer team. It turned out that someone was Fred Taylor, ISI's staff for Philadelphia at that time. It was not long until Fouad told me about the ISO plans to recruit international students to travel to Los Angeles for the Christmas-New Year's holidays. He explained to me that the ISI staff member was willing to help him make the trip possible. In checking with

Fred Taylor I found that Fred was working with his counterpart in the L.A. area, Max Kershaw. Max had lined up the Hollywood First Presbyterian Church to take care of the local arrangements, including housing and sight-seeing.

As plans developed, students who signed up for the trip flew from Philadelphia to L.A. One of the students who had signed up for the flight from Philadelphia to L.A. was the British Prime Minister Harold Wilson's son, Robin Wilson, a graduate student in mathematics at Penn. Upon arrival in L.A. the international students were assigned to different host families. A tour was arranged for the students to visit Disneyland and see some of the other tourist attractions that Southern California has to offer. An example was the Tournament of Roses Parade in Pasadena around New Years Day. They were also taken to Hollywood's First Presbyterian Church by their hosts to attend a Sunday morning church service. Needless to say, I had never seen an international Muslim student leader like Fouad who was so aggressive and creative in partnering with a Christian organization to carry out such enjoyable activities, including being hosted by church families and attending church together. Fred Taylor and Max Kershaw had teamed up to be of great help to Fouad and the ISO in showing their care for Penn's international students.

At a spring banquet planned by the ISO, Fouad invited ISI's Fred Taylor to be one of his guests and recognized him from the podium for all the help he had provided the ISO. Hearing what Fouad said were the Vice President for Student Affairs, Gene Gisburne and the Provost, Dr. David Goddard who were seated close to the platform. At the ISO's annual meeting to elect a president, Fouad was re-elected President of the International Student Organization, which was a testament to how well Fouad was respected by this ivy league university's international student enrollment of nearly 1,000.

To save money, Fouad and Wedad moved from one apartment building to another. The move turned out to be physically more than Fouad could handle. So much so, that Fouad suffered a heart attack the morning after the move. Being panic stricken, Wedad called me at the office. Frantically, she said, "Come quickly! Fouad is having a heart attack." This happened before Philadelphia had 9-1-1 service. So Bill Carr, my Assistant Director (former IVCF staff) and I jumped in the car and headed for Fouad and Wedad's apartment building, picked up Fouad and Wedad, then raced back to the University of Pennsylvania Hospital. Naturally we prayed much for Fouad during his hospital stay. Sadly, I never did find out whatever happened to Fouad following graduation. I would not have been surprised to find out that he had been elected or appointed to a high office in Egypt, much like Dr. Morsi, a Ph.D. graduate at the University of Southern California, had done in becoming Egypt's first democratically elected President.

12

Chapter

Adapting Global Missions to a Dangerous World

ACCORDING TO THE FORMER Chairman of the Joint Chiefs of Staff Gen. Martin Dempsey "we are living in the most dangerous time in my lifetime, right now." A year later he was more assertive, stating that **the world is "more dangerous than it has ever been."**[28]

Sound familiar? The assertion that we live in a dangerous world should come as no surprise to those who live in many areas of the world. In 2014, according to a Cato Institute Policy Report, the focus of the Cato Institute's 10/25/13 Conference was upon the statement just cited. Now practically all of the nation's government leaders are saying the same thing.

Following the controversial signing of the agreement between America and other nations of the West with Iran over the nuclear issue, Israel's Prime Minister Netanyahu declared that the world was much more dangerous than the day before the signing of the agreement. (Fox News Interview with Netanyahu, 2/14/15.) Also featured in the same Fox News Program was a statement from noted author and conservative commentator, Mark Levin, in which he said, "America is in incredible danger as a result of this [Iranian] regime."

TIME Magazine's cover highlighted the prospect of entering a new era with its singular caption for the entire cover: "World War III," (Cover, Time Magazine, July 2014.)

The threat of cyber space attacks and intervention has brought national fears to a whole new level. Countries including the U.S. feel nuclear threats are surfacing again, making those in America and certain other countries feel terribly unsafe.

Facing Perilous Times to be a Missionary from the West

What does this mean for Christians in North America and other predominately Christian nations who are considering whether to continue sending foreign missionaries to countries hostile to Christianity? If your church or missions organization hasn't re-examined and made some radical changes in recent years to your missions' strategy for reaching other nations with the gospel of Jesus Christ, it's long overdue.

Hardly a day goes by that the news media does not report Islamic extremists who, as followers of their religious beliefs, confront non-Muslims with the ultimatum either convert to Islam or die. While listening to world news you can't help but have picked up the inhumane ways in which Christians are held in captivity and executed by the extremists.

Take a look at what is going on in the Middle East. America's agreement with Iran on the "nuke deal" has caused senators like Lindsey Graham to say that the decision to strike a nuclear agreement with Iran has placed America in the most dangerous situation in his life time.[29] This was a hot topic for the debates of those running for the president in that election cycle.

You could not be living on planet earth if you were not aware of the nuclear threat posed by North Korea now that it is reported that they can reach the U.S. with their rockets with nuclear warheads.

Yes, sadly that's what those on the mission field and prospective missionaries face in today's dangerous world.

Facing Dangers South of the U.S. Border, Other Parts of the World

John Creasman, M.D, Chair, (Ret.), Ophthalmology Dept., Mayo Clinic, Scottsdale, AZ and highly respected personal friend made the following statements in a phone call to me on 12/5/15: "My involvement in Medical Missions in Baja de Norte, Mexico, began one Thursday afternoon in 1972. Two pastors in Mesa, Arizona, contacted me and asked if I would fly them to El Centro, California, to meet a young pastor of a 450 member Baptist church in Mexicali, Baja. Ramon Valenzuela shared his vision for the Mexicali Valley where he stated there was no Evangelical voice throughout this large agricultural area. He determined that the small village of Veracruz was a central location and began visiting it during the week while he still ministered in Mexicali. He eventually moved his family to the village and with the help of the two Mesa ministers was able to build a small home and a small meeting facility for his new church.

I was curious about what was happening, so I visited him in 1974 and began, with the help of friends and members of my church, building a medical clinic on the church property. Within twenty years, 86 individuals had spent time working on this facility and the property. A larger church was built, a basketball court was poured, Junior High kids from Trinity Baptist in Mesa spent a weekend building a fence around the property and landscaping the entrance to the medical building.

During the thirty plus years I visited Veracruz, I crossed the border almost a hundred times taking truck loads of building materials and on one occasion 3000 pounds of beans that had been given to me by a farmer friend from SW Colorado. Nine young men in a Bible Study I was leading pre-fabricated a four room house and assembled it in a neighboring village for a mission pastor who was starting a church. All of these crossings with tons of materials were never questioned when we explained to the border authorities our mission and purpose.

This has all changed in the past five to six years. Moving any materials or medical supplies into Mexico is prohibited. An expensive import license would be prohibitive today. Additionally, I have been warned by my contacts in Veracruz not to attempt to come to the village. As Ramon told me three years ago at my kitchen table, "**Juanito, you will never make it to the village, and you will be lucky if they don't kill you when they hijack your** vehicle". The 'They" to which he was referring is the Mexican Drug Cartel that controls the fifty miles south of the US border. (Dr. John Creasman's phone call to Dr. Jack Burke, 2/8/15)

"Moving any material or medical supplies into Mexico in the way we did in previous decades has become completely unreliable and treacherous. Supplying the Medical Clinic in Vera Cruz requires ingenuity and piece meal planning. It is still a dangerous part of the world, but God has given the people of the village the protection to carry on His work down a productive and inventive pathway. Years of preparing the locals to administer and provide medical care at the clinic have moved this project forward in the Lord's name."

(Notes from phone call from Dr. Creasman to Dr. Jack Burke, 12/5/15) Here is a series of stories related to missions that Dr. Creasman told me: "Walt started coming to church as a teen-ager; he came to the Lord, graduated from Arizona State and went to Indonesia as a missionary. Walt said 'The nationals are most effective.' Went to Brazil and India and continued teaching.

Malcom was a missionary who went to a tribe in Kenya that had never had any mission involvement. He and his wife taught for many years. They go back every few years.

1. Duncan went with Malcom on missions. They can't go to Kenya anymore. It has become too dangerous because of the Muslims. Duncan does not want to be known as a pastor. It's one problem why people do not want to go as missionaries. They don't see it as a life-long calling. Too dangerous. **There is need to train the nationals. They can move in and out**. Duncan is one of those guys who thinks he is immune. His wife is Costa Rican. However, he doesn't want to go to India anymore. The trains are a problem. You can travel a 100 miles, must stand the entire way. No civility. **Terrible experience.**

2. Walt was in and out of Qatar, Bahrain, and other places. Went in there with a couple of missionaries from So. Korea. Took 1 hr. 45 min. to get through customs. Others went through - no problem. (So. Koreans went through – no problem – no question.) Dr. Creasman said: "**We need to let the nationals do the missionary work. Getting harder for Americans.**"

Dr. Creasman continued by telling a problem a young man had in Kenya. On some of the roads he ran into barriers and encountered gun shots. These were not all government road blocks.

In 1971 I remember Dr. Creasman moved from Houston back to Phoenix his home city. A year later he was encouraged to become involved with a young man who was a U.S. citizen. This man went to Mexicali to do missionary work. In a few years he had 450 in his church. In visiting several of the villages he found no evangelicals. Continuing on he went to Veracruz where he established a church. In 1974 he approached people about starting a mission. People were very pleasant. After 2-3 months he noticed that the people started changing their attitude toward him. They blocked him from coming into their homes. He found out that a priest had told the people his friend was a priest from Satan.

Several years went by, Dr. Creasman got involved again. He took a pickup full of material to help build in Mexico. A lady told Dr. Creasman he could take her father's products, beans, across the border. There were several thousand lbs. of beans. People were so happy. **Now everything has changed. It's too dangerous to try doing the same thing**. People steal and make it difficult for you. In a few weeks Dr. Creasman will again take some supplies to the Mexican border. In order to get the products across the border you have to think of creative ways to do it.

By his last count 80 people from church have gone with Dr. Creasman to help build a church. However, a problem of greed arose in the 1980's. The people Dr. Creasman has to deal with "want something under the table" as a result of the cartel having taken over the border.

Dr. Creasman cited other stories of how difficult it has become for him and other Americans in his Sunday School class in Phoenix to do mission work in Mexico. Combined with the other stories the **bottom line is that it has become increasingly difficult for Americans to do mission work not only in Mexico but in other parts of the world**.

(Notes from phone call from Dr. Creasman to Dr. Jack Burke, 12/5/15)

13

Chapter

REASONS WHY SO MANY MISSIONARIES ARE RETURNING HOME FROM THE MISSION FIELD

Dangerous world and economic downturn

CHRIS AND JAMIE SUEL were commissioned by Houston's First [Baptist Church] in 2008 and began serving as missionaries to Kenya the following year, where they have served as church planters in Nairobi. Over the years, they discovered a strategic advantage in engaging university students, mobilizing and training them to reach the unreached in East Africa. "There are fewer barriers when people are trained to reach out to those in their own culture," said Chris. "We provide vision, strategy and training, then we take them on mission." The IMB funds living expenses for Chris, Jamie and their five children, ages 9 to 18. Morningstar, their Life Bible Study class, also offers moral support by writing them throughout the year, and sending e-mails and care packages to make birthdays special for the kids.

Two years ago in September, the Suels survived a terrorist attack at the Nairobi Mall. The family split up and hid as they listened to machine gunfire, exploding hand grenades and helicopters circling overhead. The family kept in contact by cell phone as terrorists tried to lure people out by pretending to be police. Eventually, Jamie and four of the children made it to safety. When Chris and a son moved to locate the rest of the family, they encountered a barrage of gunfire that ricocheted off their escalator. Two hours later the two safely joined the rest of the family. The IMB sent the family home to the States to regroup the following summer. "It's no cheap thing to send seven people to the U.S. for counseling," said Chris. "The IMB also provides living expenses, insurance, vehicles, gas for travel, even some scholarships to help our children attend college." Chris notes that when the family returns to Kenya in February next year there will be fewer than 10 or 12 missionary families remaining in his regional "cluster." Just over 10 years ago, 100 families were on the field to minister in Kenya, Uganda, Rwanda, Burundi and other East African nations.[30]

Retirement

Some missionaries make it all the way to retirement. However, the bar for retirement age has become more flexible and set lower according to friends, former Southern Baptist missionary, Dr. Kathy Kelly, and Conservative Baptist former pastor/former denomination missions leader, Dr. Marvin Webster. From what I gather the idea of a career missionary may be a thing of the past. From the perspective of those who have caught the vision of the future of global missions, there are no better people to fill this vacuum than well-trained Christian international students returning to their homelands.

For some career missionaries there is a very practical reason to return to the U.S. no later than age 66. That's the age American citizens become eligible for Medicare insurance coverage to help pay medical and hospital expenses incurred in the U.S. However, retirees can still be active in global missions. D'Ann and I were brought in by the Southern Baptist International Mission Board's V.P. Bill Wakefield to participate in a training program for missionary retirees at their headquarters in Richmond, Virginia. The purpose was to prepare the former missionaries to transition to a volunteer work with international students, some students being from the very same countries in which they served as career foreign missionaries.

Language and Culture Barriers

Despite the mission agencies attempts to provide the best possible training, there are still problems in this area that are insurmountable for some missionaries. <u>Some have returned to the U.S. because of the language barrier</u>. It is too frustrating for them. The missionaries cannot understand the people and the people in turn cannot understand the missionaries. To illustrate the problem one of my former International Student Counselors at the University of Houston, Margie (Escalera) Foster, wrote about a language problem she had when she was a Southern Baptist Journeyman in Taiwan serving under the International Mission Board as a student worker. Margie entitled it, "WHAT I SAID WAS NOT WHAT I MEANT" "The Taiwanese pastor was driving me home one evening after I had taught an English class at his church. Trying to ease the awkwardness, I asked him in my beginner's Chinese if he ever studied English. He proudly announced that he spoke Taiwanese, Mandarin, Hakka and Japanese but no English. I eagerly offered to teach him English. At least that's what I meant to say. However, he quickly turned towards me with a strange look accompanied by a "Huh?" By the time I could understand what I had said, he had run a red light, hitting the curb. He was busy trying to regain control of the car while I had my hand on the door handle ready to make my escape whenever we stopped. I had eagerly told him I wanted to sleep with him!"

Even receiving language and culture training for a year or two still is not enough to prepare some missionaries to communicate effectively with people who have learned their language and culture since birth. A friend told me that when she was a missionary her husband could not handle the language. It was too frustrating. So they returned to the states. Most people who have studied foreign languages during high school and college can fully appreciate the complexities of communicating in a foreign language. Take idioms of speech, for example. I don't think many Americans fully realize how much of our language is laced with idioms of speech. Also, we have words that sound the same. For example, take the three words "to, too, and two." Since the words all sound the same, the word has to be understood in context.

Dr. Kathy Kelly further explained, "for the missionary to understand the Thai language, he or she has to understand, among other things, the "tone" in which the words are spoken. A tonal difference can completely change the meaning of the word. In Spanish, the language I have studied the most, I have to say in Spanish, "speak more slowly, please." There are many tenses and moods involved in language communication that add to the complexities of learning to speak and write in a foreign language.

When university faculty and staff are invited to speak to newly arrived international students during orientation, they often speak too fast, often using idioms of speech that I know from past experience the non-native speakers of English will find it next to impossible to understand what the speaker is saying. That goes for jokes too because to understand humor one has to understand the cultural context of the joke. Speakers at new international student orientation that try to tell jokes are often disappointed because so few caught the humor so did not laugh.

Even for international students who have grown up speaking English as one of the languages taught in their home country, it is often difficult for them to be understood by Americans because of the heavy accent. Yes, accent. The same holds true for those in other countries who may have studied the English language but when they hear someone from an English speaking country, like America, they have problems understanding what we say. That goes for American missionaries too. When purchasing something in a London department store, I still vividly recall the sales clerk commenting on my American accent, though both of us grew up being native speakers of English. If you have ever tried making an airline reservation with a non-native speaker of English, you know exactly what I mean. That goes also with a computer resource person you contact for help with a computer problem, only to find that the person you are speaking with is foreign with a heavy accent trying to communicate with you in English. To illustrate the differences of culture that can pose a barrier to communication once I tried ordering flowers for a funeral that came a few days before Christmas. The foreign person in India whom I was speaking with did not understand my word "Christmas."

In the opinion of returned missionary, Dr. Kathy Kelly, *"cultural differences are a significant difficulty, probably even more than language, for missionaries. Culture influences our world view and our behavior. It is often the foundation for how we relate to others. Many times conflicts that arise between a missionary and a national have a cultural basis. Often neither party even realizes that culture rather than personal traits are the source of the conflict. The accumulation of many conflicts with nationals on how to work together in ministry as well as frequent clashes with the culture in general, can lead to frustration and despair for the missionary, sometimes to the point of returning home."* (Email from Dr. Kathy Kelly, former Southern Baptist missionary to Thailand, to Dr. Jack Burke – 1/24/2014).

More on Problems Living in an Unsafe Environment Abroad

Not all countries are governed by the same set of laws which most people in America obey. How many times have you heard of missionaries being captured for ransom, imprisoned or killed because of such things as not being a Muslim instead being a Christian (often referred to as an infidel) or trying to convert someone to Christianity in a predominately Muslim country? Why is that? Most often it is because the people there are living under a different set of laws, e.g. Shariah Law for Muslims.

Traffic standards are different. In some countries people drive on the "wrong" side of the highway by American standards. Missionary Dr. Kathy Kelly added, *"I have been in countries where the car horn is often honked because of people's lack of respect for the law and the need to 'bully' one's car through heavy traffic."*

Political upheavals cause people to be cautious when driving in certain parts of town. When my brother Harry was a missionary in Bogota, Colombia he had to avoid driving near a university during a politically upsetting time. His license plates showing that he was an American did not help. People tried to stop his car. At times like that you can have rocks thrown at your car or even have your car torched. In the Wycliffe group house in which he and his family at one time lived, terrorists forcibly gained entrance into the house and kidnapped one whom they mistakenly thought was the group leader. Later the kidnapped Wycliffe American was found dead. Also, people driving the highways in some rural areas where terrorists were known to be in control, were putting their lives at risk.

Not knowing the customs of the people can cause danger to those new to the culture. When my wife and I were in Cairo, Egypt, following the Suez crisis in 1956, we put our lives at risk by having an Egyptian new acquaintance ask a few farmers working by the roadside if we could take a picture of them. (Location was near the Pyramids.) When other farmers in the group saw this they came running to also be in the picture. Following the photo they immediately demanded a "baksheesh" (we found out later it was the word "tip") from us. Having just graduated from seminary D'Ann and I were traveling on a "shoe-string" budget. Plus not understanding their culture, we didn't succumb to their demands. That put our lives in danger we found out later. Fortunately, a city bus arrived just in the "nick of time." However, that did not stop one of the workers. He jumped on the bus with us still demanding the "baksheesh." When the conductor came by to collect our bus fare we noticed that he not only did not ask the worker to pay but did not even ask him to leave the bus for bothering passengers riding in the first class section. (We sacrificed by paying the extra because we felt our lives were being threatened.) We were glad that our young Egyptian new found friend, Farah, who was accompanying us, knew exactly what the custom was, so he gave the worker a tip and the farmer then exited the bus at the next stop. In asking Farah why the bus conductor did not require the worker to pay or ask him to leave the bus for harassing passengers, Farah said, "The next time the bus returned to that part of his bus route, the farmers would have pulled him off the bus and killed him."

Health Problems

Unaccustomed to living in another country where there are differences in food, poor standards of water and air purification, cleanliness, diseases transmitted by insects, perils of attack by wild animals and poisonous snakes, extreme temperature and level of humidity differences, and lack of good medical and dental care, there are many health reasons why missionaries return home at an earlier than anticipated age. Most missions-minded folks read the prayer requests of missionary loved ones, often detailing their health needs, or those of their children and co-workers. Many have to go either to large metropolitan areas in the countries in which they serve, neighboring countries, or return to the U.S. or another country to receive the advanced medical and dental care needed. Often it is more than just "turistas" involved when living abroad. Sometimes it is a deadly serious health issue that brings missionary families home for an extended period of time, which may lead to a permanent move back home.

Political Unrest

Much has been written about the communist takeover of China. At that time many missionaries were compelled to return to their country of origin. Most people who travel abroad are aware of the risks. To check out political risks it is always wise for Americans to be in contact with the U.S. Department of State before making reservations for travel abroad and with the embassy or consulate when visiting abroad.

Conflict on the Missionary Team or with Leadership

This is another significant reason according to Dr. Kelly. *"Unfortunately this is a frequent problem. People who are willing to pick up and move across the world are usually rather independent-minded. That can make it more challenging to work so closely together on teams, especially when so much of your daily life can be intertwined with lives [of] your team members."*
(Email from Dr. Kathy Kelly to Dr. Jack Burke 1/24/14)

In his experience on the mission field my brother Harry told me virtually the same thing existed in one of his mission locations.

Financial

It is understood that missionaries can only stay on the mission field as long as there is financial support to do so. If support drops from their mission agency, churches/denomination that provides support and/or individual donors to the point where the missionaries can no longer afford to stay on the field, they return home.

Children Reaching High School Age or Beyond

Missionaries can get along quite well in meeting the educational needs of their children until high school. Then they meet a bump in the road in trying to locate a high school that will meet the requirements needed by their children at that age level. Choices have to be made whether there is a place for missionary kids to be educated in the part of the world where the mission work is located or a suitable place for the student to live and attend school back in the U.S. To solve the problem it may end up requiring the family to return to the States in order for the children to attend high school. If a student who is a U.S. citizen is still living abroad by the time he or she reaches college age, then he or she normally attends college in the States.

Taking Care of Elderly Parents

When parents of missionaries reach an age where they need extra care, the children of those parents can be worried to the point where they feel the responsible thing for them to do as Christian missionaries is to return home. The Lord led them to the mission field and that same Lord can lead them to return home to give their close loved ones the care they need.

Employment is Terminated

If the missionary is not a self-employed "tent-maker" but instead works for a Christian organization, the missionary's support can be terminated if the missionary does not live up to the "job" requirements. There may even be moral issues involved. Likewise, if the mission agency closes and there is no back-up organization or individuals available to pick up the support, then the missionary may come to the stark reality that it's time to return home.

Conclusion

The difference with the foreign missionary being in the international student's country is that the missionary is a non-citizen and in most countries is living in a totally foreign environment that presents its own set of problems. The problems cited above for the foreign missionary do not apply to the Christian international student who has returned to his/her country of origin, which he/she calls "home."

14

Chapter

CRIES FOR HELP . . . RELIEF IS IN SIGHT

THE SMALL GROUP OF disciples had heard the "last call" from Jesus, "Therefore, go and make disciples of all nations, baptizing them in the name of the Father and of the Son and of the Holy Spirit, and teaching them to obey everything I have commanded you." (Matt. 28:19-20) This has been referred to as "the Great Commission" ever since.

Most disciples were fishermen. They knew what it felt like when challenged by the overwhelming odds of the stormy waves at sea. Now instead of the challenges of the sea, it was all about the global challenge of how to "make disciples of all nations." Can't you just imagine how they felt? On the Day of Pentecost Peter wasted no time when provided the opportunity to speak to the 3,000 gathered from many nations, to recruit volunteers. As a sailor and fisherman he most certainly cried out to any believer and potential believer in sight, "All hands on deck . . . all hands on deck!!!"

The Ethiopian eunuch in charge of all the treasury of Candace, queen of the Ethiopians, upon hearing Philip's explanation of the Scriptures on his return from Jerusalem to Ethiopia, committed his life to Jesus and wanted Philip to baptize him. (Acts 8:26-39) In returning to his country a believer in Christ and "man of influence" he was in position to influence his nation for Christ. The strategy was beginning to take shape of how to make disciples of all nations. It was through foreign people of influence returning to their home countries as followers of Jesus. (Acts 8:26-39)

Throughout the centuries the ripple effect of the Day of Pentecost has been observed. In a study of church history it is exciting to see the many ways in which the gospel has been advanced. However, there are still all too many lonely outposts, especially throughout Asia and Africa, awaiting reinforcements. They are cheered on by thoughts that "the cavalry is coming . . . reinforcements are on their way." But all too often the recruits are just a few lone but dedicated stragglers.

Now, like the Day of Pentecost, we have the chance once again to "make disciples of all nations" through those who return to their own countries with Christ embedded in their hearts. Yes, a golden opportunity has arrived for a potential mighty force far greater than the 3,000 gathered on the Day of Pentecost. God in His sovereignty has opened the flood gates for a potential force of hundreds of thousands to be reached with the gospel, then trained and equipped and sent back to their homelands. We have the opportunity of a lifetime with the over one million of the world's best and brightest who have arrived on intercontinental jet airliners from all over the world to study at our nation's colleges and university campuses. Having the reputation of being the most desirable country in the world to seek a higher education, many of the over one million are the sons and daughters of the world's leaders in government, business, and education. Thousands are scholars who come to do research and teach at our American universities. Additionally, many students come to study English and American culture. What more can you want God to do than to bring a mission field filled with the future world leaders right to your own doorstep?

The facts show that America is by far the nation with the highest number of international students.[31] This amounts to America's modern Day of Pentecost. But what is the church's response? Unfortunately, too little. We are still caught up in the momentum of past centuries. This amounts to recruiting citizens from our own country to learn foreign languages that Christian international students from the countries we are trying to reach already know. Also to learn foreign cultures that Christian international students from those countries already understand. Further, to do this we are bearing an enormous price tag when there are Christian international students available who could share the Christian gospel message to their own people at a fraction of the cost.

To spread the gospel to the other nations more effectively, efficiently, and more economically we need to encourage Americans feeling a call to missionary service to prayerfully consider instead of going overseas to stay at home and minister to international students at colleges and universities loaded with international students. Many of these students who are or become Christians, as we have said before will be returning home to positions of great influence for Christ.

At the same time we need to retool our missionary training centers from preparing Americans to go overseas, to training Americans or permanent residents (or now American citizen internationals) to work with international students on our nation's campuses. Instead of the Americans going overseas it would be the international students returning to their homelands as effective and efficient witnesses for Jesus Christ. It would be Christian international students going to the very same countries American missionaries were planning to go. Instead of supporting American missionaries to go overseas we would be supporting the American missionaries to reach the future world leaders right here on our home turf, at a college or university nearby. Our churches and mission agencies would still be supporting American missionaries. But these missionaries would be training internationals here in America who would be the ones doing the traveling and missionary work, i.e. returning home to countries where they would be doing a much more effective and efficient work for Christ than would the American missionary counterpart if he/she had gone.

On our part we need to recruit Christians from our own country, both professional missionaries and volunteers, e.g. friendship families, campus workers, to be volunteer missionaries to the international students who are on nearby campuses to work with the Christian international students and seekers. We do this by equipping the Christian internationals with training in Biblical-theological studies, preparing them for the rigors of re-entry to their homelands, then sending them out and following them up.

Also, because there is the ecclesiastical 9-1-1 call, it is fellow American citizens who are being recruited to go to certain countries on short-term mission trips lasting from a few weeks to a couple of years, even without fluency in the language and relatively little knowledge of the culture of the country to which they are going. That's all well and good and certainly to some extent should be continued. After all, we still have the problem cited in the Scriptures, the fields are white unto harvest but the laborers are few. (Matt. 9:37)

In conclusion, whether professional or short-term missionaries, it still does not take into consideration the fact, as stated before, that a massive number of the mission field's best and brightest have come to America on temporary student visas, are enrolled in America's colleges and universities, and for the most part, regrettably, are completely ignored by the church. We as Christian Americans need to be aware of this golden opportunity and to awaken to the fact that the world's future "movers and shakers" have come to campuses relatively close to where most of us live. Where are the mission strategists occupying our denominational mission boards and churches when it comes to placing a high priority on designating funds and personnel to reach this strategic mission field that is right on our very doorstep?

On behalf of the relatively small, but growing number of Christian leaders and volunteers who are vigorously involved in ministry to international students we strongly believe that the church for the most part has gone AWOL in reaching out to this most strategic mission field. It has been our experience that most churches have failed to see the potential for global missions that is theirs in reaching, training and equipping international students who are right here before our very eyes. It is surely the church's greatest "blind spot" when it comes to global missions. Let me add, I'm the last person who would ever want to be critical of the church in the decisions it makes. In this case though, I hope you understand. After my 60 years of experience in ministry to international students, this is my conviction as well as that of many others.

Meanwhile, we keep encouraging Christians in those lonely outposts in 10-40 window countries, and other countries in Asia, Africa, and Latin America with the words "the cavalry is coming . . . reinforcements are on the way." Brothers and sisters in Christ, we need to open our eyes to the vision that the potential reinforcements are Christian international students who now are on our nation's campuses. The countries we refer to as "foreign," the students call their homelands.

Christians should recognize that those engaged in ministry to international students are also in reality foreign missionaries themselves who are fulfilling the Great Commission. The big difference is where each group works and with whom they work. The foreign missionary works through traditional channels of reaching the workers of a society with the Gospel. No question but someone needs to continue going through the traditional channels. However, to reach a nation for Christ it makes a lot of sense to begin with those who are Biblically trained Christian international student leaders committed to returning home with the purpose of reaching their nation for Christ.

The ones who are reaching future world leaders are in what's called international student ministry (ISM). They are on staff of some churches but more than likely found working for international student ministry parachurch organizations. They are the ones who are in outreach programs designed to care for the needs of international students, the sons and daughters of the world's elite. Those students have the potential of becoming world leaders themselves after their return home.

It is exciting that these future "movers and shakers" of their own countries are on our nation's campuses today. Therefore, the churches and denominations are given the God-given opportunity and responsibility to share Christ's love with them. For this to be done what should be our first step? We need to move these future foreign leaders up toward the top (ideally the top) of the priority list of global citizens who most certainly need to be reached with the "good news" about our Lord and Savior Jesus Christ while they are still in our midst.

Some might say, "but I had the idea that the international students do not return home at the end of their studies." Some don't but the pendulum is swinging the other way. As the economy improves back home, an increasing number are being lured back to their homelands. I distinctly recall one of my student leaders from India coming to my office at the University of Houston to tell me he had succeeded in his pursuit of the coveted "green card" granting permanent residence in the U.S. following graduation. Despite receiving permanent residence status in the U.S., he also wanted to tell me that he was coming to say "good-by." His father wanted him to return home to take over his business, so the student was moving back to India. As countries improve their economic status, students return home because that's becoming the place where the jobs are. We all know many of the jobs that used to be in America have moved to their countries.

15

Chapter

OTHER CHRISTIAN INTERNATIONAL STUDENTS WHO RETURNED TO THEIR HOMELANDS WITH THE "GOOD NEWS"

I ALREADY SHARED WITH you in chapter 8 about the three Christian international graduates of the University of Houston whom I knew personally before they ever left the University to do great things for the Lord in their homelands. There were stories of two others, one being from the same seminary I attended who upon returning home had a major impact in his ministry upon the entire continent of Africa. The other was one well publicized for his incredibly successful evangelistic ministry in India. There were others who returned home to carry out highly significant ministries. Altogether the institutions attended by these Christian graduates represent a small number of the 4,726 degree granting institutions of higher education in the United States. Think what the total impact for Christ would be if we were to survey every returning Christian international student from the other 4700+ degree-granting U.S. institutions of higher education.[32]

As you read previously, top professionals knowledgeable about the state of the world are saying this is a dangerous world. Now things are growing worse. We are constantly bombarded with these news features every day. There is nothing new about this news.

Before sending our missionaries out to areas where it is dangerous for Americans, we should explore ways in which we can send the message of the gospel out to these countries at less risk. At this point decision-makers whose job is to make decisions on where to send missionaries and whom to support should pray and think more strategically as to best ways to get the message out. Sound like a "tall order?" We believe it can and has been done. The question is "what is the best way to do it?"

Through my 60 years experience as a professional or volunteer in working with sons and daughters of the world's "people of influence" who return to their homelands to eventually become their nations' leaders I am convinced that there is a "best way." That is, as Benjamin Schmoker, one time Executive Secretary of the Committee on Friendly Relations Among Foreign Students (CFR), 1946-1969 (name changed to International Student Service) said in a CFR meeting I attended in 1956 in Pasadena, CA, "the best way to send a message anywhere is to wrap it up in a person." In this context he was referring to sending our message through international students we befriend. Former four-star general and President Dwight Eisenhower (1953-1961) also embraced this idea through his founding of The People-to-People program in 1956 in order to release world tensions and promote peace.

Now who is that person or people who should take the message back to their own country about what they learned during their studies in America? My wife D'Ann and I, together with tens of thousands of others, believe the best of the "people-to-people" scenarios is through an international student or scholar returning to his or her homeland who can share heart-warming stories about friendships developed. We as Christians would hope they would not only be filled with stories about life at the university but also stories to share about close friendships developed with Christian students and Christian families whom they met through a friendship family program at the university or community based, such as the church. Through these friendships many international students have also become followers of Jesus.

Has this method been tried before? Most certainly. When? During the Cold War America invited the best and the brightest of the world's university students who showed promise of being merchants of American idealism and democracy, to come to America to attend its colleges and universities through the U.S. State Department's Exchange Visitor Program, often as

Fulbright scholars. Through the State Department's Bureau of Education and Cultural Affairs, grants were given to the Institute of International Education (IIE) and to NAFSA. NAFSA used the State Department funds to provide support for the national Community Section (COMSEC) for the purposes of strengthening Friendship Family Programs across NAFSA's 12 regions in the United States. The purpose was to achieve peace through cross-cultural programs aimed at bringing international students together with American families. I had the honor of being elected as chair-elect of COMSEC and served as the national chair in 1969-70. Also actively involved in COMSEC was my wife D'Ann. She was elected chair-elect 20 years later, serving as national chair in 1990-91.

The following stories were sent to me from others about Christian former international students who returned to their homelands with the "Good News." Consider this a sequel to chapter 8.

MEET JOHN GABRIEL

International Student at Boise Bible College (Idaho),
Returned to India – established churches, English School,
Bible College, Homes for Orphans

Charles A. Crain, D.Min, Assoc. Minister, Eagle Christian
Church (Idaho), former President, Boise Bible College

International students studying in America are making a big impact for Christ in their home countries. One example is John Gabriel from Pampady, India. John originally came in the 1960's to learn how to manufacture plywood, but ended up building Christ's church.

John came to a mill in Arcata, California managed by Erville Buck a graduate of Boise Bible College. Erville's son was writing a school paper on India. The Buck's invited John to church and Sunday dinner. This became the normal Sunday event for the rest of John's stay.

John became friends with Doyle Farnsworth the preacher. When John returned home Doyle gave him a Bible and urged him to study Acts and Romans. John found a close friend who studied together with him. They became convicted of their need for Christ and together went to the river to confess their faith and to baptize each other.

Hearing the news Doyle encouraged John to return to study at Boise Bible College. John came, graduated, and now is Dr. John Gabriel.

When John returned to his home his father arranged a marriage for John with a beautiful young Indian lady, Kunjamah. John taught her and she also gave her heart to Christ. Together they minister in India.

They have begun more than thirty-five churches, Crossroads English School, Pampady Bible College and several homes for parentless children.

These are fine Christ centered churches. Crossroad English School has over 2000 K-12 students who study English from the Bible. They have rated number one in scholarship out of over 5000 public certified schools.

The Bible College has a nice campus, dormitories, classrooms and cafeteria. The children from the homes study at Crossroads School and attend the churches.

The Gabriel's two daughters Lynn and Liz work in the mission. Lynn has become principal of the school and Liz head of the children's homes. Their Christian husbands are a real help with the mission. Both daughters have earned masters degrees from the university.

I have visited these places three times and found them dynamic, biblically sound, works. This mission is a fine example of the value of welcoming foreign nationals to our homes and churches when they come to study in America.

(Sent by postal mail, Dr. Charles Crain to Dr. Jack Burke, 1/19/2014)

MEET PROF. PETER UBOMBU-JASWA Ph.D.

Former African Students Christian Fellowship leader
University of Wisconsin – Madison
Returned to So. Africa - professor & consultant,
preached at local churches; involved with IFES

Ned Hale, former InterVarsity ISM Director
ACMI Staff Volunteer

Peter, a Ugandan, came to the Univ. of Wisconsin at Madison in the early 1980's to start a PhD in Sociology. He had been part of the Christian East African Revival movement in eastern Uganda, **http://en.wikipedia. org/wiki/East** [he] had gone to Ghana for a masters degree in education and to teach in a high school, and there had met and married Susan, a native of Ghana. They had three daughters in Ghana before he felt the need for more higher education in the field of Sociology. He enrolled in the University of Wisconsin at Madison in the early 1980's, but because of visa issues, had to leave Susan and their three daughters in Ghana when he came to Wisconsin for his Ph.D.

Shortly after arriving at the UW Madison, he became the primary leader of the African Students Christian Fellowship (ASCF) group at the University. (This group had been founded in the mid-1970's by a Kenyan, Watson Omulokoli, while Watson was an IV staff worker serving Wisconsin "IV chapters." Prior to that Watson had been a "traveling secretary" for Scripture Union in East Africa. Watson had been recruited by InterVarsity's President Dr. John W. Alexander, with the help of Kenya's Christian leader, Prof. Kenobi, to help the IV-USA movement become more internationalized and multi-ethnic).

Peter's involvement in the ASCF at the UW Madison brought him into contact with Ned Hale, InterVarsity's National International Student Ministry Director. These two met for prayer and mutual encouragement during Peter's four years of study at UW Madison. Peter endured these years without his family (for the sake of getting his PhD), and was finally rejoined with them when he graduated and got a teaching position at the University in Botswana.

While teaching there he preached in local churches and collaborated with the International Fellowship of Evangelical Students (IFES) to begin a student-led ministry at the University of Botswana, considered at the time a pioneering situation for student ministries in Africa. Later he got a teaching position at the University in Durban, S. Africa. By 2006 he had become a consultant on "Population and Development Integration" with the following address:

Prof. Peter Ubomba-Jaswa, PhD
Population & Development Integration Specialist
[Independent Consultant]
P.O Box 39163
GARSFONTEIN EAST 0060
Pretoria South Africa

(Email from Ned Hale to Jack Burke, 11/07/13)

NORTHEAST INDIA

FORMER INTERNATIONAL STUDENTS INTERSECT AS REDEMPTIVE CHANGE AGENTS IN A TROUBLED BORDER REGION

Bob Osburn, PhD
Wilberforce Academy

The young international student who began his studies in 1958 at Northern Baptist Theological Seminary in Chicago hailed from India's Northeast, worlds apart from the capital city of New Delhi. Tuisem Shishak's home is in a lightly-populated region, a geographic misfit where seven Indian states are linked to India's mainland by a tiny thread of land at one spot only 13 miles wide.

Major civilizations intersect here: China on the northern border and Myanmar on its eastern. And it is here that Shishak, a member of the feared Naga tribe, would intersect a generation later with Thangboi Haokip, a member of a rival tribe called the Kukis. What unites their stories is that, as international students in the USA, both caught God's call to be redemptive change agents who apply a Christian worldview to deep regional problems of poverty, tribal conflict, corruption, and violent insurgencies as Christian educators.

When Shishak ventured abroad for studies in the USA, he was a surprise for most Americans who expected features akin to mainland Indians: dark hair/dark complexion and features like those of Europeans. Instead, they were shocked to find an Indian, like most from the Northeast of India, who look like Chinese (in the sometimes naïve way that Americans perceive cultural difference). Few could have anticipated that he would become the author (in 2007) of a daring and courageous public "confession," in a well-read regional newspaper that focused on the issue of cultural difference.

As the founder, in 1974, of Paktai Christian College, one of Northeast India's most respected undergraduate institutions (and soon to become a full-fledged degree-granting university), Shishak knows the meaning of deep sacrifice and courageously carrying his Cross. The courage to write the article is borne out of deep faith in Christ, but also in part a product of thoughtful and loving mentorship by leaders in International Students, Inc.

(ISI) with whom he also served as a staff member for several years during the tumultuous 1960s.

In his confession, Shishak lamented the way his particular branch of the Naga tribe had inflicted suffering on others in the region. Openly confessing his faith in Christ, while appealing to the legacy of St Augustine who had said that confession is good for the soul, Shishak wrote of his people: "Most of our so-called Christian politicians are morally bankrupt." He also accused his fellow tribes people of corruption and arrogance.

Courageous public leadership like this is a mark of a Christ-animated change agent. Always willing to "despise the shame" (Hebrews 12:2), redemptive change agents like Shishak speak the truth because they know that the complex problems of the Northeast thrive in the shadows offered by lies and dishonesty.

Little did Shishak realize that about the time he was making his 2007 confession, one of his former students at Paktai (1978-80), and the link that forms the intersection between him and Thangboi Haokip, was also trying to rescue truth from the shadows, and almost lost her life doing so. Haokip's wife Kimsi was a bank manager in a large regional city called Imphal. Insurgent leaders threatened her life if he would not accept their bribes to offer them bank loans. Fast forward two years, and Kimsi's husband Thangboi (whom she wed in 1995) lands at the University of Minnesota in the middle of one of Minnesota's notoriously cold winters. A guest of the United States government, Thangboi was commissioned for six months of study in the USA by the US State Department. Forlorn in the bone-shivering cold of the Land of 10,000 Lakes, Thangboi, whose walk with God had come alive some ten years earlier, longed for fellowship with American Christians. God answered his prayers in two remarkable ways. In a way that can only be described as miraculous, God led Thangboi to a church (Central Baptist of St Paul) that had links to a missionary whom his father had known over 50 years earlier. God also led him to a meeting of Christian faculty at the University of Minnesota where he met the author of this article, and began a systematic process of preparing to return to India (in Summer 2009) as a redemptive change agent.

Like Shishak (his wife's former college president), Haokip had come to America for studies and was returning emboldened with an education-centered vision for God's Kingdom that was greater than he could have ever imagined. Upon his return, he launched Cornerstone Academy of Manipur, a K-10 Christian school to educate some of the poorest of India's children. Still a government employee, he also leads a government school in a sensitive border town with nearby Myanmar and serves on a powerful committee of Christian educators in the region. During the past couple of years he has mediated a conflict that could have exploded into a tribal war. He regularly leads evangelistic meetings (he effectively reaches Hindus, as well as local tribespeople, for Christ), while also training church leaders part-time through the Center for Evangelism and Leadership.

MEET CHIKAKO ONISHI

FORMER INTERNATIONAL STUDENT BECAME CHRISTIAN IN USA RETURNED TO JAPAN - TAUGHT AT CHRISTIAN HIGH SCHOOL NOW PASTOR'S WIFE

Dr. Carl Selle, The Lutheran Church-Missouri Synod

Chikako Onishi came to the United States as an undergraduate to receive her bachelor's degree. She left her home in Chiba, Japan, venturing out into an unfamiliar world. Her arrival at the university was like traveling to a new country. She had only been at the university for a short time when she realized that help with English would be critical in the pursuit of her degree. A friend told her that conversation partners at Peace Lutheran Campus Center (Stevens Point, Wisconsin) were willing to help international students improve their English skills. Bob, a retired college basketball coach, was there to meet with Chikako each Wednesday afternoon. They grew to appreciate each other so much that even difficult topics became easy to talk about.

One day Bob stopped at the pastor's office with a concern. "Would it be appropriate if Chikako and I were to speak about spiritual and religious topics?" Assured that it was fine, Bob and Chikako began to talk about God's love for all people. Chikako was also intrigued by a Christmas break visit from Ruby, a Christian woman who loved to bake cookies. The gift of cookies spoke clearly to Chikako in her loneliness since she had been unable to travel home for the winter vacation and she ended up spending much time alone in the residence hall. It was another evidence of God's love.

Shortly after the Christmas break, Chikako began to faithfully sit in the back row for Sunday worship; singing, learning, and listening to what was happening in that morning hour.

An American Christian, Tim, had by now come to know Chikako as a very special friend. They dated and learned much from each other. At graduation time, both chose to go separate ways: Tim to complete his ROTC training in Oklahoma and Chikako, back to Japan for a job. But this really is just the beginning.

Their correspondence brought them to the realization that changes needed to be made. Chikako returned to the States so that she could be touched by the water and the Word in the sacrament of holy baptism. What a wonderful celebration! Several weeks following the baptism, Tim and Chikako were married.

God's Spirit moves quietly, quickly, and often in unpredictable ways. Tim soon was led to accept a position in Japan with the Lutheran Church Missouri Synod's Overseas Volunteers in Youth Ministry (OVYM), a two year teaching stint for Lutheran college graduates. Chikako stood by his side as both traveled to Japan. But for Chikako, the Spirit had a unique and special place as she became administrative secretary to the Japan director of OVYM. Here Chikako had opportunity to interact meaningfully with the American teaching volunteers (V'ers) both as a friend, a sister, and a "mom." Chikako's knowledge of the Japanese language and culture was God's way of using her as a profound blessing to the work of the Japan Lutheran Church and to the support of the V'ers.

The Drawbaugh family returned stateside in late spring 1998 when Tim began four years of study at a seminary. Tim and Chikako served the Lord in New Jersey for a time (campus outreach worker at New York University and among the Japanese business community). After serving there for several years, God called Tim and Chikako to return to Japan to serve at a Christian high school. Their son, Joshua, graduated from college this year and will soon become an international student in Indiana. And the Spirit is still moving.

As a pastor's wife, Chikako took on special roles. Now, in Japan, Chikako continues sharing faith as a wife, mother, neighbor, friend, and counselor.

It all began when a campus center offered English conversation opportunities. The story continues to evolve and is not nearly complete, but many have already come to see the powerful love of God in Jesus Christ through the witness of Chikako.

Chikako now is Jesus' mouthpiece in her own country among her very own people. (Attachment to email from Carl Selle,* 3/15/14, now deceased, to Jack Burke, Message confirmed by Carl's widow, Karol Selle – 7/17/2018)

TESTIMONY ABOUT INTERNATIONAL STUDENT [NAME *W/H* <u>FOR SECURITY REASONS</u>] CAME TO CHRIST IN AMERICA, RETURNED HOME TO BECOME OUTSTANDING CHRISTIAN LEADER

Dr. Robert Osburn, Executive Director of Wilberforce Academy, wrote: "As you can imagine, I can't let her name and institution be used in a book, but I can tell you that she is a professor in the most prestigious institution (equivalent of Harvard) in one of the world's 10 most important nations, that she is a leader in her church, that she is a relentless evangelist, and that she came to Christ through the ministry of an ISMer at a large university in the USA."

(Email from Dr.Robert Osburn to Dr. Jack Burke, 2/11/2014)[33]

SIMILAR <u>TOP SECRET STORY</u> ABOUT FORMER STUDENT, NOW COUNTRY LEADER

Jack Burke, Ph.D., M.Div.

I am in contact with a former international graduate student who had originally agreed to permit me to write his story in this book, but recently his situation has become so politically sensitive for understandable reasons that he asked me not to print his story. He holds dual citizenship.

I would like to write the name of the country whose citizenship he holds other than the US, but at this point in time it is inadvisable. All I can say it is a middle eastern country. This former student for some reason continues to tell me of his deeply held respect for me. He attributes it to the way I dealt with him when he was a new student at the University of Houston. Today, spiritually speaking, if you knew him you would call him a "seeker," although he does not discount his Muslim heritage. It's amazing how he operates. As a graduate student he developed relationships with the university President's Office as he did mine and an international affairs office that did contracts with foreign governments. After he left the university with Ph.D. in hand, the next time I saw him to my great surprise was at the annual Presidential Prayer Breakfast in Washington, D.C. He came from his country just to attend this event since he had key contacts within the Presidential Prayer Breakfast leadership. He would like to get together with me to pray. I could go on and tell you stories you would be most fascinated with, but I will leave it and say that as Christians we have the opportunity and great satisfaction of getting to know these internationals, some of whom are natural born leaders. Because of the positions this former international student has held following graduation, both countries benefit from his being in each other's presence as a strategic partner.

"Pray that 1000 hear about Jesus!"

"This is a quick prayer request [I received], because Kevin West had an opportunity to talk to up to hundreds or even more than 1,000 people tomorrow in Kobe, [Japan]. The West family will attend an event that commemorates the Kobe earthquake of 1995.

Kevin has been given about 5 minutes to talk about "miracles," especially God's salvation in Christ. Then he will sing "You were born to be loved" (kimi ha ai sareru tame umareta).

Please pray that many of the crowd will choose to come listen to Kevin and **Nozomi** at their particular stage, that they will have the full attention of the crowd, and that God will use Kevin's preaching to work in their hearts to draw them to faith in Jesus! **(Kevin's wife, Nozomi came to Christ as an international student in Omaha 20 years ago. They are now missionaries in Japan planting churches and leading scores of Japanese to Christ).** (Email – Julie Arant to Jack Burke, "Pray that 1000 hear about Jesus!" Global Friends Omaha, http://www.globalfriendsomaha.weebly.com, 3/14/15)

TEARS FLOW WHEN FORMER INTERNATIONAL STUDENTS RETURN TO U.S. FOR 40ᵀᴴ REUNION - INTERNATIONAL CHRISTIAN FELLOWSHIP (ICF)

Wichit and Miriam Maneevone, ISI Staff, International Christian Fellowship (ICF) directors; Escondido, California

We just want to say thanks for the prayers for the ICF 40th Reunion 12/27-31/2014. Amazing to see many came all the way from Australia, Indonesia, Malaysia, Brazil, Singapore, Korea, Japan, Cambodia, Taiwan, Thailand and one Japanese lady came from Germany. <u>Most who came to the reunion accepted the Lord in ICF and were discipled here. They were the first in their families to know Jesus. Many have family members and friends who have accepted Jesus.</u>* (Underlining by author.) The dream became a reality. We had a full and fun schedule:

12/26, Friday. We had a pre-reunion Fellowship Dinner at our home for about 50 who arrived early from overseas. We cooked together and enjoyed fellowship by worshipping God together.

12/27, Saturday was the first reunion day. Over 120+ came to our home for dinner and brought all kinds of food to share. Everyone sang the "Welcome Song" gustily, some with tears, remembering how much that song means to each of us. We worshipped God together. It felt like heaven with strong voices from all over, worshipping our Savior together in love and unity. I (Miriam) couldn't sing for the tears and "lump" in my throat; it touched me in a deep place in my heart. Harry and Sang Hee, now in Korea, shared about their moving to Indonesia to serve the Lord full time.

12/30. Tuesday, December 30, was our last night together. EFCC hosted our Celebration Dinner. Pastor PY Young, pastor of Salt and Light, spoke the closing night. He challenged each one to go out and live as a witness for Jesus. We saw a few with tears as he shared. About 120 came even though it was cold and raining that evening. A lot of Chinese food, fun and fellowship. Wanida lead us in worship with people from each generation of ICF being part of the worship team. Amazing spirit-filled worship. Lots of tears as we said good-byes because of the love we shared together and because we don't know when we'll see each other again.

Amazing how our God is faithful and good. He knows what is happening in the lives of these returnees, some were among us 20+ years ago. What binds us together all these years is love - the love of God for each of us and the love we share together. Wow! Overwhelming.

They came as young students not realizing that God would find them at ICF and it would be the turning point of their lives. Knowing God and making Him known was the challenge from the start, and it continues today*

We made a significant observation. Those who accepted Christ in the US and returned as believers and are still serving God, and living a Christ-like life over the long run, and are actively making Him known and impacting their world for Christ were almost all (95%) involved in weekly one-on-one discipleship and active participation in ICF. They were leading and involved in serving during their early Christian lives here in an interactive Christian community (ICF). What they did here, they continued to do, and even more, when they returned home. Those who did not serve or lead here, still do not serve or lead back home after they return. Discipleship takes time, but it works. We have lived long enough to see the fruit![34]

16
Chapter

OBSTACLES FOR CHURCH & DENOMINATION TO OVERCOME FOR ISM TO EXPAND

ALL OUTREACH MINISTRIES BEGIN with having a heart for God and for people. Christ's number one command was that his followers should love God and second that they love people as they should love themselves. His last command was that his followers should spread the gospel, i.e. good news about Christ's life, death, and resurrection throughout the world. At that time it was virtually impossible to do this for many reasons, mainly because it was logistically impractical, if not totally impossible. Another hurdle was the linguistic barrier. People from other parts of the world had their own distinctly different languages. We have a parallel situation which exists today. Just like the Day of Pentecost, people throughout the known world have come to our country. Instead of coming to celebrate a certain day, they have come to study in our nation's colleges and universities. It's linguistically possible to communicate with them because only those who can speak English are accepted. Those who do not speak English or have a partial ability to communicate in English are placed in English as a Second Language classes in order to bring their written and spoken fluency in English up to speed.

Many enrolling from abroad in our nation's higher education institutions are the sons and daughters of our world's leaders. They are the future leaders of the world. Having the opportunity staring us in the face where we can be world-changers simply by becoming acquainted with those from other countries, we need to get involved. Whether as a professional, such as being on the international student office staff at one of our nation's campuses or one who works off-campus with a church or Christian organization, or simply as a community volunteer, the best way to become involved is through cultivating friendships with our overseas visitors. While befriending international students we are not only fulfilling our service to Christ but also we are serving as unofficial ambassadors of our country.

Although most denominations or churches which I am familiar with do not consider international students to be a part of "foreign missions," they do consider international students organizationally to fall under the umbrella of either "home missions" or "student missions." Mission leaders are beginning to realize the strategic importance of this most vital mission field. It involves the sons and daughters of leaders throughout the world who come to the United States for a college education. It also involves those who will become tomorrow's world leaders who are studying right now here in America and living in our own communities.

Since missions outreach to international students is vastly different from the traditional methods of reaching out to the world with missionaries going abroad, new modes of outreach will be explained involving the total Christian community in America.

Why Some Churches Are Slow at Catching the International Student Ministries (ISM) Vision

For those who have not been involved with the leadership of a church, there is often a lack of understanding of the decision-making process. I remember when I first became interested in a ministry to international students I was completely unaware myself as to how decisions were made and the impact of the priorities of the church on those decisions. I couldn't understand why the church leadership would agree to support one mission request but not another. On the surface the request that was denied appeared to be an equally fine program, if not even a more sensible request for the church to support. What drives the leadership to fund one mission project but not another?

1. The church already has more than it can handle.

When young Christians become pastors they may have an agenda that is limited to: preach, teach, marry, and bury. That agenda meets their needs and qualifications. After all, they may have just graduated from a theological seminary. Very soon though, they find that they are also expected to be administrators of a business, "church business." I don't know how many times I have heard fellow seminary graduates who became pastors say that their seminary education did not prepare them adequately for all the organizational details of running a church. I assume there have been changes to help budding pastors.

2. The church already supports foreign missionaries.

So when you come along and ask the pastor to support your international student ministry, the pastor may be thinking to himself, "Oh no, not one more thing to do." He might say to himself, "To be honest, foreign students are not my passion or a concern of the church. Our people seem to prefer going on short-term mission trips rather than be tied to a long-term friendship relationship with an international student. (Church members going on a "short term" mission trip should first be assigned to a student from the same country to be visited.) Further, our mission budget doesn't have enough money to support everyone who has a mission project they want the church to support. Look at the map of the world on our church bulletin board showing where our missionaries are located all over the world. Isn't that enough?"

3. ISM is not a church priority.

The big three excuses are:

- We're (husband and wife) too busy.
- The church does not support this program. (Talk about a "discouragement" for a person who is enthusiastically involved in

this ministry. Although you don't give up, it's a pretty huge burden to carry.)

- I don't feel comfortable and/or have any desire to be involved with:

  1. a ministry to foreign people
  2. a ministry to university students
  3. having a male international student around my teen-age daughter. If I agree to participate, it would have to be a female student.

4. The pastor may be faced with a conflict of interest.

If the church is in a denomination, there is another layer – and possible barrier – to the church becoming actively involved in international student ministry. In a denomination there undoubtedly is an established way in which missions is handled. There may be a foreign missions department and also a home missions. The local church is expected to support the goals and objectives of the denomination, which might be in conflict with some of the church's own goals and objectives in doing missions. The Southern Baptists have a very strong denominational International Missions Board (IMB). In recent years the IMB was known to have 6,000+* missionaries on the field. From what I have been told many times in the past by church leaders, the Southern Baptists sponsor more missionaries than any other Protestant denomination in the world. Southern Baptists are known for their Cooperative Giving Program which gathers support from Southern Baptist churches throughout America. These funds are used to support a number of Southern Baptist organizations, including the International Mission Board (IMB) and the North American Mission Board (NAMB). Because these organizations are so well established in Southern Baptist circles, there is pressure for the pastor to support these highly successful denominational structures. Many Southern Baptists who are involved in international student ministry, are concerned that there is no longer any centralized Southern Baptist missions organization that supports a ministry to international students. There once was, through the National Student Ministries Department/Division. Through those years I cooperated with Benton Williams in the 1970's. Later it was Nell Magee in this ministry that covered many parts of the nation. From what I can gather, other denominations and non-denominational churches are also still lagging behind in their support of international student missions. The ones that have been most active besides the Southern Baptists are the Presbyterians, Assembly of God and the Missouri Synod Lutherans.

*Recent information indicates that those numbers are receding.

17

Chapter

THE BIBLICAL MANDATE FOR INTERNATIONAL STUDENT MINISTRY

A PRESENTATION BY DR. Bob Taussig, professor of Veterinary Medicine, Kansas State University, held at an ACMI Conference, Azusa Pacific University, 5/30/09.

I have provided many reasons why ministry to international students is so important and urgent. The Biblical basis in this chapter was a presentation by a distinguished speaker and friend, Dr. Bob Taussig, who like myself worked for a secular university but who God had also called to be strategically involved in ministry to international students.

THE WHOLE BIBLE REVEALS GOD'S DESIGN

Isaiah 60:3 (NIV) "Nations will come to your light"

Presentation, ACMI Conference, Azusa Pacific University,
Dr. Bob Taussig, Professor of Veterinary Medicine, Kansas State University, May 30, 2009
We who serve God in the area of international student ministry understand that it is God's design to send students from many nations to

us here in order for them to hear His message. God's Word mandates that His people would share their lives and the Good News with these people. God's Word must be taught and explained to God's people as we seek to build a passionate, obedient army of volunteer workers.

It is my purpose today to point out the necessity that we, who serve God in ministry to international students, must share with the church of Jesus Christ these biblical truths and concepts. Our effectiveness and efficiency depends on our doing this.

A PARTIAL LIST OF ESSENTIAL BIBLICAL TRUTHS
GOD SENDS PEOPLE FROM THE DARKNESS TO THE LIGHT IN THE OLD TESTAMENT.

> Genesis 12:3 (NIV) is God's covenant with Abraham. "...and all peoples on earth will be blessed through you."
> Leviticus 19:34 (KJV) "Love the stranger who resides with you..."
> Psalm 67:2-3 (NIV) "May the peoples praise you, oh God, may all the peoples praise you."
> Psalm 96:3 (NIV) "Declare His glory among the nations."
> I Kings 8:60 (NIV) "...so that all the peoples of the earth may know that the Lord is God..."
> Isaiah 60:3 (NIV) "Nations will come to your light."

LIKEWISE, GOD SENDS PEOPLE FROM DARKNESS TO THE LIGHT IN THE N.T.

> Matthew 28:19 (NIV) "Therefore go and make disciples of all nations,..."
> Acts 2:5 (NIV) "Now there were staying in Jerusalem God-fearing Jews from every nation under heaven."
> Acts 8:26-40 (NIV) God sends an African who heard the Truth and took it back to Africa. (Dr. Taussig's comment, not a Biblical quote)
> Acts 10 (NIV) The Roman military officer, Cornelius, hears the Truth from Peter. (Dr. Taussig's comment, not a quote)

Question: What country might this officer later go to for his next assignment?

> Acts 13:2-3 (NIV) The Church begins to send prepared people from the light to the darkness. (Dr. Taussig's comment, not a quote)

RECRUITING OF VOLUNTEERS TO SERVE IN ISM

In Mark 13:10 (CEB) Jesus reminds us, "The Good News must be first proclaimed to all the nations."

A) Enthusiastically remind them that Jesus commanded them to make disciples of all nations.
B) Fervently and skillfully use the Bible to show them that God sends people to us.
C) Pray that the Holy Spirit will take these Biblical truths to persuade them to volunteer to serve God in ministry to international students.

An army of laborers is needed to reach the international students coming to us. It is the Scripture itself that is the first and most effective recruiting tool. These Scriptures should become the curriculum for new laborers. Those we recruit must base their service upon these teachings in the Bible.

18

Chapter

REACHING INTERNATIONAL STUDENTS - WHY IT'S THE CHURCH'S JOB

Ellen Livingood

PERMISSION GRANTED BY ELLEN Livingood; Postings, the Missions Mobilizers' e-newsletter November 2012/ Vol. 7, Issue 11. Book Author's Introduction: rarely does one find such a well-written article which defines the local church's responsibility for ministry to international students.

Imagine a city the size of San Francisco populated entirely by future global leaders. While its citizens come from almost every nation on earth, they all speak, or are quickly learning English. The boundaries of this city likely reach all the way to your back door. Then imagine that in four years, most of the city's population will be gone, but another 800,000 plus new citizens will take their place. This "city" is the international student population studying right now in the US. (If you live in some other Western nation, or any world-class city, you likely have a similar influx of international students.) Where once the vast majority of these internationals were clustered in graduate programs in the top universities, today thousands are enrolled at community colleges and small universities, bringing them to virtually every church's doorstep.

A Unique Window

For two, four or more years these students are detached from the controlling influences of their religious environment back home. These cream-of-the-crop young adults are open and curious about Americans and their religion. Many are lonely and looking for friends. Yet during their years here, the vast majority of these international students will never be invited into an American home, much less make a Christian friend.

Missing: An integrated Church Strategy

It is amazing that many churches focus large amount of time and money to penetrate closed countries around the world. Yet they fail to take advantage of the barrier-free opportunities they have to reach the future leaders and influencers of those very same countries during the time they are living next door.

While some church leaders believe it is important to reach international students, they choose to take an outsourcing approach. When asked how international student ministry fits into their global missions strategy, they reply that they leave that ministry up to parachurch specialists in organizations such as ISI (International Students Inc.) or InterVarsity. Many churches that do engage in ministry to international students separate it from their global missions efforts. This segregation robs both students and church of maximum benefit.

God's Missions Strategy

The book of Acts reveals God's two-pronged missions methodology. He both sent witnesses (example, Paul and Barnabas) to where the church did not exist, and He sent unreached people to where the church already was (example, the international crowd at Pentecost). Church history demonstrates God's ongoing commitment to both approaches. The unprecedented flood of global peoples He is moving to the West today emphasizes His commitment to that strategy. . .

Strategic Reasons the Church Should Engage International Students

The friendship equation

Valuable as they are, full-time para-church workers cannot provide a sufficient quantity of the one ingredient essential for reaching internationals-personal friendship. Many international students crave friends, particularly to improve their English through conversation with a native speaker. "Conversational English and free suppers are your ticket to meet students, especially undergrads," says Derrah Jackson, Midwest regional field director for ISI. Typically, after about three or four contacts, these students begin to ask why their new American friends are reaching out to them. Sharing faith then comes very naturally, a matter of answering the questions of the new international friend. Usually it is much easier to talk about spiritual issues with international students than with an American neighbor because internationals are curious and don't have the cultural taboo that frowns on discussing religion. One student told her American friends, "You built a bridge from your heart to mine, and Jesus walked across it!" However, not all international students are responsive. When churches are strategically engaged in the outreach, their leaders can provide encouragement and support when ministry is challenging. Cross-cultural passion and skills "Missions" seems unrelated to real life for many believers. But a friendship with an international student translates the Great Commission into a real, live person. Prayer is transformed when "the lost" are now represented by someone whom believers know and care about. And the challenges missionaries face in crossing cultures are suddenly appreciated in a new way then church members wrestle themselves with understanding and being understood by a new international friend. Missions takes on a whole new meaning and importance. Some churches require that any adult applying to participate on a short-term trip first develop a friendship with an international student. This helps potential short-termers understand that the key to ministry is relationship rather than task. And with good preparation, it sensitizes future short-termers to at least some of the cultural issues they will face overseas.

Family ministry

Many churches look for short-term family missions opportunities because parents want their children to have a cross-cultural experience. While the options for overseas ministry with kids are sometimes limited, one of the most effective and easiest family ministries is international student outreach. Host families don't need to add additional activities-they can just invite international students (and their families, if they are here) to participate in what their family is already doing. In the process, children learn a lot about other cultures.

Non-threatening beginnings

Crossing cultures can be intimidating, but international student ministry has easy, one-time events where church members can experience this type of outreach and overcome initial fears. Picking up new arrivals at the airport, helping to host a Thanksgiving dinner at the church, or delivering furniture to newcomers are just a few examples.

Hospitality practice

Rich Mendola, director of International Friendships, Inc., said "I believe that a lifestyle of hospitality is the greatest key to mobilizing Christians for involvement in fulfilling the great commission." The New Testament lists hospitality as a prerequisite for church leaders yet developing and practicing hospitality is not usually an intentional church activity. International Student Ministry allows church members first to watch others practice hospitality and then do it themselves in the context of high-impact ministry.

Discipling future church leaders

The local church is a place where international students who become believers can come to understand how the body of Christ functions. Of course, Western church practices are not the normative pattern for churches in other parts of the world, and most students will return to places where the church will look very different for a variety of reasons. Yet international Christians can still learn much in their adopted Western church that they can apply back home where many of them will become key leaders. For example, could they sit in on elders' meetings to understand how leaders make decision and shepherd others? Could they learn from exposure to the church's children's ministry?

Ellen Livingood ends her excellent article with

- a list of International Student Ministry Resources (Author's comment: Ned Hale has written extensively on this topic toward the end of this book in the ADDENDUM.)
- instructions regarding ministry to international students if you are a church missions leader, and a suggestion for consideration of an under-used Missionary House by redesignating the space for international student housing and/or ministry.

19

Chapter

WHY IS IT SO IMPORTANT FOR THE CHURCH TO HAVE OUTREACH PROGRAMS FOR COLLEGE STUDENTS LIVING AWAY FROM HOME IN GENERAL AND INTERNATIONAL STUDENTS IN PARTICULAR?

Answers:

1. College age students away from home are more open to explore new life styles, religious and political ideologies than students who live at home? Being away from the influences of home, family and the cultural environment, the student is most apt to become an independent thinker.

2. At that age college students are so impressionable. The Christian philosophical genius and film maker, Dinesh D'Souza, made that observation in a TV interview on Fox News when he cited his

own experience in coming to America as a student from India to attend Dartmouth College. In that interview Dinesh D'Souza told Megyn Kelly on her October 16, 2014 TV program "Kelly Files" that he made many friends and "**at that age you are so impressionable,**" (According to Webster's New World Dictionary impressionable means "*easily impressed or influenced . . .*"

3. Being away from home and family and <u>living in university housing with students who were raised with different values often causes the student to re-evaluate his/her own cultural values.</u> The same goes for students sitting in classrooms of favorite professors who at times also share different values. I remember a church minister who often blamed a UCLA university professor for his part in causing his son to return home with religious values which were not the same as his parents and sister. Often the student ends up integrating values of those he respects into his own set of values. That includes friendship families whom the international student has grown to admire and respect. They contribute enormously to the student's set of core values.

   To illustrate the impact of classroom professors and fellow students on one's cultural values, an international student came to my office and told me with tears streaming down her face that she did not see any point in continuing to live. In her studies of English literature she had come across literature that showed there was no purpose in life, no reason to live. There was no meaning to life. To continue living was pointless. At the conclusion of our time together the student gave me permission to pray for her. Also, I made several referrals to help this student. One was the Baptist Student Union staff. They had wonderful leadership and students, in their relatively new building on campus, who showed the love of Jesus. Another was to arrange for a loving, caring friendship family for the student. Two weeks later D'Ann and I were delighted to see this same international student at the end of a Sunday morning church service walk down the aisle to accept Jesus as her Savior at Houston's First Baptist Church. No one could ever convince me that developing a personal relationship with Jesus does not bring meaning to life. For this international young lady it surely did.

   How many of you have known students who as college graduates had modified their core views about life, including religion and politics from the time they entered as new freshmen? I certainly have and most probably you have too.

Having worked at two major universities in my career, I found <u>students are open to discussing and considering new ideas about the important values and purposes of life</u>. A new student from China came to my office to talk about her arrival the previous Saturday and what she did on Sunday. She said that since **she had never been to a church before**, out of curiosity she attended a church service. When I shared with her that I was a Christian, she looked completely surprised and with a questioning look of bewilderment she exclaimed, "You are???" It left me with the impression that she had never met anyone with a Ph.D. who was a Christian. Being from China, that easily could have been the case. Later in the conversation she indicated an interest in having a friendship family. We were only too glad to assign her Carloss and Doris Morris, a prestigious Houston Christian family (head of Stewart Title, a national company) whom we knew personally, to reflect the love of Jesus.

4. Throughout my life I have witnessed many revolutions and rebellions within countries. Inevitably who were the leaders and followers in the civil uprisings? It was college students. Why is that? <u>College age students tend to be idealistic</u>. They are open and willing to fight for new ideas, plus they have the conviction, energy, confidence and ability to do so. Look at the uprisings on Beijing's Tiananmen Square (remember the college student willing to risk his life by standing, immovable, in front of the armed tank?) How about the uprisings in the Middle East, Hong Kong, and Venezuela to cite a few more examples? **Even in America, when there is civil strife more often than not it is predominately the college age students that are carrying out the demonstrations.** Born out of a sense of idealism, students are often disillusioned with the *status quo* and want change. Some are so dedicated to their causes that they are willing to do whatever it takes to bring about change. That brings us to the point. International students too are idealistic, open to new ideas, willing to be a part of a movement that is capable of bringing about change. **Many have found Jesus to be that which is found in the "Hallelujah Chorus of George Handel's Oratorio, the Messiah."** "He is "King of Kings and Lord of Lords and He shall reign forever and ever." King

George rose to his feet. Others followed. Hearing a great choir and orchestra during the Christmas holidays singing with great passion the majestic words found in Isaiah 9:6 "and His name shall be called Wonderful, Counselor, The mighty God, The everlasting Father, the Prince of Peace" brings ones emotions to a crescendo, evoking tears, an indescribable sense of awe as one stands with a grateful heart and ponders the greatness of our God, our Lord and Savior. Surely a serious investigation of who Christ is will bring many international students, who have not yet discovered the Greatness of our incomparable Lord and Savior Jesus who has brought meaning to life to untold millions of followers, to the point where they at least ask "Am I missing out on something here that I did not hear about in my own country? If Christians have been willing to die a martyr's death for their faith through ages past, then I too should find him worthy of a serious investigation on my part."

5. Last, but far from being least, is the matter of **access**. We as Christians have access to students who live on or near the college campus during the 2 – 4+ years that students normally attend the local college or university in the area in which we live. That is not only true for outreach programs to American students, but the same holds true for contacting international students. That is done best either through student to student programs or friendship family programs sponsored by churches or parachurch organizations. Even on occasion one can gain access through a university International Student Office employee who is a Christian.

Why is that? In the case of international students that are new they are faced with culture shock (after the honeymoon stage of having arrived in America has worn off). Don't for one minute underestimate the damage of culture shock. Many stories could also be told of other students I have counseled personally who encountered deep-seated problems associated with loneliness. **I found out assigning a caring friendship family and/ or the student to a Christian on-campus group where other students would share the love of Christ, was the best way to provide ongoing support to students through the adjustment phase of their experience in a new country so far away from home.** Being in America is often the

<u>first time</u> some students have ever been out of their own country or region and away from their families. Can you imagine what heartache that can bring a young college student? What better way to convey God's love than for a Christian friendship family or fellow student to befriend the homesick international student.

When I was a student at the University of Oregon, as has been mentioned elsewhere, in my first contact with an international student, after introducing myself I asked the student from Baghdad, Iraq, if he would accompany me on a trip to the Oregon coast that weekend to attend a conference sponsored by InterVarsity **Christian** Fellowship, an on-campus **Christian** group. After only knowing me a couple of minutes he replied, "Yes, I would like to go with you."

If I was meeting an American student for the first time and asked the student the same question, you guessed it, the answer would probably have been a "Thanks but I have other plans for the weekend." Goes to show how you have access to a lonely international student and how important personal invitations are, especially to new international students. On top of that I found out later Aziz was a Muslim. Yet, he accepted an invitation from someone he did not know to a religious event that was completely different from his own. It was Christian. Think about it. This would never have happened in Baghdad. Being a foreign student, far from home, lonely, he was willing to take the risk, Aziz accepted. This can be repeated in your life if you too will be willing to share Christ's love to an international student who is far from home, lonely, and starved for friendship.

Question: By contrast what kind of access do missionaries have with international students once the students return home and become busy with their careers?

Answers: I will give you several examples. One is from my brother Harry who spent a lengthy career as a missionary in Latin America. He told me that if you went door to door in the upscale neighborhood where international student returnees lived, you would more than likely be greeted at the front door by a servant who would only offer to take what literature that you had into the house. Many missionaries go to countries where they encounter this challenge. Sorry to say, these missed the golden opportunity of reaching those who had been international students from those same countries, when they were students in predominately Christian countries like the U.S. As mentioned earlier, D'Ann and I have friends who had been missionaries to international students in Houston, Texas. They had a great ministry with easy access to international students, particularly those from Hong Kong. When they decided to become missionaries to Hong Kong, for some time they found access to the former international student returnees much more difficult than it was in Houston. The former students were preoccupied by advancing their own careers.

D'Ann and I had a similar experience. When I was the university administrator in charge of services to international students at the University of Houston, it was relatively easy to get in contact with any of the 2,000 international students. But years after my retirement when D'Ann and I tried to set up an appointment to visit former student Patrick So, we found it somewhat difficult, even weeks in advance to our arrival in Hong Kong.

Another example of the problem of gaining **access** to the countries' leadership, involves the late Ralph Winter, known for his founding the U.S. Center for World Missions in Pasadena, California. Dr. Winter was a leading missiologist and cross-cultural studies professor at Fuller Seminary. In 1983 Dr. Winter, the main speaker at an ACMI Conference in Houston, Texas, referred back to the time that he was a missionary in Central America. He contrasted the people that he had access to, such as the unemployed and young people, with the outreach those who are involved with friendship family programs and singles programs on U.S. campuses have here in America with international students. By comparison my experience has been that the Latin American students here are usually from the influential and affluent families of Central American countries.

Another illustration comes from D'Ann's and my visit to the home of two brothers in Damascus, Syria, whom we had the privilege of leading to the Lord when they were college students in Pasadena, California, and I was a seminary student. In taking them to visit a missionary compound in Damascus, **as previously mentioned, the two missionaries we met said that they would never have had access to people from that high level of society had we not brought them for a visit to the missionary compound.**

Many missionaries I have spoken with throughout my adult life have referred to their mission as being to those who are available. That normally means to young people, orphans, low-level employees or to those unemployed. Someone needs to attend to their needs. But this book's objective is focused on the people of influence because they often are in positions which will effect change making it easier to reach more people with the Gospel. The pastor of the church I attend goes on a short-term mission trip once a year to Beijing to train pastors who need theological training but he has to do it through an interpreter.

When missionaries show their pictures to church audiences in America they often show pictures of the streets filled with the extremely poor who live in very simple dwellings in areas where they minister. In their reports to the supporting churches following the mission, short-term missionaries often tell about their visits to the orphanages. That's all well and good, and certainly Biblically inspired. One problem though, they are limited in their outreach because they don't normally have ready access to people of influence, those in high positions of government, business, and education in their societies, commonly referred to as the "movers and shakers." By contrast, Christian international student returnees in such high positions make an impact for Christ upon the decision-makers of their societies. Look at former international student Sam Tin who is cited earlier in this book. He has made a significant impact for Christ in the Chinese regions of East Asia. If we add the names of pastors like Patrick So or other indigenous ministers involved in ministry on the "mission field," trained in America, the list could go on for pages.

Chapter

THE RELEVANCE OF FACTS, GOALS AND OBJECTIVES WHEN IT COMES TO SETTING THE CHURCHES' GLOBAL MISSIONS PRIORITIES

EVERY PERSON, EVERY COMPANY, and every church should have a list of goals and objectives, if that is not already the case. When I was working at the University of Houston, our top administrators would tell the department heads periodically to update and submit our goals and objectives. Goals are the ultimate final objective of what we are trying to accomplish. Objectives are the road map showing the way to get to the destination.

What is our ultimate goal as a Christian?

Whatever the creed, it all comes down to this: to know Christ and to make Him known. Once we receive Christ as our Lord and Savior, we are to make Him known so that others may have the same opportunity. Jesus gave us the ultimate goal of what we as Christians are to do. That is to make the gospel (the "good news") known to every person on planet earth so that every person would have a chance to become a follower of Jesus and finally to receive the ultimate reward, heaven as a final destination.

What are our objectives?

People in the business world are all trying to reach a goal. In the travel industry it is all about getting people from point A to point B in the most efficient, effective, comfortable, and least expensive way possible. As has been cited earlier Henry Ford looked at people going from point A to point B on a horse. He thought to himself "there's got to be a better way to do that." So he came up with the idea of a machine, an automobile. At first there were scoffers. Any time you talk about change, there is going to be a large segment of the population who are going to resist change. They want to do things the same way that their ancestors did.

As was cited earlier Orville and Wilbur Wright developed a machine that would transport people from point A to point B even faster. It was a flying machine. A model of that first airplane developed by the Wright brothers is even featured hanging from a ceiling inside the international airport in Hong Kong.

Have you noticed that with each step of change in the transportation industry, it has impacted the way the gospel gets out to people in other nations? First, it was done by horse, donkey, and camel. Look, for example, at the "wise men" or "kings" who followed the star which led them to Bethlehem where they could witness Jesus, the King of Kings, as an infant. When they returned to their homelands to share news of this historic event, they were transported by animal. Throughout the Bible, people were transported by animal or boat with sails, not a motor.

As we fast forward through the centuries, the boats became larger and faster with more advanced sails. Eventually missionaries could cross the oceans in a month with the invention of steam engines and fuel-driven motors. With the introduction of airlines for overseas travel missionaries could reach any place in the world by airplane. As jet airplanes came on the scene and began flying between continents, they largely replaced passenger ships as the mode of transportation. But, in so doing, note this, intercontinental jet travel made it possible for the mission field to come to America and other countries where Christians are in the majority.

How intercontinental jet travel and growing world economy have brought a burgeoning mission field of future world leaders to enroll in America's universities

Significant changes were reported in the number of international students who enrolled in American universities, the country of choice for those venturing overseas for study. For example, in 1950-51, only 29,813[35] students showed up to enroll in American colleges and universities. By the end of the century (2000) that number had skyrocketed to 547,867[36]. By fall 2016, the number enrolled was markedly higher with more than a million students desiring an American higher education, with 50% coming from China, India, and South Korea, all Asian countries, making the U.S. their destination of choice for higher education. (The UK is in second place, but with half the number who come to America.)[37]

In 2014/15, there were124,861 international scholars who taught and conducted research in the United States. From my experience, those who do research and teach are most responsive to the offer of friendship by American families. Not to be overlooked were 126,016 international students who enrolled in intensive English.[38] In the 1950's international student enrollment used to be measured by the hundreds on American campuses. Today it's measured by the thousands. For many years the University of Southern California was acclaimed to have the largest international student enrollment with its 9,000 - 10,000 international students. In 2016 New York University was #1 with 15,543, followed by #2 University of Southern California (13,340) and six other universities with numbers over 10,000).[39]

American pastors whose sole focus for foreign missions is to allocate 100% of the missions budget for sending American missionaries to foreign countries have not been on the nearest American college or university campus lately. I remember having a few discussions on mission priorities with my pastor in Houston, Dr. John Bisagno. Once I had the audacity to say to Brother John, as we affectionately called him, "What is it going to take for the church to realize that the mission field has moved to Houston? Do we have to circle our megachurch with international students carrying the flags of their nations so that it will be plain for everyone to see when they come out of church following the morning services?" I tried to get the point across as effectively as I could because my university office suite waiting room was often filled with international students, the future leaders of the world, needing my office's services. It makes you realize that much of the mission field which was once "there," is now "here."

When you consider that we are talking about internationals on our doorstep who, many in all probability will be the world's future leaders, it should make international students a top global missions priority for every church and mission organization. Whether serving as a friend to an international student, or in a decision-making role in a denomination or church regarding the allocation of personnel and financial resources for missions, we should clearly be aware that missions to international students is a God-given opportunity to impact the world for Christ.

21

Chapter

APPLICATION OF TWO OVERSEAS SECULAR WORKPLACE MODELS TO ISM. TRAINING COUNTRY'S UNIVERSITY STUDENTS TO DO MISSIONARY WORK, "WORKS BEST"

Application of the Overseas Business Model

DURING YOUR TRAVELS OVERSEAS you may select an American brand hotel to stay in but the staff who welcomes you and registers you are most likely nationals from the country where you are staying. If you dine out at a restaurant with an American brand name, those with whom you come in contact are nationals from that country. If you are there to do business with an American company, there is a good possibility you will be meeting with a national from that country. That's the way it is all the way up to the top. Now why is that?

In an article entitled "How can we differentiate international and global marketing," it gives the advantages of international marketing:[40] "The executives are usually native to the country and so are familiar with customs and ideas that are best suited for the area."

"The nationals still make most of the marketing and business decisions." Whatever you want to call it, this is a basic argument for having returning Christian international students, well trained and equipped, be the ones that the church in America should primarily focus on for recruits to carry the gospel message of hope back to the countries from which they came.

Are we missing out on something?

Lessons learned from use of nationals with language & culture skills for overseas military operations <u>found useful for ISM</u>

The most effective way to wage war with the ISIS military is for those in the region of the newly formed Caliphate State to take the leading role. Gen. Mark Clark's analysis was based on the fact that they "know the language and culture. America's role should be primarily supportive." (Source: Juan Williams interview of Gen. Clark on the O'Reilly Factor segment of Fox News, 8/22/14)

When the stealth bomber was being built, there was a shroud of secrecy around that operation. As we know, the stealth bomber was an introduction to a new weapon system. The goal was for the bomber to complete its objective without being detected or at least to minimize detection.

Although traditional missionaries try to go into a country with as little fanfare as possible, there are still signs of this person being a foreigner, which to some raises questions as to why they are there. Compare that with the international students returning to their respective countries from a study abroad experience. For starters, that person upon entering the airport security area proceeds to the area marked "citizens" to be checked in. There is less reason to be suspicious about that person than the one who stands in the line for foreigners to be approved for entry by the country's immigration officials. The degree of scrutiny the foreigner receives during his/her stay depends much on the relationship between the two countries. Also, the returning Christian international students being citizens have more advantages than the noncitizen to share their faith. When the scriptures say "be wise as snakes [serpents] and innocent [harmless] as doves," (Matt.10:16) the person who speaks the language fluently and understands the culture is more apt to be the person that this scripture best describes.

Missionaries find training country's university students to do missionary work, "works best." As previously mentioned Chris and Jamie

Suel* were commissioned by Houston's First Baptist Church in 2008 and began serving as missionaries to Kenya the following year, where they have served as church planters in Nairobi. Over the years, they discovered a strategic advantage in engaging university students, mobilizing and training them to reach the unreached in East Africa. "There are fewer barriers when people are trained to reach out to those in their own culture," said Chris. (Author underlined)

22

Chapter

YOU DON'T HAVE TO GO TO A FOREIGN COUNTRY TO SHARE THE "GOOD NEWS" WITH INTERNATIONAL STUDENTS - YOU CAN DO THAT RIGHT WHERE YOU LIVE.

A NATIONALLY WELL-KNOWN BAPTIST pastor with many years experience, Dr. Charles Stanley, addressed the subject by saying "I've heard every reason you can imagine for avoiding missionary service: 'I haven't been to seminary. I'm too old. My family won't go for it.' On and on the list goes. Let me tell you that there are thousands of active missionaries who once thought that God couldn't use them either. I often have the privilege of hearing their stories of how the Lord turned resistance into enthusiasm . . . People can offer God plenty of reasons why He shouldn't call them to spread the gospel. But His call is not issued for our consideration; He expects a response of obedience and surrender." (Dr. Charles Stanley, <u>Christianity.com@crosswalkmail.com</u>, February 27, 2014, program – In Touch).

One way and certainly the easiest way to be a global missionary is to make contact with an international student or two, right there in the city in which you live. A campus nearby that has lots of international students enrolled could be your "mission field." Look at the advantages. First, it doesn't involve going to seminary where you might be required to take Greek and Hebrew, as I was, and leaving home for a couple of years for language and culture training. The international student has already done that in order to study in an English speaking university. For the American Christian who turns his house into a place of contact with international students there's no asking others to help you financially so that you can serve overseas as a missionary. You are spared the heartache of homesickness and frustration of culture shock that comes with living in an environment that may be completely alien to what you are accustomed.

As a positive, it will provide you with the opportunity of developing a friendship with someone who will respect you, enjoy your company, and want not only to share his/her life's story with you but also to find out who you are and to learn from you about your background and values you hold near and dear. This could easily include reasons why you pray before your meals, go to church, and relish time spent in private prayer and studying the Scriptures.

Take a page out of the book of thousands of others who have learned the joy of making friends with an international student. I have heard countless stories of Americans who traveled to the countries and homes of international students whom they had befriended while they were students at the local American college or university. Just recently D'Ann and I learned of a couple whom we had introduced to the friendship family program years ago who had just returned from a visit to their students in Korea. In this book I have cited stories from our own experiences of developing close friendships with international students in which D'Ann and I followed them up by going to their homes in their countries. In our retirement we have come to cherish their friendships. You have met some already whose stories are in this book. We have Presbyterian friends, one being a former staff member, Jane Dunham, and her husband Cleon who have hosted more than 1,000 international students who have signed their guest book, near the entry way to their home. Additionally, they have visited a number of them who had returned to their homes in other countries.

Together D'Ann and I have had the privilege of befriending many international students during my 30 year career of serving in a university position which required my office to offer special services needed by international students. D'Ann, as a volunteer, was in charge of one of those services, the university's International Friendship Program. I have come to find that as a category, international students in many respects are more interesting than American students. For example, I worked on the same floor for most of my career with those in charge of services to American students. I think the students I dealt with had such interesting backgrounds and certainly added much to my understanding of the world in which we live. Also, they were very respectful.

- D'Ann was given the University of Houston's "Volunteer of the Year" award by the President in 1994 for her voluntarily directing the International Friendship Program and arranging friendship families for the university's international students. The President presented the award at a special university luncheon involving corporate leaders of downtown Houston. We found area churches to be far more responsive in supplying friendship families than other community organizations. Especially helpful was our home church, Houston's First Baptist Church.

23

Chapter

HOW TO IDENTIFY INTERNATIONAL STUDENT FUTURE WORLD LEADERS AT A CAMPUS NEAR YOU

INTERNATIONAL STUDENT LEADERS ARE best identified by looking at the roster of leaders who are campus student body officers, presidents of the international student organization, nationality associations, council of ethnic organization leaders, or any group on campus that appears related to the United Nations. While serving as the International Services Office (ISO) director at the University of Pennsylvania and later director of the International Student and Scholar Services Office (ISSSO) at the University of Houston, it was my wife D'Ann's and my privilege to get to know a number of student leaders and scholars who were to return home to positions of leadership in their respective countries' governments, leading businesses, educational institutions, and other organizations.

Where to find information on international student leaders? Because of government and institution restrictions on releasing information on students and scholars, it will help if you know someone who works at the college as faculty or an administrator. Even being an alumnus in some cases could help. To secure this information I would suggest you start with the campus office that provides services for international students and scholars and/or go to the university's campus student organizations' offices found in the campus activities department. Where I worked, the campus activities department would provide a list of student organizations, their leaders and contact information. The presidents of the International Student Organization were more often than not blessed with leadership talent and some were connected to leadership in their own countries. The same would hold true for those who were presidents of their nationality group organizations, particularly the larger groups. Sometimes the university public relations office can come up with a few names.

At Penn the first student I met who was to return home to be a leader in his country's government was Nabil (last name withheld). Nabil was President of the Organization of Arab Students. As a student leader Nabil had a winsome personality, was very bright – going for a Ph.D. - and was a good leader. Some years after his return to the Middle East, I saw Nabil on our national television news, not once, not twice, but a number of times. He had become the Minister of Communications (the spokesperson) for the Palestine Liberation Organization (PLO) leader Yasser Arafat. Remember Arafat winning the Nobel Peace Prize? Since Arafat was not exactly known as a peace maker, I have often wondered to what degree Nabil made it possible for Arafat to receive that distinguished award.

The best known Christian Chinese alumni of the University of Houston who returned to Hong Kong continue to be Patrick So and Sam Tin. As was pointed out previously Dr. So is the senior pastor of the Yan Fook Evangelical Free Church, a 19 story mega-church in Hong Kong, quite possibly one of the largest in any predominately Chinese country. Sam Tin as was previously indicated returned to Hong Kong to eventually take over the manufacturing empire and philanthropic foundation established by his famous father, Tin Ka Ping. Both as you have noticed are highlighted in this book.

Another group to be identified are those known to be connected in some way to world leaders, either by being a relative or friend. As you have previously read such a student at the University of Pennsylvania when I was there was Robin Wilson, the son of British Prime Minister Harold Wilson. At the University of Houston, another example would be from India. When it became known that the immediate past president of India was coming to Houston to have open heart surgery at the St. Luke's Hospital in the Texas Medical Center, Sanjay (fictitious name) came to my office and asked if I would like to meet the president. As you have already read, Sanjay's father, an Indian army general, made the necessary arrangements for my Associate Director and me to meet with the immediate past President of India. As was previously mentioned also, a student from Taiwan, Cheyenne Gao, was the son of the Mayor of Taipei, Taiwan, at the time of D'Ann's and my visit to the Mayor's office and home in Taiwan.

There are also students who are natural born leaders but held no campus student organization positions. Most likely the Director of International Student and Scholar Services and/or staff will know of international students who have <u>natural born leadership qualities,</u> though they might not hold a campus student organization leadership position. I was always impressed by students who portrayed leadership qualities. I could name a number who were student leaders and also those who were not, but showed every sign of being natural born leaders. I have kept up with some but did not have the foresight to keep up with all.

Regarding where to make contact with the university's distinguished international scholars, the **university's International Student and Scholar Services Office, campus public relations office and faculty departments that have large research budgets, often found in the hard sciences and engineering should be able to help.** Foreign scholars often come to the U.S. sponsored by their governments or ours and/or the university departments that extended the invitations.

If all else fails, go to the university cafeteria during lunch time and sit at the table of some internationals who look like and/or talk like those from the part of the world in which you are most interested. Someone there may be able to tell you the information you are looking for.

24

Chapter

PREPARING CHRISTIAN INTERNATIONAL STUDENTS TO RETURN HOME AS AMBASSADORS FOR CHRIST

Recommendation by Rev. Patrick So
in Hong Kong interview

Dealing with Attrition Rate of Students Receiving Christ Abroad, Dropping out Back Home

IN A MAY 23, 2013 meeting with Patrick So in Hong Kong, he estimated that 80% of the international students who made a commitment to Christ abroad, lose that commitment after they return to their home country. He said that their "faith was too shallow." He went on to say "We need someone to pick up the responsibility to nurture them, equip them, and disciple them. Without that they will be lost. Between the U.S. and Chinese Church there is no communication. Two years ago I started a program between OMF [Overseas Mission Fellowship], Navigators, Campus Crusade for Christ [now CRU], Ambassadors for Christ, and a number of other parachurch organizations. One of our co-workers will take up the post working half-time to be the coordinator of this kind of program – called "**ministry for the returnees.**" (Dr. Jack Burke interview of Patrick So in Hong Kong, 5/23/2014)

We talked to Patrick about our thoughts on urging Christian Chinese students to include in their plans of returning to China and Hong Kong the opportunity of spending time studying the Bible and receiving theological training at the Yan Fook Church's seminary. Suggested time is from three months to a year. His response:* "**In many ways it is more advantageous for them to take Bible and theological classes in the Chinese languages and be taught by those who can make applications within the context of Chinese culture.** Besides those who are returning to do full-time ministry, it is also important for those returning to secular positions to spend time in Bible study and theological training." We all agreed that it was important to provide guidance to returning Chinese to find a suitable church. Some parachurch organizations are providing that service not only for students returning to predominately Chinese countries but also to many other countries as well. Patrick's observation does lead us to believe that Christians need to do a better job of preparing Christian international students to be well-equipped with Biblical and theological knowledge before they ever return home.

Patrick So informed us that he has also initiated the idea of seminary training by television and a new web site for this purpose. It is called 'Bible Initiative.' There are 40 professors. It is a Bible Seminary to equip people for full-time ministry. Also, this training is for lay leaders in the church.

Professors include those from Wheaton College and Dallas Theological Seminary. Students just starting their theological training "must get the recommendation from their pastor . . . Students serve practical training in local churches. Courses are granted credit until the practical training is completed. They are doing this because of the entire world's need for this training. In China 95% of the Christians do not have theological training in seminary. 80% of pastors in Germany do not have theological training." Patrick said he "preached there at a joint retreat in which 350 Chinese students attended. More than 40 dedicated themselves for full-time ministry. This is connected with Yan Fook Church in Hong Kong."

Secret to growth

"There are 8,000 people involved in Evangelism Explosion (EE). More than 1,000 are group leaders. The church started the Yan Fook Bible Institute for the church people. It's been exciting to see the growth of the Bible studies, with people being trained in doctrine. More than 1,000 people signed up. I would like to see 5,000 more. This is an indigenous church that is completely paid for."

*(Dr. Jack Burke's interview of Patrick So, Sr. Pastor, Yan Fook Church, Hong Kong, May 23, 2013)

LITERATURE TO PREPARE INTERNATIONAL STUDENTS FOR RETURN HOME

Ned Hale
Former InterVarsity ISM Director, Former ACMI Staff

Resources for Returnees: *Back Home* (IF in UK) and *Think Home* (ISI) by Lisa Espineli Chinn, *Home Again* (Navigators) by Nate Mirza, and a returnee booklet (ISI) by John Eaves are some individual ISM workers' contributions to provide training for reentry/returnees:

For Lisa Chinn's recent booklet *Back Home*: info@friendsinternational. org.uk

For Lisa Chinn's workbook *Think Home*; https://store.intervarsity.org/think-home.html

For Nate Mirza's book *Home Again*: www.navpress.com/Product/9780972 902304/Home-Again

For John Eave's booklet: *"Preparing Your International Friend for Life Back Home"* http://store.isionline.org/products/Preparing-Your-International-Friend-For-Life-Back-Home-%252d-PDF.html

25

Chapter

PERSONAL WORD WITH YOU, BELOVED CHURCH PASTOR, CHURCH AND DENOMINATION MISSIONS LEADERSHIP

AS YOU CAN SEE in the reading of this book I have tried my best to convince you that ministry to international students in the area in which you live or serve as pastor or missions' agency leadership should be a top priority in your budget for global missions. Under ideal conditions I would make an appointment with you to meet and discuss the tremendous opportunities that are available to share Christ's love with international students among us who are on the path to leadership in their own nations. To make my case I would assume that you are already convinced that there is scriptural mandate documenting the case for involvement in ministry to international students, as was pointed out in an earlier chapter. Also, you are undoubtedly exploring new ways to increase the effectiveness of your foreign missions program. To summarize I would:

1. make sure that you understood the advantages non-immigrant Christian international students have in reaching people in their

own homelands with the gospel message of hope, peace, and love through Jesus, as has been pointed out in this book.

2. review the facts of there being more than one million international students on our nation's campuses and that they are the sons and daughters of the world's people of power and influence. Further, upon their return home they gradually will follow the trend of moving into positions of leadership themselves.

3. share facts of the international student enrollment in colleges and universities nearby. Demographic data covering number of international students, where they are from (many being from closed countries to missionaries), what they are studying, level of instruction, and where they are attending classes in colleges and universities nearby, would all be a part of the discussion.

4. want to know what you see to be the priorities of your church. Having degrees from universities and a theological seminary myself, I would assume that your seminary or Bible college training probably included very little, if any, information about the unparalleled opportunities that exist with international students. Most startling is that many may be enrolled in your local as well as your state's colleges and universities.

When mission options were discussed, it was most probably about local, domestic, and foreign using Americans as the missionaries. (My recollection is that there was very little, if any, mention of international student ministry from seminary administrators, faculty, or staff. I assume that has changed.) What little I heard about international student ministry was from a few students who had heard of an organization called International Students, Inc. and these few invited me to join them in serving as a conversation partner to international students attending the local community college.

In this book I have shared my story of how I became involved in international student ministry. It all began with a friendship with a student from Baghdad, Iraq, while attending the University of Oregon. During my first year of seminary what began as pleasant memories of my Arab student friend in Oregon, Aziz, ended with my receiving an instantaneous full-blown "calling" to ministry to international students. So I assume:

- in the seminary or Bible college where you attended (or are attending now), as just mentioned, you probably heard very little about developing friendships with the local college or university international students.

- if you are a denomination pastor I am sure you are aware of the need to support the home or foreign missionaries commissioned by the denomination, but very little about a ministry to international students.

- there is denomination and peer pressure to be a team player and support the denomination's carefully screened and trained domestic and foreign missionaries who are in training now or are already on the "mission field."

- you may have found very little encouragement among the church leadership or parishioners to initiate a friendship family program to bring church families and single adults together with international students. For those who need some type of foreign missions experience, you may have found that for your church's purposes a short-term missions program fulfills that need.

- if some member has brought information about international student ministry to your attention you may have had thoughts at times that this is just another church program which I am expected to support but will draw people's attention away from the other many fine missions programs which members of the church participate in and support.

- you may have also heard talk about the foreigners who take up space, do not join the church and do not contribute financially to the support of the church.

- on the other hand you may have considered the wonderful opportunities an international student missions program would provide the church and future world leaders who would benefit from this ministry.

Through friendships with international students, new life will be breathed into the missions program of the church. At this point your people need to know that "no sponsorship" is involved. Students for the most part do not live-in the homes. No overnight stays are expected. The goal of foreign missions can take place right in the living rooms of members of your church. The bonus for the church is that Friendship Family Programs enhance the missions program of the church.

Need more information about this ministry? Just check out the chapters toward the end on the various churches and parachurch ministries that are already involved. Or, turn to the Addendum on resources for added help. Please strongly consider recommending this book to those in your congregation to read. Any church member who cares about missions should have a copy of this book. They would find out about the wonderful missions opportunities they are missing out on if they do not already have a friend or two who are international students. I say two because it is often easier on the host to invite two students to their home. They can entertain themselves when the host is away from the table. Dear Pastor and mission leader, people do not realize how interesting international students are. I can tell you from personal experience most are the "cream of the crop" from their countries. As mentioned elsewhere D'Ann and I accompanied two brothers on their return home to Damascus, Syria, at the end of their school year and my graduation from seminary. They had committed their lives to Christ when they were students. While staying with the family we took the two brothers to a missionary compound. The missionaries said they would never have met people from an elite family in Damascus if we had not brought them to their missionary compound. (The brothers' father was the General Motors dealer in Damascus.) Further, it is typical for international students when they come to an American university to make the highest grade point averages (GPA) of any category of students regardless of race, color, or national origin. How do I know? While serving as Director of International Student and Scholar Services at the University of Houston, an academic research study was done on grade point averages of undergraduate students attending the university. Among undergraduate students, the category that had the highest GPA's were international students. This was verified also while serving as a National Association for Foreign Student Affairs (NAFSA) consultant at other colleges. In meeting with student leaders the number one complaint was that the international students made the highest grades, thus when graded on the "curve" American students who normally made A's found themselves making B's instead. The "A's" went mainly to international students. One American student leader complained that it seemed like the only thing international students do is study. At the University of Houston it was commonly known that Chinese students occupied a large room in the library for study every evening.

An added advantage that has not been discussed is built-in help for those who would like to receive some personal coaching in the language the student speaks or in understanding more about the culture of the countries from which the students come.

In spending a career working with international students, I can honestly say I would rather be in a profession working with international students than American students. As a category international students are more interesting, can talk on global issues more fluently, and in my opinion are more respectful than most American students I dealt with on campus. They are fun, inquisitive, and great to be around. Regardless of their religious heritage this is perhaps the one time in their lives that they are open to talk about faith issues with "outsiders," in this case Americans who have befriended them. If you show yourself open to hearing them out about their religious heritage, you have an open field to discuss your personal experiences about your faith.

When I became involved with international students, I found a whole new world out there. International students have broadened my horizons about the world and have brought me into contact with the sons and daughters of some very distinguished and famous people, many of whom I have met and would not have had the honor of meeting had it not been for choosing to be in a work with internationals from all over the world. This can happen to anyone who is willing to get out of their comfort zone of American friends only, and experience the world vicariously through contact with students from every country and continent you can imagine.

I prayerfully hope that people, especially Christians like you, will not miss out on this golden opportunity of getting to know some international students personally. The most exciting time of the year outside of holidays like Christmas, Easter, Thanksgiving, and the Fourth of July is to be around a university's international student office during the time right before a semester begins. You see international students arriving, some with luggage in hand, tired but excited after having come straight from the airport from a flight that started on the other side of the world. They are ready to "check-in" at the university office they were told to report to upon arrival on campus.

As a Christian when you become involved with international students you feel that you are involved in an Acts 2 setting. It's not uncommon for any major university in America to have students from more than 100 countries enrolled. It's exciting. Once you have become involved yourself, you will not want any of your people to miss out on this opportunity of a lifetime. If you are a "possibility thinker" there is no end to the limit of possibilities which are out there for the Christian who dares to become involved with international students. Interestingly, you may find some who also want to be followers of Jesus. How exciting can it get!

Why International Students are so Strategically Important to the Church's Great Commission Ministries?

All outreach ministries begin with having a heart for God and for people. As you know Christ's number one command was that his followers should love God and second that they love people as they should love themselves. His last command was that his followers should spread the gospel, i.e. the good news about Christ's life, death, and resurrection throughout the world. At that time it was virtually impossible to do this for many reasons as was cited previously from Dr. John Bisagno's sermon. To review, one of the seven reasons cited earlier for being impossible was that it was logistically impossible.

The logistical and linguistic problems were solved at least temporarily on the Day of Pentecost, just 40 days before Christ's ascension into heaven. How was that? When the Holy Spirit came upon His disciples on the Day of Pentecost, Jewish people who had come to Jerusalem from "every nation under heaven" witnessed a mighty happening that grabbed everyone's attention. Then they heard his disciples who had been filled with the Holy Spirit, speak in other tongues [languages] as the Spirit enabled them." These Jews were bewildered because each one heard them speak in their own language. Peter then stepped forward and explained what had just happened. During his speech Peter made a clear explanation of why Jesus had come to earth and why it was so important for those in this international audience to follow Him. (Acts 2)

Those enrolling from abroad in our nation's higher education institutions are the sons and daughters of our world's elite. These students are the future leaders of the world. Having the opportunity staring us in the face where we can be world-changers simply by befriending those from other countries, we need to get involved. Whether our involvement is professional, such as being one who works with international students on one of our nation's campuses or one who works off-campus with a church or Christian organization, or simply as a community volunteer, the best way to become involved is through cultivating friendships with our overseas visitors. While befriending international students we are not only fulfilling our service to Christ but also we are serving as unofficial ambassadors for our country.

Since international student missions is a relative newcomer to the scene of national and global ministries, missions leaders are beginning to realize the strategic importance of this most vital mission field. It involves the sons and daughters of leaders throughout the world who come to the United States for a college education. Many will return also to become tomorrow's world leaders. It's an awesome thought to know that they are studying right here in America and living among us in our own communities. Since missions outreach to international students is vastly different from the traditional methods of reaching out to the world with missionaries going abroad, new modes of outreach will be explained which potentially involve the total Christian community in America and for that matter, the world.

26

Chapter

"YOU HAVE MADE YOUR POINT" "WHAT ARE THE SPECIFICS OF WHAT OUR CHURCH AND DENOMINATION SHOULD BE DOING?"

IN ORDER OF PRIORITY you should consider starting with these recommendations:

1. **Appoint a staff member to be responsible for the church's ministry to international students**, ISM Coordinator or Coordinator of Ministries to International Students are appropriate titles. See the list of churches toward the end of this book that have such a position on staff. If possible make that staff position full-time. If you need to work up to that level, start at least with a half-time staff person. If all else fails after putting forth your best effort, appoint a willing and capable denominational or church volunteer to carry the same title. In case the church clearly is not at the point of setting up a position, is to ask one of the parachurch organization international student ministry leaders to step in and offer assistance.

2. **Organize a Friendship Family Advisory Committee to help the person who ends up with the international student ministries responsibility.** Whether staff or volunteer, that person should be made a member of the missions' council of the church. The job description should be free from other church-related responsibilities. Its main focus should be to recruit, assign and provide orientation for friendship families. (Orientation should include that this is not a live-in program) and should recruit international students to be assigned to the friendship families. This could be done through the cultivation of a relationship with the college or university's International Student and Scholar Services Office Director or staff designate. Another resource is the International Student Organization and nationality organizations on campus. The coordinator would also be in charge of planning church sponsored activities for international students. As was pointed out before, if a church staff or volunteer is not appointed to carry out this responsibility, then the only logical alternative is to team- up with a parachurch ISM organization leader who works with local international students. The contact information for parachurch ISM leaders is listed toward the end of this book.

3. **Make support for International Student Ministry a line-item in your church budget.** For starters, the person in charge of the International Student Ministry program would work with the Minister of Missions who should provide support for the programs needed to minister to the international students

4. From D'Ann's and my experience, **the most effective way to recruit volunteers from the church to become international friendship families is for the pastor to present the need from the pulpit.** A brief form explaining the program should be inserted in the church bulletin with a tear-out section where people interested could then fill in their contact information and drop it in the offering plate or hand it to the church friendship family coordinator at the front of the auditorium at the end of the service. We have found that a rousing enthusiastic endorsement of the friendship family program by the pastor at the end of the service helps tremendously.

5. Also helpful is to **have the appropriate pastor's approval for giving an announcement to adult classes on the following Sunday**

to recruit friendship families. At that time a person who has had a good experience serving as a friendship family and/or an international student who has had a good experience with a friendship family usually are very effective recruiters.

27

Chapter

SHARP INCREASES IN INTERNATIONAL STUDENT ENROLLMENTS: OPEN DOORS FOR SERVICE BY THE CHURCH

Michael Brzezinski,* Ed.D.
Dean of International Programs, Purdue University

ENROLLMENT OF INTERNATIONAL UNDERGRADUATE students will continue to be a key strategic goal for US universities during the 21st century, in fact, for many institutions, it already has reached a level of significant importance. Declining US non-resident student enrollment among public institutions has forced such schools to earnestly seek full-fee paying non-resident students from abroad to achieve overall enrollment targets. The result - institutions have seen unparalleled increases in international undergraduate populations, particularly from China, starting from as early as 2008.

The surge of Chinese student enrollment is a unique phenomenon unfolding before our very eyes. Never before in the history of international student enrollment in this country have we seen such a rapid increase of sojourners from a single nation. Several Big Ten schools have experienced international undergraduate enrollment increases of more than 50% since 2008, with the primary, if not sole increase, coming from China. Such increases are not of the 200 to 300 student variety, but are rather significant increases, in some cases, 2,000 or more students.

Despite a trend of enrolling a declining percentage of the world's international students, the US continues to experience numerical increases of students from abroad. Baring catastrophic political changes, this trend will undoubtedly continue for the foreseeable future as the quality of our country's tertiary education system is still viewed as second to none by the intellectual class in nearly every nation. We are, beyond a shadow of a doubt, the educational destination of choice by many of the world's intellectual elite. Few, if any world leaders or educators would argue this point.

Given these trends, what challenges do US campus administrators and faculty alike face as they seek to meet the needs of international students? Frankly speaking, international student offices need volunteer assistance in order to provide a full range of services to large numbers of international students. Very few offices have the human resource capacity to offer the full array of the kinds of social and cultural helps that new arrivals to our country seek and require. Arrival pick-up at the airport, planned social events such as picnics, and becoming friendship partners, are but a few ways that volunteers get involved. Churches and para-church groups are generally welcomed to team up with university international student offices when they display the proper attitude and approach, an approach of "friendship first." Persuading students to attend church should not be the primary goal of Christian volunteers who desire to assist an international student office. Volunteers should rather be friends first and foremost [with] the new arrivals from abroad realizing full well that during the course of becoming friends, that conversations about other topics will naturally follow.

At Purdue University, **if it were not for parachurch groups and churches, international students would have far less meaningful experiences upon arrival.** (Author added bold print.) Properly trained volunteers meet students upon arrival and shuttle them to their place of residence. Students are treated to numerous free picnics. New student arrivals are also matched as friends with community residents through an international student friendship program. From time to time volunteers provide emergency housing for a few days for the less prepared foreign sojourner who arrives without a place to lay his/her head to rest at night. Some volunteers even offer trips to Wal-Mart, sell used bikes at discounted prices, and offer rides to students to go shopping. With more than 2,000 new students arriving [on] campus every August, extended help beyond an international student office, is still desperately needed and appreciated. Community residents, primarily Christian church goers and parachurch group personnel, meet these needs. They are both encouraged to do so and recognized for their contributions. The town and gown relationship is strong and both sides have great respect for one another. Christian churches and para-church groups offer invaluable service to our international student office.

Young men and women considering international student ministry as a career should not underestimate the key role played by the leader of a university's international student office. Such an individual can open community doors to recruit and train Christians in his/her community who can then reach out to international students. (Author added bold print.) Few positions are as strategic to the cause of serving international students living in our midst.

Chapter 28

MISSION STRATEGIC THINKERS: HERE'S THE CHALLENGE FOR YOU NEED BETTER STRATEGY OF HOW TO REACH THEM WHEN THEY ARE HERE

Where are the Students - Where are the Workers?
A geographic analysis of international students
and the ISM labor force in the USA
Dr. Beau Miller, Executive Director, ACMI

Grasping the Dilemma

IN THE SPRING OF 2012, I was at the Bridges International staff conference in San Antonio, Texas. Bridges is one of the world's largest ministries to international students. While there, I was gripped by a presentation made by Bill Horlacher, who served as Executive Director of the Bridges ministry for nineteen years. Bill spoke candidly about the need for ISM workers in important U.S. locations. From that presentation (and a subsequent conversation with Bill), important issues related to International Student Ministry (ISM) in the USA came to my attention. Foundationally, there is a geographic disparity between where international students in the USA are residing and where ISM workers are ministering. In addition, there seems to be an "inverse relationship" between major U.S. universities and our capacity to place ISM workers there. In other words, at locations where there are sizable populations of international students and/or the most influential international students it is difficult to place ISM-focused staff there. The reasons for this conundrum are:

1. Economics (which Bill attributes as being 75% or more of the issue). Generally, one has "to pay the big bucks to live in the big city."
2. Schooling of children of ISM workers (he pointed out that the home school movement is helping to decrease this).
3. A general aversion to crowded and *perceived* unsafe urban communities.

Bill went on to list what he thinks are the key cities that are fulfilling this "inverse" challenge: New York City, Boston, the San Francisco Bay area as well as places like Chicago, Philadelphia, Washington DC, and Los Angeles. In addition, he made the point that there is a direct correlation between these (comparatively unengaged) cities and the cities that draw the most influential (future national leaders) of international students (Horlacher 2012). Examples of this phenomenon are Harvard and MIT in Boston, Columbia in New York City, Stanford in the San Francisco Bay Area, Northwestern in Chicago, etc. Of course, there are exceptions to this since influential international students also attend universities outside the metro areas named.

I came out of the meeting in San Antonio thinking, "we need a graphic that visually demonstrates this challenge." Something visual that can be shown to others—dots on a map that indicate where the masses of students are, compared to where the ISM workers are. I discussed the concept with an associate who was attending the same conference, Carmen Bryant, who affirmed the value of such data. Carmen served as the Acting Director of the Association of Christians Ministering Among internationals (ACMI). ACMI is the primary networking body of ISM-engaged workers, churches, and volunteers and it was in my capacity as a board member of ACMI that I was attending the Bridges conference.

In my zeal for the project and interest in having such tool to demonstrate the need and cast vision, I eventually decided to take it on myself—not knowing what I was getting myself into!

The Opportunity and the Vision

International Student Ministry in the USA and beyond is a tremendous opportunity as it relates to Christ's directive in Matthew 28 to "make disciples of all nations." International students, and scholars also, come to us as temporary visa holders to study at North American universities. These students represent "people groups" of the world—often people groups that are rather unreached. A study at a nearby university revealed that two-thirds of its students there come from countries in the "10-40 Window" (using the revised definition of the Window).The best and the brightest of these students coming to North America represent a tremendous opportunity for the Church to befriend them, demonstrate the love of Christ and proclaim His good news. Bridges of communication are in place since these individuals are required to achieve a level of English language proficiency before being admitted into degree programs or work positions. In addition, these internationals among us often desire friendship with Americans.

Many missions-minded believers residing in the USA have already "made the connection" about the significance of international students. My vision was to be able to geographically demonstrate where we (ISM-engaged Christians) are in terms of physical contact with the students. Or, better stated, where we are *not* in contact. Gospel ministry to internationals is highly relational. Though other means can be effective, there is no substitute for relationships—in which members of the Body of Christ demonstrate unconditional love for these dear people. In seeking to find where we *are* located, I started with the ISM workers. These are generally staff members of organizations such as Bridges that are dedicated to reaching internationals. I did not get far into the project before realizing that I also needed a measure to demonstrate where the local churches are positioned. In other words, what is the location of the evangelical churches that are intentionally—and in an ongoing fashion—reaching out to the international students and scholars who God has sovereignly placed near them (see Acts 17:26, 27)?

Gathering the Data

In the fall of 2012, I began to work on gathering data in three primary areas: the locations of the international students residing in the USA, the locations of ISM workers in the USA and the locations of ISM-engaged evangelical churches.

The primary agency that gathers statistics on international students living in the USA is the Institute of International Education (IIE), which produces the *Open Doors Report*. Each year this non-profit agency publishes very helpful information that provides many specifics related to the presence and impact of international students at American educational institutions. According to their research for the year 2011, there were over 723,000* students studying at colleges and universities in the USA. From the *Open Doors Report* information is available that lists the locations of these international visitors by educational institution Institute of International Education 2011. I took that information and isolated institutions that have 100 or more international students enrolled. Of course, all international students are important, yet since research and data collection are time intensive, I chose this threshold for the project. This step yielded a list, by institution location, of over 637,000 students.

The next step was to "plot" the location of the students—where they are located as one looks at a map of the United States. For this purpose, co-worker Jacob Jasin researched and found a very helpful internet resource, TargetMap, a product of MapGenia (TargetMap, 2013). This online product allows one to enter data via Excel spreadsheets and graphically demonstrate locations of the subject. The data is tracked by zip code, so after adding the zip codes to the educational institutions we uploaded the spreadsheet and achieved the desired result—a visual that demonstrates locations of students (at least ones at institutions that enrolled 100 or more that year). The beauty of the product is that the maps are dynamic—allowing us to easily zoom in and out of the U.S. map, looking at cities and states. In addition, the product lists the data entered by selected graphic in a column/spreadsheet format at the bottom of the screen. Thus, we ended up with a database in addition to the ability to show the graphic. The outcome was a powerful demonstration of international students spread across the United States. Yet particularly, and when using the zoom function, one can see *a preponderance of these students in major urban areas such as Manhattan, Boston, Chicago, Los Angeles, etc.*

The next step was to determine the locations of "ISM workers" in the USA. This includes staff workers and volunteers who are intentionally ministering to international students and scholars. Since workers around the country are able to give varying amounts of time to this very strategic ministry, I decided to use twenty hours or more per week as a threshold. Who are these workers? They are largely staff members of international student ministries, whether national, regional or local in focus. Also, this measure includes church-based workers.

To get updated information on where the workers are, I personally contacted the leaders of national, regional and denominational ISMs in the U.S. The result was fourteen responses from these ministry directors with the geographic location of ISM workers within their organizations that met my criteria. From my own association with ACMI, I knew there are other ISM workers who are not on staff with or regularly volunteering with these larger bodies. Thus, I worked with the ACMI office to get location information of other ISM workers such as those employed by a local church, working with a localized ISM or laboring independently. ACMI staff member Ned Hale had previously completed a similar research project and produced a list of those working a minimum of fifteen hours per week in ISM, which I felt was close enough to my measure to include them (Hale, October 2012).

In the spring of 2013 I sent a request to the ISM ministry leaders seeking to update my initial findings. The yield of these requests is a list of 959 workers—staff or volunteers working in direct ministry with internationals at least fifteen or twenty hours per week. Though I do not claim that this list includes every ISM worker in the U.S., I ended up with a good level of confidence with what had been compiled—a robust list that includes workers with many of the larger ministries and denominations or that have connected themselves with others in the ISM community through ACMI.

Subsequently, I took this ISM worker information in spreadsheet format and created a new plot using the TargetMap software. I can now display, by zip code, the locations of the known ISM workers in the U.S., and again, the dynamic nature of the software allows the user to zoom in and look at states and cities in particular to see the labor force represented there. Again, I ended up with not only a graphic yet also a spreadsheet correlating to each state or zip code graphic selected. This time the graphic displays the locations of the workers.

As I progressed in the project, I soon realized that the picture would be somewhat deficient if I did not also represent local church involvement in international student ministry. Believing in the importance of the local church and being aware that there are many churches in the U.S. that are significantly involved in ISM, I knew I needed to represent that work also. Since there is no known exhaustive list of evangelical churches involved in ISM, I had to go find the data. Again, the ACMI office was extremely helpful and was able to supply locations of many churches that are involved in ISM (Hale October, 2012). Since that time I have solicited key ISM-engaged people across the country to submit to me the name and location of evangelical churches that "are intentionally reaching out to international students in a consistent way toward the end of students encountering Christ and the Gospel." The yield of this data gathering is a list of 218 churches involved in ISM. Again, the list is not exhaustive, yet it does contain many of the known churches that are doing significant work among the nations who have come to us as international students and scholars. Similarly, I am able to plot on the dynamic map the locations of these churches, a significant measure as it relates to intentional outreach to the 700,000* plus students among us, as well as the international scholars.

Do these two "groupings" of ISM workers and churches represent all of the intentional outreach to internationals at our universities? Certainly not. There are university employees around the country who value Gospel outreach to international students, not to mention students and others such as marketplace professionals who are engaged. Also, there are ISM workers and administrators who are engaged and making tremendous contributions, yet do not meet the twenty hour per week measure I chose. The point is that all ministry to internationals is important. An example of this is the church family that has committed to be "host family" to an international student and is able to give a few hours a month to the relationship. The Word calls us to love the stranger among us (Leviticus 19:33) and there are many ways to do this that were not measured in this particular project.

The Outcome

What was the outcome of my research? First, we (connected leaders in the U.S. ISM community) acquired a sharp, dynamic tool and database that shows where the students are, where intentional workers are and where ISM-engaged churches are. What about the premise of the project and assessment of Bill Horlacher as it relates to the dearth of ISM workers in strategic, urban locations? Did the research confirm his claim? After the student location and worker location maps were created I was able to put them side by side. Each shows many dots across the landscape, indicating a fair dispersion of the respective parties. It was after I zoomed in that the problem became so visible. Take Manhattan for example—my map shows over 28,000 students and only 9 ISM workers. The District of Columbia with such universities as American University, George Washington University and Georgetown University has drawn its share of influential international students. In DC proper, my map and database of 959 workers shows only one person laboring there. San Francisco, Chicago and Boston also have disparities in the number of students compared with the number of workers.

In short, the data collection and map demonstrates that there is a chronic situation as it relates to the number of ISM workers in such important areas. I wish I could say that the church location map and database served to "fill in the gaps" of where the broader ISM community is "short" on workers, yet that is not the case. Even with the known churches and their valuable ministry added to the ISM labor force equation, there remains significant needs in most of the key areas.

Meeting the Need at Hand

So we have a tremendous need, and a tremendous opportunity as it relates to international students in major urban areas. The question is, "will the American Church rise up and meet the challenge?" Surely there are many "domestic" needs and ministry opportunities before our evangelical churches in urban areas—so much remains to be done among American citizens. Churches that are actively seeking to meet such needs with ministry of Word and ministry of deed are to be commended. Yet, at the same time local churches and the broader Church need to be reminded of the opportunity—and dare I say responsibility— before us as the nations have come to our doorstep!

Many of these students go on to be national or global leaders. Years ago, the U.S. Department of State published a list of "world leaders" which lists country of origin and office held by former international students in the United States. This fascinating resource contains the names of presidents, secretaries, [prime] ministers, etc. I culled through the list to see which U.S. institutions had drawn larger numbers of leaders. Harvard, Columbia, California-Berkeley, Stanford, Princeton, Yale, M.I.T., Georgetown, American University, Cornell, USC, Univ. of Minnesota, Univ. of Chicago, Univ. of Illinois and others topped the list (U.S. Department of State Bureau of Education and Cultural Affairs n.d.) Note the geographic locations of those institutions—places like Boston, New York City, San Francisco Bay area, DC, Los Angeles, Chicago. So, we are right back to the same issue. Some of the *most populated* metro areas with international students are the same ones that draw the *most influential* international students. And these tend to be the same areas with the much lower, comparatively speaking, amount of labor force toward ISM.

What is needed is more intentional focus on this strategic segment of people as it relates to global outreach. The beginning point is for local churches to engage the issue in a deeper way. There are hundreds of churches across the U.S. that are within geographic proximity of international students and scholars. Also, we must consider the reality that, generally speaking, churches have more resources than ISM agencies. The question is *"will more of these outreach-minded, gospel-bearing churches in such key cities engage the issue of international students and scholars among them?"* Beyond that, will the regional and national ISM agencies be able to place an increased amount of laborers in such key areas? From dialoguing with some of these leaders, I believe they want to. Yet, as previously alluded to, they face challenges putting workers in such urban areas. But the opportunity at hand is not just for local churches and large ISMs. Such needs can be met by outreach-minded Christians who are near these universities. Whether it is the university employee, university student, host family, marketplace professional, seminary personnel or other—we need a more global effort toward the tremendous opportunity at hand. May God use us to be a blessing among the nations whom he has sovereignly placed among us (Genesis 12:3).

*ACMI – Association of Christians Ministering Among Internationals

Beau Miller, Executive Director of ACMI, served as International Pastor at Briarwood Presbyterian Church (PCA) in Birmingham, Alabama, for 13 years. He previously worked with CRU as a campus staff worker stateside and overseas missionary in Eastern Europe. Beau received a

Master of Divinity (Missions) from Reformed Theological Seminary and Doctor of Ministry (Global Studies) from Columbia International University, with dissertation topic on church-based international student ministry. Beau previously served as Chair of the Board of Directors of ACMI, the Association of Christians Ministering Among Internationals.

*In 2016 the total number of international students increased to more than one million.

References

Hale, Ned. October 2012. Association of Christians Ministering Among Internationals (ACMI) Office.

Horlacher, Bill. 2012. Presentation and subsequent telephone interview.

Institute of International Education. (2001-2011). "International Students at All Institutions, 2001/02-2010/11." Open Doors Report on International Educational Exchange. Retrieved from http://www.iie.org/opendoors.

TargetMap: Knowledge Beyond Borders. http://www.targetmap.com/. [accessed July 2013].U.S. Department of State Bureau of Education and Cultural Affairs. n. d. Foreign Students Yesterday World Leaders Today.

29

Chapter

Considerations for Mission Planners in Churches, Denominations and Parachurch Organizations for the Location and Funding of Ministries to International Students

IN ALLOCATING RESOURCES FOR ministry to international students a major consideration should be to determine which universities the sons and daughters of world leaders choose to attend. There is a good possibility that they will end up being world leaders themselves. The following chart shows top American universities attended by international students who ended up being world leaders:[41]

TOP AMERICAN UNIVERSITIES ATTENDED BY INTERNATIONAL STUDENTS WHO BECAME WORLD LEADERS

Compiled by Jack D. Burke, Ph.D. December 3, 2002

University	Number of World Leaders
1. Harvard	31
2. Columbia	10
3. MIT	9
4. Univ. of California/Berkeley	6
Univ. of Chicago	6
Stanford	6
5. Cornell	5
Georgetown	5
Univ. of Illinois	5
Univ. of Michigan	5
Princeton	5
Yale	5
6. Arizona State	4
John Hopkins	4
7. Howard	3
New York	3
Northwestern	3
Univ. of Southern California	3

Since this data was collected some years back, these numbers have most certainly multiplied since then. You might find it difficult, as I did, to receive updates on this specific kind of information.

American universities with highest number of international student alumni who became world leaders

Harvard has been by far the top choice of those who became future world leaders. There is no question but that Harvard could easily fill its freshman class with nothing but "straight A" students. However, in looking at the admission requirements for a student to become admitted to Harvard, one can see that Harvard is looking for more than just students with high I.Q.'s and high GPA's. I have heard it said that Harvard begins thinking of students as alumni when they first enroll. Harvard and other prestigious universities are looking for students who can enrich the student environment. (My nephew Timothy Neville was admitted to Harvard partly because he was a world class swimmer who could (and did bring recognition to Harvard's swim team.). Harvard looks to the future. As a former Ivy League university administrator myself, I became involved with the concerns of admissions officers, alumni officials, and the development office. I could easily see that Harvard's admissions offices (Undergrad and Grad) would choose students with strengths to be good students. But they also want those with promising careers ahead who could enhance Harvard's reputation as a top world class university.

Knowing that every international student walking across Harvard Yard has been carefully screened and hand-picked by skillful university administrators, the church has a strategic responsibility. It only seems logical that denomination and church leaders would desire to place Christians in Boston, as an example, with the skills necessary to become effective witnesses for Christ to these future global leaders attending prestigious Harvard and MIT.

The ISM leader I know best in the Boston area is Southern Baptist, Michael Dean, who also serves as a Chaplain at MIT. At this time I only know two Christians who work in Ivy League international education offices. When I was director of the International Services Office at the Ivy League University of Pennsylvania we had many students who were the sons and daughters of some of the world's elite. For example, one whom you have already read about, a guest in our Philadelphia area home many times was British Prime Minister Harold Wilson's son. As an added benefit, D'Ann and I were invited to Philadelphia's Consul General's home to spend an evening with the Prime Minister and Britain's First Lady. We found that only friends of the son were invited to meet his father. (Has a great Biblical application, doesn't it?)

It is hard to hide one's disappointment, as has been noted in the previous chapter written by Dr. Beau Miller, Executive Director of ACMI, when he made the salient point that there are relatively few engaged in ministry to international students at highly prestigious universities especially those located in densely populated areas. As a review and for added emphasis I would like to focus on what Dr. Miller cited when he wrote "**Many of** these students go on to be national or global leaders. Years ago, the U.S. Department of State published a list of "'world leaders' which lists country of origin and office held by former international students in the United States. This fascinating resource contains the names of presidents, secretaries, [prime] ministers, etc. I culled through the list to see which U.S. institutions had drawn larger numbers of leaders. Harvard, Columbia, California-Berkeley, Stanford, Princeton, Yale, M.I.T., Georgetown, American University, Cornell, USC, Univ. of Minnesota, Univ. of Chicago, Univ. of Illinois and others topped the list (U.S. Department of State Bureau of Education and Cultural Affairs n.d.) Note the geographic locations of those institutions—places like Boston, New York City, San Francisco Bay area, DC, Los Angeles, Chicago. So, we are right back to the same issue. **Some of the *most populated* metro areas with international students are the same ones that draw the *most influential* international students. And these tend to be the same areas with the much lower, comparatively speaking, amount of labor force toward ISM."**

We as a church and/or denomination must dig deeper into the income ledgers of our annual budgets to make it possible for supremely qualified Christians engaged in ministry to international students to live in these most strategic, but expensive populated places of opportunity.

"**Armed with U.S. Education, many leaders take on world**" is another article which lends further documentation to international students who returned home to become leaders in their respective countries. (The Washington Times, August 19, 2012).

Why a special strategic ministry focused solely on international students and scholars?

Christians should recognize that those engaged in ministry to international students are also foreign missionaries who are fulfilling the Great Commission. The big difference is where and with whom each group of missionaries works. Those who work with international students and scholars may be equated with the Harvards of this world who go after those who are highly strategic for kingdom purposes.

The ones who are sharing the love of Christ with the future world leaders are in what's called international student ministry (ISM). They are on staff of some churches but more than likely found working for international student ministry parachurch organizations. In addition there are Christian individuals ministering independently to international students. Because of my own sensitivity of having worked in university offices for 30 years, where my office was responsible for offering the services needed and sometime required by international students, I wish to re-emphasize that Christians in these offices also consider their work with international students as highly strategic. All together, they as a team are the ones who are in outreach programs designed to care for the needs of international students, the sons and daughters, in many cases, of the world's leadership. These students have the potential of becoming world leaders themselves after their return home. It is exciting that these future "movers and shakers" of their own countries are on our nation's campuses today. Therefore, once again, what should be our first step? We need to move these future foreign leaders up toward the top of the priority list of global citizens who most certainly need to be reached with the "good news" about our Lord and Savior Jesus Christ while they are still in our midst. Because of recent world developments I want to re-emphasize the words "while they are still in our midst."

30

Chapter

RECRUITMENT OF INTERNATIONAL STUDENTS – A HIGH PRIORITY FOR AMERICAN UNIVERSITIES

International Students are Needed to Internationalize our Universities and Help Pay the Costs

THE SHRINKING GLOBE HAS made the world interconnected like it's never been before. One nation depends upon another to buy their products as well as to sell their goods. Countries are in competition with each other for power, wealth, influence, things to sell at home and abroad that make life easier, more enjoyable, and more secure.

Outside of certain federal agencies, there is no greater interest in the strategic value of international students and scholars than American universities. Gradually through the years universities have come to recognize that international students are of great value to the university. Many examples could be cited. I have selected the following:

1. What better way to internationalize the American university is there than to enroll international students and scholars? They

are recognized as a great resource for making America more competitive in the global market place. Having international students in our classrooms makes American students and teachers more aware of what is going on in the rest of the world. Schools of Business Administration are particularly sensitive to this need. They want their students to have the competitive edge in developing, marketing, exporting and importing products which can increase our country's economic prosperity. No longer is the focus just on the American economy. It's now global. My son, David, having grown up in a family whose focus was on international students, coupled with a major in Business Administration from Whitworth University, makes it understandable why he could launch out into a successful career in the global high tech industry.

2. By providing services to international students through the university my career, I found that many international students grew up in societies where there is great emphasis on classroom academic performance, in contrast to the school's athletic ratings. Also, good grades are given a higher criterion for advancement in their country. This has given international students the competitive edge. By now you should remember the University of Houston's study I cited earlier which showed academic performances of undergraduate students according to their ethnicity. Ranked in first place were international students. Eva, a bright student from Hong Kong, told me that in growing up she and her friends studied all the time. The school had no athletic programs. There were no after school activities, so the students would go home and study until bed-time. They brought that academic discipline with them to the U.S.

3. International Students are seen as a rich source for enrollment-driven universities. I can vividly recall a meeting at the University of Houston's College of Engineering when one professor emphatically stated "if it were not for the substantial number of international students enrolled, many of our graduate level classes would be closed." Of the 1,078,822 international students enrolled in U.S. higher education institutions in 2017, there were 230,711 enrolled as engineering majors. That's 21.4% of the total engineering student enrollment. For many years more than 50% of graduate-level engineering students were international students.

Universities that recruit students from other countries find China to be the most fertile ground for recruitment. The 2017 enrollment data shows 350,755 were from China. That's 32.5% of the total international student enrollment. Next is India with 186,267 or 17.3% of the total. As cited before, my enrollment figures are derived from the Institute of International Education's well documented publication, Open Doors.

4. To recruit international students is admittedly quite self-serving. International students attending public universities bring more money into the university than do resident students. Non-immigrant internationals pay the higher out-of-state tuition rate. For international students to receive nonimmigrant visas, government regulations require that they have sufficient funds to pay the expenses for their college education. That means more scholarship funds become available for American students. Also, since states like Texas pay their universities more for each graduate student credit-hour enrolled than undergraduate, especially in majors like engineering, it helps colleges within the university, like engineering, to receive more funds. It appeared that private universities to some degree are also helped on the income side of the ledger by students who are classified as being international students.

5. **Some international students bring world-class prestige to the university. Among the International students enrolled, there are students who are the sons and daughters of world leaders.** This helps the prestige of the university much the same as when **international students return home and eventually surface as leaders of their respective countries.** This gives a university "bragging rights" to have alumni who are distinguished world leaders. Therefore, they want to take good care of these students and future alumni, some of whom become world leaders.

Why internationals are so attracted to America's Colleges and Universities

One area where America still takes the lead is its higher education system. That's why students from other countries are beating a path to our nation's door. They want to enroll in one of America's universities and colleges. An American college degree still carries the significance of prestige and is a symbol of good training in an environment where freedom reigns.

America has for many years had a corner on the market for educating the world's elite who come from powerful families, families that are in the higher ranks of government, industry, and education. America's role in higher education is now being challenged. Other countries have seen the light. They too see the importance of developing an educational system for the lower grades through college that will make their countries' students more globally sophisticated. They too would like to enjoy the financial benefits of countries like the United States.

Other countries have discovered America's secret. Do it through education. Now America has some competition. What are our nation's universities doing about it? **Many universities are working at a feverish pitch to internationalize. They want to stay on top.** The government, both federal and state, is pumping money into the nation's school systems and universities. This is the way many of our country's leaders see how America can continue to maintain its economic role of leadership. Until universities from many of the other countries get up to speed in delivering a comprehensive, quality college education available for all, America will still continue its leadership role in educating college students from countries world-wide. **That's why private and public universities are now in competition with each other to internationalize - for some its fierce competition.** By internationalize I mean that the universities and colleges are taking a close look at their resources to see how they can use them more effectively and efficiently to help faculty and students think more about global needs. They need to apply what they have learned to meet needs through their teaching and learning. Awards are given to universities that do the best job of internationalizing the cultural environment of their institutions. Two of the headlines on the website of NAFSA: Association of International Educators (3/10/2012) were (1) "Eight U.S. Campuses Recognized for Excellence in internationalization" and (2) "Getting Students involved in Solving Global Issues."

31

Chapter

MINISTRY OPTIONS FOR THOSE FEELING "CALLED" TO WORK WITH INTERNATIONAL STUDENTS

HOPEFULLY BY NOW YOU can easily see the critical need for mission outreach to international students and may be wondering whether God's calling might be upon your life. Christians should recognize that those engaged in ministry to international students are also, to use church language, foreign missionaries who are fulfilling the Great Commission.

I am pleased to share with you the following excellent articles written for this book by Christian leaders for those seeking information about ways Christians can become involved in a ministry to international students. The first is by Bridges International's Executive Director, Trae Vacek, with Bill Sundstrom, Director of Publications. It's written for Christians who would like information about ways one can work for a church, denomination, or parachurch with international students. The second is by Charles Olcese, Director of the International Student Services Office at the University of Kansas, who shares his experiences past and present working with international students in several venues, both Christian and secular.

A third is the story of veteran pastor, Rev. Al LaCour, who changed to a campus ministry for internationals. God used incredible circumstances to miraculously bring favor from the administration on his work with international students.

Fourth is an article written by Anita Gaines, Director of International Student and Scholar Services at the University of Houston. Anita started as a student assistant in my office at the University of Houston. Through the years she worked her way up to the director position of the ISSS Office upon my retirement. For those who want my own advice on ministry options for service to international students in higher education, read my three articles which include "My Advice for Christians Seeking Employment Working with International Students in Higher Education as a Ministry." They are borne out of 30 years of experience in professional leadership positions at two secular universities and 30+ years of volunteer service in ISM prior to and after retiring.

3 PATHWAYS OF MINISTRY TO INTERNATIONAL STUDENTS: PARA-CHURCH, LOCAL CHURCH, AND DENOMINATIONAL

Trae Vacek, Executive Director, Bridges International
With Bill Sundstrom, Director of Publications

Each year, thousands of students from around the world attend universities. In fact, more than 1.3 million students from the top academic, economic, and social levels in their countries have come to pursue the "American Dream". What they really need is Jesus Christ! This vast mission field is at our doorstep. We don't have to go to them because they are coming to us. I first discovered this strategic opportunity as a sophomore in college, when I befriended a post-graduate student from China. Despite our age difference, my friendship with "Xiang" was life changing—for both of us! Seven years later I sensed that international student ministry was my full-time calling.

Looking back, it was a handful of international student friendships that compelled me to serve long-term with Bridges International. The return on an investment in the life of an international was staggeringly high. Although students today, they may be world leaders tomorrow! My call was to glorify God and proclaim His name to the nations—especially those least reached by the gospel. When I realized that the nations had come to American campuses, that they spoke English, and were future world leaders, I knew was no better place to invest my life and resources!

What about You?

You may be thinking about doing something similar. You want to make your life count through reaching international students. There are chapters which discuss options within the context of a university, but what about other options? Three main pathways exist—parachurch ISM mission, denominational ISM mission, and the local church.

Before getting into these, however, let's take a look at what it takes to succeed, no matter where you serve.

First you need to embrace the **vision**. Ministry to international students is compelling! They want to experience American culture, and often, they want to be our friends. We have the opportunity. However, ISM takes God's calling and dynamic determination. The reality is that although God is working among international students, not all are eager to learn the message of Jesus. Things move more slowly to share the love of Jesus with students from places that foreigners can never enter. The potential is overwhelming!

Slowly, due to language barriers, cultural barriers, spiritual barriers. And it takes time – time for you to get to know a new friend, and time for them to consider a new understanding of how to approach God.

So God calls us to take the long-term view. We need perseverance and a bigger perspective of what He may do in the lives of our international friends. Such a vision will carry you through the tough times.

Secondly, you need **servant leadership**. International students are the first to sense if they are your ministry project. We love them because Christ first loved us! Much of the time, that love is displayed through simple acts of service like practicing English, helping run errands, navigating a new community or making new friends. As we serve our international friends, the Lord uses us to help students consider the gospel.

Then there is the **team**. Success in international student ministry can be discovered in the African proverb, "If you want to go fast, go alone. If you want to go farther, go together." ISM is best accomplished in community.

Involve others who share your vision for the nations. Don't pursue this mission without others in your church or community who will labor alongside of you.

Finally, you need **Spirit-led creativity.** ISM is extremely fun! Days can be filled with friends from Africa, China, India, Saudi Arabia and Japan. The wide range of relationships forces us to walk in the power of the Holy Spirit and to be creative. Patience, flexibility and being teachable are important - you don't approach friendship with a Latvian the same as someone from Lebanon.

Learning daily about culture, and a willingness to feel uncomfortable, will help you depend on the Spirit of God to be effective.

By this time you might be asking, "What does an ISM worker actually do?" It varies by organization, but most emphasize three areas: showing hospitality, meeting physical and social needs, and, most importantly, discussing the spiritual side of life.

A common denominator is building friendships with students. It helps to have some ministry experience, so as students want to know more, you are equipped to share the gospel in a culturally appropriate way, lead Bible studies and answer questions.

Three Pathways

As I mentioned earlier, if God is calling you to work full time with international students outside the university context, three main pathways, or models, exist. First would be a *parachurch* organization like Bridges International. "Para" means "alongside," so in Bridges we see ourselves as a complement to the church, with a specialized mission. Parachurch staff members are part of a nationwide network, with training and conferences to support individual staff members. Usually staff members are part of a campus team and need to raise their own financial support.

A second pathway is to work on the staff of a *local church*. Though relatively few churches have the resources to hire somebody for ISM, those that do can have effective ministries. My friend Paula Parker, who served many years at the First Evangelical Free Church in Fullerton, Calif., had more than 1,000 international students involved. A local church has resources, facilities and a congregation of people to help.

In fact, local church ISM staff can multiply their efforts by training members of the congregation. This is critical, according to Paula. And to do this well, one needs strong administrative gifts, plus a willingness to sacrifice personal time with students in order to train and mentor Americans.

The final pathway—*denominational ISM*—lies somewhere between church and parachurch. Four groups have their own ISM – the Presbyterian Church of America, the Southern Baptists, the Assemblies of God and the Lutheran Church – Missouri Synod. If you belong to one of these, you may be well advised to look into your denominational ISM. Qualifications vary – the PCA requires their ISM team leaders to be ordained ministers, while AOG staff members usually join through the local Chi Alpha campus group.

One strength of the denominational ISM is their connection with a recognized church. This can help in dealings with the university, or in sending new believers back to their home country, or in raising support.

The three pathways each take a slightly different approach to ministry. Al LaCour, coordinator of RUF-I, the Presbyterian ISM, has developed a good summary of the main approach of each:

- The parachurch uses a missionary model – going to the campus as a registered student organization
- The local church uses a hybrid missionary/community model — "going" to the campus and "coming" to the church
- The denominational ISM model (at least in RUF-I), is "the church going to the campus."

My prayer is that each international student would have an opportunity to respond to the gospel. Every graduate will go somewhere carrying a message. We must ask ourselves: "Where will they go?" and "What message will they take with them?" Would you join us in reaching these students?

Although the Lord is working in powerful ways through ISM, we are touching only 20 percent of the international students in America. My hope is that you would join us in this strategic missionary endeavor!

It is as easy as making a new friend.

Join us

(Email from Trae Vacek to Jack Burke, 1/31/16)

Professional Opportunities for Christians to Work with International Students

Charles Olcese, Director
Office of International Student Services
University of Kansas

I've been told that my professional journey among international students may be unique, in that it has included a variety of professional settings and experiences. I'm not sure how unique it is, but it did allow me to have some personal insight into at least three options for professional service opportunities. Most importantly, from the beginning I have pursued each of these opportunities with a clear sense of vocation. That is, the primary and most singular aspect of my journey is that I have had an understanding from the beginning that God would use me in a particular way and that my professional career would have this underlying sense of ministry about it.

This point is key for two reasons. First, it has given clear direction at each decision point of my professional career. Each time I've been at a crossroads in my career, I've been able to recall why I entered this field in the first place. This has given me confidence to know when it is time to make a move professionally. Rather than relying on personal ambition, or professional positioning – although those are not necessarily negative aspects in decision making — I have also been able to rely on a deeper sense of following the Lord's leading. This assurance gives a confidence that can overcome doubt in the most troubling times. Secondly, this sense of calling has provided a direction for my day-to-day work. When I am lost in the paperwork and minutiae of regulations (the least inspiring part of my job), I can put that into perspective of what my greater purpose is, and why the paperwork may be important.

My career has had four particular positions that can each be seen with advantages and challenges in the differences. I began my work among international students with InterVarsity Christian Fellowship, a campus ministry organization which I had worked with for several years focusing primarily on the American student population. I took a year leave to join my wife, Camille – an ESL teacher as we stepped out on the adventure of teaching English in China. After a year in China, I returned to work with InterVarsity. I found myself spending and enjoying more time with international students on campus in the US. I then got more professional training and have worked as a university administrator in two distinct settings – at a Christian university, and also at two different state universities. Each move could be seen as taking me further from direct ministry. However, each move was informed by my sense that I was pursuing my vocation.

It was at the juncture of moving from staff work with InterVarsity to pursuing a position on a university campus that I first really identified how God had been using me and how I got real joy out of ministry. My gifts and key experiences have always been more in encouraging and challenging growth among others. For example, when Camille and I went to China we told some friends what we were going to do and three of them decided to join us on the experience. While working with American students with InterVarsity, I was always encouraging them to do summer mission trips and challenging them to engage in a more global Christian experience, and they did in significant numbers each year. Understanding how God had used me was the key to receiving my calling. When I began International Student ministry on campus and was enjoying it so much, I realized that there was an office at the university that often served as the gatekeeper for my ability to work with students. My ability to work freely with the international students was very much dependent upon my relationship and mutual respect with the International Student Services office on that campus, and the director of that office in particular. I began to see that this office operated much like I had done ministry – encouraging and challenging others to respectfully volunteer and create cross cultural friendships with international students. The more I pondered that, the more I felt the call to step into that role. That was my defining moment to pursue a profession as an international student advisor and eventually a director of an international student office at a university. That was my calling – to encourage and challenge others to become global citizens with students from around the world, and to do so in a respectful way to both the university and the students involved.

Now that I've outlined the main points of my journey and my calling, let's look at some of the specific professional opportunities that I have experienced. Again this is not an exhaustive list of opportunities that exist, just what I have experienced. Perhaps this can be an encouragement for the reader to see the joys and challenges of each of these avenues of service as you go through your own decision making process. I'll describe each professional role and then give the benefits and challenges of each one as I see them.

Ministry with a US Church or Para-Church Organization

My time in formal international student ministry (ISM) with InterVarsity, was a direct result of being changed by my China experience. I found relating to international students – especially Chinese – to be easy, enjoyable and challenging at the same time. International students seemed so much more interested than their domestic counterparts in deeper conversations. This interest probably was because they were having a very profound experience in a foreign land, just as I had done. The students were also very eager to have an American friend with whom they could process their encounter with American culture. A typical day for an ISM worker could be three or four very stimulating conversations with students from several different countries, followed by a Bible study with one or several students interested in finding out about the message of the Bible, often for the first time in their lives. Planning retreats and special trips on weekends is also a great way to meet and interact with international students who are eager to have as many American experiences as possible during their time here.

One of the aspects of this work that I liked the most – in keeping with my calling – was helping other Americans to get involved in the work. I really enjoyed presenting the opportunity to form international friendships with others in the community, often through local churches or clubs. It was always very satisfying to see someone else catch the vision for ISM, and then to see how international friendships changed their lives. I remember one couple from our church that befriended a young man from the Middle East. They really enjoyed him and took him on many family outings. He was only in the US for one year, but after he returned home he kept in touch with them and vice versa. They had a true friendship. Soon after his return, the 1990 Gulf War broke out. The couple were very concerned that their friend might be in danger. What previously would have been only events in the headlines became personal. Now they knew someone "over there."

I found that ISM yielded benefits to international students, to members of the community, and to me. In addition to what I've mentioned above, the ability to engage in direct ministry was very invigorating and was not bound by some of the restrictions I now face in my current position. The challenge for me was more on the financial end. I was in a position of needing to raise my own support each year in order to continue this very valuable ministry. Over time it became more of a burden than a pleasure. Not everyone in this ministry feels this way. I have friends who have continued to work in the ISM field with InterVarsity and other organizations for many years. They continue to greatly enjoy the ministry and the independence they have to relate with so many interested internationals.

While I grew weary of raising support, there was an even stronger motivation to change my role. At this point my calling began to be very clear and definite. I realized that my role in international student ministry would be to create opportunities for others. I saw that the international office had real challenges in budget and personnel that restricted them from doing all they wanted to do with the students. They were dependent upon people like me who understood the office mission to both help international students acculturate to America, and to also help American volunteers expand their worldview. The most significant way I saw was to be in the international student office at a university and to be in a place of building respectful relationships among volunteers who would be able to recruit other volunteers.

Ministry at a Christian University

When I committed to following the Lord's call to be an International Student Advisor at a university, I needed first to get the appropriate graduate degree to qualify me for such a position. I was able to do this fairly easily while still working part time with InterVarsity. After graduation and a very beneficial internship at the University of Houston with Dr. Jack Burke, I began the search for a permanent position. The opportunity opened at a Christian college in Chicago that was affiliated with my home denomination, North Park College. I had never thought I'd work at a Christian college. My experience with InterVarsity was always at state universities where the calling to be "salt and light" was clear and necessary. However, it was clear that God had a plan for me at North Park.

The field of international student advising (ISA) is made up of two main parts. The part that has the most obvious value to the university (and possibly the international student) is working with the various immigration regulations that govern the relationship between the school, the US government and the student. This is really very technical, detail-oriented stuff. It is not necessarily fun, but it is very valuable. The ISA needs to be able to interpret some very vague regulations that keep the school compliant with federal regulations, and help the students know what the rules are for their time in the US. As I said, it isn't fun but I learned to enjoy being a resident expert and helping students in difficult situations. For example, I could guide them through the process of getting permission to work an internship, or I could help them see what their options were for getting financial assistance if they were having financial difficulties.

The second area for an ISA is that of creating programs to help international students adjust to American culture and also help Americans appreciate the value of having international students and a diversity of cultures on the campus. North Park was a great training ground for me as I was able not only to begin new programs and experiment with creative ways to get others involved, but I could do it on a blank canvas. While the College had about 87 international students, they had never had an ISA before. North Park allowed room for a lot of creativity in the programmatic aspect of the job. It is also the case that you can affect a whole campus quickly, just by turning a spotlight on the value of international students and cultural learning on campus.

The relatively small size allowed me to establish the office and the programs very quickly. This is not the case at larger state universities. Another benefit was the relative ease of "doing ministry" while still being an employee of the university. I didn't have to raise my own support, but I was able to do many of the community outreach programs that we had done with InterVarsity to get others involved. I was also able to engage with interested American students who learned to expand their worldview and internationalize their degree because of their international friendships.

Alas, after seven years it seemed I had done just about everything I could do in that context. Smaller settings can sometimes be more limiting as well. In an effort to continue to be challenged in my job, I moved from the director of the International Office to the Dean of Students and then to a unique position overseeing five cultural study centers. It seemed I was moving further from my calling. Consequently, I began to look for what God would have for me next. An opportunity came when a friend informed me he was leaving a position at a state university in Kansas.

Ministry and Work at a State University

From the somewhat protected environment of North Park, I moved to a regional state university, Pittsburg State University in southeast Kansas and later to the University of Kansas, a major research university and the flagship school for the state. While the job remains much the same – immigration regulations and international programming, the two functions play out very differently in a secular context. To begin with, I am an employee of the State, not of a religious organization. This status comes with some challenges and also some privileges. Another difference is that both of these universities have larger international student populations. Again this presents its own set of benefits and challenges.

When I first arrived in Kansas at Pittsburg State University, I was introduced to an ISM worker on campus who had worked well with my predecessor. This was a match made in heaven. Don was a great partner to work with and my calling to allow him to do his work on our campus was effortless. This came from a clear understanding of our roles and respect for each other. Don recognized the restrictions that I had to pay attention to and he respected that. He never asked me to do something that would jeopardize my position in the university. I recognized Don's gift for relating with internationals in a very deep and caring way. I was sure that he would not abuse his position and would not offend students by being overly aggressive about the Christian faith. We partnered on various programs together.

One of the most successful programs we ran together was called the International Gathering and it was a perfect example of how we could complement each other in our roles and fulfill each of our callings professionally. This was a simple concept of hosting a monthly gathering for students and community members that had two parts – a simple meal and an informative presentation about a country. The international student office would identify a group of students from a particular country that wanted to tell people about their home country. We would work with them to prepare a PowerPoint presentation with sights and sounds from their country. Often they would also want to prepare some samples of food from their culture. Don organized the local churches to prepare a simple meal – soup, bread, fruit, dessert, drinks – that would supplement the food the international students made. Students loved to come out and get a free meal. People from the whole community enjoyed hearing about different countries around the world from first-hand experience. Many friendships were formed around the tables. The program grew so large that we had to move the venue to a lecture hall on campus and serve the food in the hallway and lobby of the hall. The university had no problem with us doing this since the program had become so popular and was seen as a staple of the internationalization program of the university.

With larger universities come greater opportunities like the International Gathering. There is also the increased bureaucracy and larger office staff to manage. This means I have become less involved with the students than I was at North Park and especially with InterVarsity. However, I have been able to be true to my calling to an ever-increasing extent. With InterVarsity I helped a few families to get involved with international students. Now at KU I deal with several networks of families that relate with many different community groups, and over 2200 international students from about 100 different countries. One last story about my calling and what brought me to leave Pittsburg State University for KU.

As I was pondering the offer to come to KU to direct the International Student Services office, I had two meetings just days apart that made my decision for me and reiterated my specific calling in this profession. As I sat having lunch with Don at PSU and discussing my opportunity to move to KU, he said something interesting. He said, "Chuck, we are in such a position now at PSU that nothing we do as ministry will stop if you were to leave. We are firmly established and enjoy the blessing of the Administration." I should mention that Don had just received an award from the University for the support he offered to all international students. I took Don's words and turned them over in my mind. It was true and it was very satisfying to see that come to be. Days later, while on a visit to KU to investigate the opportunity, I sat having coffee with an ISM worker there. He said, "Chuck, everything we are able to do at KU is dependent on who sits in the director's seat of the ISS office." I instantly was taken back to when I first refined how God was calling me to this profession. My decision was made for me and I can confidently say I was "called" to this position. No looking back, no doubts. Even if something else should keep me from fulfilling this job, I know where I am supposed to be today.

These are but a few examples of ways in which the church, denomination and parachurch organizations may work together with Christians who work for universities with international students to make these events not only successful but also provide a mutually satisfying experience. All options have their downsides. The downside for many in parachurch organizations as Chuck Olcese pointed out is having to raise one's own financial support. JDB

How God Called Anita Gaines to a Fulfilling Career Working for a Secular University With International Students

Growing up in a rural town in the southern part of the United States during the 1950s appears an unlikely start for a young African American girl who years later would work with university students from all over the world. But it was through those humble beginnings that I learned tremendous lessons about faith and perseverance. Fortunately I had a nurturing family and solid Christian teachings at my church where I accepted Jesus Christ as my Savior and Lord. In retrospect I can now see how God was planting seeds of curiosity about the world and the desire to branch out beyond the border of my small town experience. Public school was a wonderful outlet for me. I especially enjoyed world geography, history and music. My parents encouraged me to take piano lessons and later because of that interest, I decided to study music teacher education at the University of Houston.

During the start of my first semester at the University of Houston my dormitory roommate and I were invited to visit the Baptist Student Union (BSU). I really enjoyed the Christian fellowship there and the opportunities provided by the BSU for spiritual growth. For the first time in my life I met students who came from diverse backgrounds and experiences from the local area, from other parts of the U.S., and also from many other countries. I felt drawn to international students, and wanted to learn about their cultures and their countries. I was grateful for their friendships. Soon I was taking on leadership positions in the BSU, singing in the BSU choir, and going to Christian conferences. Through God's prompting I chose to spend several of my summers doing mission work through BSU programs in Texas, Arkansas and New York.

The BSU provided loving support and friendship to the international students and it was there that I met Dr. Jack Burke who was the director of International Student Services. He let me know about an opportunity to be a student worker in his office. Since it provided some much needed income and more importantly the chance to work with international students, I excitedly accepted the job.

As I approached the end of my studies I was uncertain about what to do next. I really enjoyed my experiences working with international students but my degree program had prepared me for a career in music. BSU had also developed my love of missions. These three options seemed like very different directions I could take. The opportunity that opened up for me was with the BSU for a nine month work assignment in campus evangelism at East Texas State University.

This experience involved working with BSU students to share God's love with others across campus. God graciously helped me to reach out to others and to create long lasting friendships while I was there. I felt that this experience prepared me for what was to come next: I was approved by the Foreign Mission Board of the Southern Baptist Convention to participate in a two year experience called the Missionary Journeyman program. My assignment was to be a music teacher with elementary school students at the Colegio Bautista in Temuco, Chile.

The experiences at Colegio Bautista were very special and fulfilling. I was able to use my music skills in a cross cultural setting to glorify Christ. My Spanish language skills learned in high school were quickly accelerated as I taught music in Spanish. The two years went by very quickly and I was very sad to leave. Upon returning to the United States I experienced reverse culture shock as I saw that so many things had changed, including me. I thought about the opportunity to continue in long term missions. For a brief period of time I taught music in the public schools. I also remembered the wonderful experience I had working with international students and decided to pay a visit to Dr. Burke. Through his counsel I began to see the puzzle pieces coming together. I had always wanted to work in an international environment. I now had cross- cultural experience through my mission experience. God had now opened a door for me to further my education so that I could work full time with international students. Dr. Burke told me that to work with international students it is helpful to have counseling skills. I quickly got my admissions application in and was approved to study Educational Psychology at the University of Houston.

Two years later I received my master's degree and was able to enter a position at the University of Houston as an International Student Counselor. With God's help I was able to be promoted to Associate Director and later became Director when Dr. Burke retired in 1994. God has also blessed me to be able to take on leadership positions in the professional organization NAFSA: Association of International Educators, culminating in receiving one of NAFSA's highest awards, the Homer Higbee Award for Distinguished Service to NAFSA.

As I look back on my life from where I started, I can now see how God has directed my steps and affirmed the career He has had for my life in working with international students and scholars here in the United States. I Samuel 16:7 holds a very special meaning for me. "...The Lord does not look at the things man looks at. Man looks at the outward appearance, but the Lord looks at the heart.

Figure 12 Anita Gaines, University of Houston International Student and Scholar Services Office advisor to government sponsored students, 1991

Where is the Hall of Tyrannus?

Rev. Al LaCour, Coordinator, RUF International

After thirty years as a pastor, I found myself (to my surprise - but no surprise to God!) as a fifty-six year old campus minister for internationals at Georgia Tech. My new "parish" was my own alma mater. I had served as the pastor of a multi-cultural Miami church. But I knew nothing about international student ministry (ISM). During my first year on the campus, I spent hours "prayer walking" the campus, asking God to give me "eyes" to see the harvest, and seeking the Spirit's guidance to structure my new ministry.

Observing (locally and through ACMI) other ISM's, I noted the many opportunities to serve internationals through deeds of love and mercy. Airport pickups, excursions, furniture or clothes closets, offering transportation - these are all ISM ministry staples. Having served as a campus staff member with an inter-denominational ministry, I also recognized a need to disciple and train internationals who were already following Christ. But, I sensed a missing component in this ministry to which God had now called me.

Toward the end of my first year on campus, I realized what was missing. I could spend most of my time in ministries to help students and to train the Christians. ISM is highly relational and very unstructured. But, as a full-time, ordained chaplain for foreign students, I was not doing the work of an evangelist. I realized God wanted me to structure my ministry around three broad missions:

- To WELCOME students from all nations. God commands us to show hospitality, to reflect his love for the stranger and foreigner. This meant sharing the gospel in deeds, not in words. For example, celebrations of cultural holidays would never be used to share the gospel (risking an unethical bait-and-switch).
- To EXPLORE the Gospel with internationals. This was the missing component.
- To EQUIP Christian internationals to be servant-leaders for Christ's kingdom in their home countries when they returned.

But, what was the best way to share the Gospel in Word? International students are some of the world's brightest. Most have little exposure to the Bible. It seemed that short gospel presentations, or preaching biblical sermons (a pastor's typical ministry) were not appropriate for ISM. God began to draw my heart to Acts 19:8-10: Paul's ministry at Ephesus. After the apostle was rejected by the synagogue, he moved to the "lecture hall of Tyrannus." As John Stott notes in his commentary on Acts (*The Spirit, the Church, and the World)*: "If religious people can be reached in religious buildings, secular people have to be reached in secular buildings."

Where was a suitable "Hall of Tyrannus" at Georgia Tech? This became my adventure, and also a work of God. As ISM workers know, registered student organizations (RSO's) may reserve university spaces for student meetings. But it is often difficult to reserve the same room for consecutive weeks. If you want to serve food (as we desired), most universities require the use of designated caterers. That becomes expensive for a series of weekly, semester-long meetings. So, I was presented with many obstacles.

We launched a "Dinner and Discovery" program (a meal followed by an optional Bible discussion) at a campus café owned by a Christian friend. But, the setting was a highly visible, public space. Muslim international students were easily scrutinized by friends.

After one semester, we moved to an off-campus private residence hall owned by another Christian friend. Here, we self-catered to a dozen internationals for a reasonable price. One evening, a Turkish student said to me privately, "You know, I am criticized by fellow Muslims for attending your program. I have told my friends I don't always agree with you and I don't plan to become a Christian. But I learn more here than from the Imams I have known. So, I have a suggestion. I know public universities cannot 'endorse' any religion. But, if you can find a meeting place in an on-campus facility, your meeting will look 'legitimate.' I may be able to invite more Turkish students to attend." Again I began to pray, to seek an on-campus "Hall of Tyrannus." A dramatic turn came early Fall, 2005, when Hurricane Katrina slammed New Orleans. All registered student organizations received a notice that Georgia Tech Student Center rooms would no longer be available for student group meetings until further notice. All of Tulane University's international students were being evacuated to Georgia Tech, to be temporarily housed in Student Center meeting rooms.

Personal flash back to 1992, 13 years earlier: 30 families in my Miami church lost homes to Hurricane Andrew. Church members often asked me an unanswerable question, "Why did God let me lose my home and all my belongings?" As best I could, I counseled, "If I understand the book of Job, you may never know God's reason for this. But, in the years ahead, you may begin to discover God's purpose for this in your life."

It was now time to apply those words to myself! I set an alarm for 5:00 AM to meet the buses filled with Tulane international students as they arrived at Georgia Tech. I wrote on a name tag: "Campus Minister for Internationals / Hurricane Alumnus."

What I had not prepared for: the Dean of Students, the Director of the Food Service, the Director of the Student Center, and the President of Georgia Tech were all standing on the same curbside. It was never my intention (but it was God's plan), that I received extraordinary "Nehemiah favor" from university administrators. Today, "Dinner and Discovery" meets in the Georgia Tech faculty dining room: a private dining space where faculty advisors host international students for lunch, to affirm their hard work. 65-85 international students gather each Tuesday night for a free hot meal, catered by Georgia Tech, but paid for by Atlanta area churches. After dinner, there is an optional investigative Bible study. Local area Christians serve as dinner hosts and table discussion leaders.

God has provided a "Hall of Tyrannus" at Georgia Tech, where internationals EXPLORE the gospel in a respectful, private, hospitable campus venue. The LORD is good, and he has done far more than we asked or imagined - for his glory!

MY ADVICE FOR CHRISTIANS SEEKING A CAREER WORKING WITH INTERNATIONAL STUDENTS IN HIGHER EDUCATION - AS A MINISTRY

Jack D. Burke, Ph.D., M.Div., M.S.
President, International Student Ministries Assistance, Inc.
Director Emeritus,* International Student and
Scholar Services, University of Houston

AS HAS BEEN SAID earlier there are three routes a Christian can take if you desire to work with international students. One is to <u>work in a church as a Minister of Missions or Minister to International Students</u> (currently not many openings for the latter). It has been my observation that working with international students as an employee of the church is most fulfilling for those who have the senior pastor and other senior church staff as well as the church lay leaders solidly behind you. That means encouraging you, and seeing that you have a salary and benefits that cover administrative and operating expenses at a fair and reasonable level for professional administrative staff.

Most employment possibilities will come through working for a parachurch organization, e.g. International Students, Inc., Bridges International, International Friendships Inc, InterVarsity, and InterFACE just to name a few. Having worked with many in parachurch ministries I see people who have a lot of job satisfaction, except for the continual burden to raise their own support. I have a great deal of admiration for all, but especially those in organizational leadership positions.

All those involved in church and parachurch professional positions should join ACMI (Assoc. of Christians Ministering among Internationals) which will provide access to the membership on the internet. Plan to attend the annual ACMI conferences. All possible contacts for employment will be there. Inquire also about churches and parachurch organization internship possibilities for working through their organizations with international students.

The other is to work for a university. "Way back when," I had to make the same decision. With God's guidance I decided to go the university route. Working for the church or parachurch organization is most satisfying for those who need a more direct approach in sharing their faith with international students. It also frees them from an office structured secular work environment unless they work for a Christian college. Also, there is not quite the same emphasis on higher education requirements for advanced degrees. Of course, you have to raise your own support; whereas in working for the university you do not. Both have their advantages and disadvantages.

What is needed to be effective in a position working with international students - starts with **Vision** for the job that needs to be accomplished, *prayer* for guidance in carrying out the mission, plus **courage, wisdom and hard work** are the keys to accomplishing great things for God and His Kingdom. I am thankful that God gave me the *vision* for doing ISM as a university director in charge of administering services to international students, initiating the Consultation (conference) at ISI's Star Ranch in 1981to bring those involved with ISM either outside or inside a university together. With ISI serving as the host, I am thankful for the opportunity to serve as co-founder of ACMI, and having the *vision and perseverance* to gain the NAFSA Board's approval for Christians to meet under the umbrella of the newly formed NAFSA Christian Specific Interest Group (SIG) at the national and regional NAFSA conferences. Benefits received from NAFSA were free hotel meeting rooms and publicity Opportunities

<u>for Serving Christ Working in a Campus International Student and Scholar Services Office, English as a Second Language (ESL) classroom; Study Abroad Program or as Faculty</u>

A strategic position for any international educator to hold is to be the Director of the International Student and Scholar Services Office (ISSSO) or Dean of International Programs. Either position holds tremendous influence over the campus international student community. As examples, they can:

- control, to large degree, who becomes employed, services offered, and the quality in which they are offered.
- develop a friendship family program for interested international students. (In my experience I found that families most often come from churches interested in sharing Christ's love with the students). I found it difficult to recruit families from secular sources.
- organize the 2-4 day orientation program for new international students.
- decide on which requesting groups and individuals may gain access to international students.
- promote relationships with student and community organizations that show ethical concern and care for the welfare of international students. Again, I found that it most often is the Christian groups, both on and off campus.
- select who serves as counselors and advisors to international students.
- serve as liaison between the student and government agencies, both U.S. and foreign.
- provide documentation so that the student can receive U.S. dollars from his/her own country and documentation so that the student may receive U.S. Government authorization for off campus employment or transfer to another university.
- employ and train future International Student Advisors through an internship program. In essence, a Christian leader of a campus International Student and Scholar Services Office is in a power position having control over:

  1. all services required by law and other services known to be helpful to international students.

2. access to the international students through the office's channels to publicize events, community services, international student enrollment statistics, office bulletin boards, and tables for handouts. (One year when I was the ISSSO director at the University of Houston I raised funds from Houston's First Baptist Church to rent a bus for ISM staff, Tom and Diane Lawrence and InterVarsity staff, to fill it up with international students who wanted to attend Inter-Varsity's International Student Christmas House Party (conference) at Bear Trap Ranch in the mountains high above Colorado Springs. Our office publicized that trip, as well as other holiday activities for international students. Of course, by virtue of my being one of the passengers I'm sure it could be interpreted that I approved of the organization's activity by joining the students for the overnight bus ride to Colorado Springs and conference experience. D'Ann and our children joined us after the bus's arrival. These students were all provided an opportunity to find out about Christianity and reasons for the celebration of Christmas, along with having a good time involved in Winter sports and other social activities. Sure beats loneliness back on campus.

3. Additionally, the universities' ISSSO offices are required:
   a) to help groups and individual international students through crises situations.
   b) to be the university's designated office for helping:
      (1) government agencies, faculty, students' families, students' friends, host families needing university assistance with a student overburdened with problems, meet the needs of families and foreign diplomats whenever student deaths occur, students who incur serious injuries or medical or psychological problems, victims of accidents and financial crises, e.g. students who are cut-off financially because of countries at war or suffering other forms of devastating crises.
      (2) to resolve serious problems which occur between students and professors or with other students, also their landlords, and, yes, even run-ins with the law.

These situations present unique opportunities for the office director and designated staff not only to be the spokesperson for the university but also to show compassion, integrity, and understanding. What a marvelous opportunity for those known to be Ambassadors for Christ. In many situations, especially during hospital visits, I felt like a campus chaplain ministering to the various serious needs of the students. As an option to help hurting students during times of crisis, I offered to pray for their needs. The answer was always "yes," regardless of the students own religious persuasion.

4. Here are other possibilities I found for serving Christ at a secular university:

    (a) Together with colleague Jerry Naylor, we developed a new campus organization, the Faculty-Staff Christian Fellowship. Weekly meetings were provided in the campus Religion Center and annual banquets in buildings with large rooms.

    (b) I was asked by the Religion Center program council to address the luncheon audience of university faculty, administrators, and students at annual Religious Emphasis Weeks.

    (c) At the request of the International Student Organization and nationality associations I served annually as their "chief guest" at programs they had organized in which I was requested to provide the university welcome to the audience.

    (d) D'Ann and I were on the guest lists at functions of on-campus religious organizations

    (e) I was asked to be a panelist representing Christianity at a joint weekend conference sponsored by the University of Houston Muslim Students Association and the Islamic Society of Greater Houston. (The other two invited panelists were a Muslim theologian from Temple University in Philadelphia and a Jewish Rabbi in Houston.)

    (f) Speaker at a number of churches in the Houston area, as well as throughout Texas, and in other states - denominational and independent, some were on behalf of the University's Friendship Family Program, others were to challenge the audience of the need to be involved in ministry to international students.

(g) invited speaker at churches and ISM parachurch organizations on and off campus, in Texas and other states to provide support with their ministries to international students.

(h) Chapel speaker at Fuller Theological Seminary and missions emphasis speaker at Golden Gate Seminary in San Francisco.

(i) Opportunities extended me to serve Christ by various Southern Baptist organizations

- National Student Ministries (NSM) asked me to speak at back-to-school conferences annually at Glorieta, NM; serve as a plenary speaker before an audience of 1600 at a back-to-school conference at Ridgecrest, NC, and speak at state-wide international student conferences in a number of states. In addition, National Student Ministries requested me to write an article on befriending international students for their national publication to students and to be a speaker at a seminar which involved the International Mission Board [Global Missions], North American Mission Board [Home Missions] and National Student Ministries at NSM's national headquarters in Nashville.

- Baptist Student Ministries invited me to speak, as did other parachurch campus student organizations on the University of Houston campus, and other campuses.

Southern Baptist Deacons national network invited me to write an article on ministering to the needs of international students for meetings at national and regional conferences.

Advantages of working as a university English as a Second Language (ESL) teacher

Since these instructors work with international students also, I have found distinct advantages for a Christian to work in this profession. The instructors normally work with small classes, so you get to know the students personally quite well. The students, lacking in English proficiency, provide opportunities for teachers to find families and students who can help the students practice conversational English. Christian families and student organizations are often the best resource (most often, the only resource available). Since Christians come from a culture where we are told to help the alien (foreigner) who is in your midst, "love your neighbor," be a "good Samaritan" by showing compassion where there is a need, we try to be of help. Naturally opportunities arise where both student and teacher will exchange views regarding their faith, as do people from the community who are engaged with the student in a regular conversational English program.

The disadvantage is that the ESL teachers have the students for a limited time, usually only a semester or two.

Advantages of working with international students as a university Christian professor

Since so many universities now have an international student enrollment that numbers in the thousands, chances are if you are a professor who teaches STEM courses (refers to sciences, technology, engineering, and mathematics) it's highly likely that many of your students will be international students at the graduate level. As examples:

Throughout my career, along with being a director of an International Student Office, I found that professors are usually accorded great respect by international students. Therefore, if you are considering an occupation where your influence will be widely felt by international students, try being a university professor, especially one who teaches STEM courses. Professors who are academic deans, department heads, and/or are full-tenured professors (especially if they carry a title as a "chaired professor" in a prestigious academic department) often wield great influence on a university campus. As an example I cite my good friend **Dr. Bruce MacFadyen**, former surgery department chair at the University of Georgia

Medical School. Prior to the position in Georgia, Dr. MacFadyen served as professor of surgery at the University of Texas – Houston Medical School. He returned from Georgia to UT Medical School in Houston years later where at the time of the writing of this book he continues his work as a professor.

Dr. MacFadyen was the catalyst who organized a weekly dinner and discussion program for the doctors and medical specialists from China who are at the world famous Texas Medical Center in Houston. Dr. MacFadyen first became interested in Chinese students through serving with his wife Rosemary as a friendship family to a Chinese student (and as it turned out also the students' friends) at the University of Houston. For years the Chinese ministry at the Texas Medical Center grew so fast that a Chinese minister was recruited to lead the group's activities. Added to his resume, Dr. MacFadyen has served as

- First Baptist Houston's Missions Committee Chair
- an ACMI Board member and
- a member of the International Student Ministries Assistance (ISMA) Board of Directors.

Another professor who became highly involved in international student ministry was the late **Dr. Bob Taussig**. While still living, "Dr. Bob" worked as a professor of Veterinary Medicine at Kansas State University. With a heart for God and ministry to international students he and I together with Art Everett were appointed as ACMI's first executive committee whose job was to organize the Association of Christian Ministries to Internationals (ACMI) – the title has since changed to Association of Christians Ministering among Internationals. Dr. Bob was a Board Chair early in the life of ACMI. He also developed a ministry for international students in Manhattan, Kansas, called Helping International Students (HIS). His wife Mary worked at his side in ISM. These are but a few examples of ways in which the church and parachurch organizations may work together.

Another Christian professor who served the international student community with distinction was the University of Southern California's **Dr. William Georgiades**. Now deceased, Dr. Georgiades served as the Chair of the International Student Office Advisory Committee when I was a graduate student at USC. Dr. Georgiades was not only a distinguished professor in his Secondary Education Department but also served as

Interim Dean of the School of Education at one point. He became very influential in my life by gaining approval for me to serve a one-year foreign student advising internship in USC's International Student Office following completion of my masters degree. Some years later he served as one of the professors on my doctoral committee. During the years I served as director of International Student and Scholar Services at the University of Houston Dr. Georgiades became Dean of the College of Education at the University of Houston. With the power of his position and backing, I felt like I had just been granted tenure. He served as a wonderful resource to my office. He also served as one of our Faculty-Staff Christian Fellowship annual banquet luncheon speakers, as well as speaker at a university-wide banquet honoring friendship families of international students sponsored by my office. On the personal side D'Ann and I became very close friends with Bill and his wife Ruth Georgiades. When Bill died Ruth gave me a call when D'Ann and I were in Hong Kong asking if I would give the eulogy at Bill's funeral. Of course I said I would and we caught the next flight back to Houston to be there for our good friend Bill Georgiades' funeral.

Yet, another Christian in academia of distinction at the University of Southern California was **Dr. Bob Mannis**, a Christian member of the faculty and former Assoc. V.P for Student Affairs at the University of Southern California. Dr. Mannis, the campus faculty advisor for InterVarsity, together with his family spent their summers serving as staff at InterVarsity's conference site on Catalina Island. When my wife and I headed up an InterVarsity Christmas House Party for international students at Lake Tahoe we invited Dr. Bob Mannis to be a speaker. Upon his retirement from the University Dr. Mannis was honored with great respect by the USC Community for his outstanding service to the University and its students. No one could miss Bob Mannis at the annual June commencement. A tall, handsome figure, Bob was the one who was often asked to lead the procession. He took on the appearance of a grand marshal leading top university administrators, the faculty, and graduating students to the front of the outdoor library plaza where they were seated, all to the music of the mighty Trojan Marching Band, awaiting the commencement to begin.

*Director Emeritus title conferred on me by University of Houston President James Pickering following my retirement banquet March 31, 1994.

33

Chapter

How God Opened My Eyes and Called Me To This Strategic Field of Global Missions

AS A YOUNG 14-YEAR-OLD I gave my life to Christ and later, still a teen-ager, dedicated my life to missions. In those days I was thinking only of the traditional ways of going into all the world to make disciples of all nations. That is, you sign up with a foreign mission board, raise your support and go to the "mission field" which always meant to a foreign country. If you were "Stanley and Livingston" types you went to the jungles of Africa.

When I was in college I thought I would be signing up with the "New Tribes Mission." When I became a seminary student at Fuller Theological Seminary, that was my mindset. All the chapel speakers from foreign mission boards always approached missions from that perspective. It wasn't until I began reflecting back to my college days at the University of Oregon did I begin thinking "outside the box." That was when I had befriended a student from Baghdad, Iraq. The way this came about was somewhat of a miracle itself. When Rosalind Rinker, an InterVarsity Christian Fellowship regional staff director, came to campus she wanted the IV chapter students to sign up for appointments in which each would join her for coffee at the Erb Memorial Student Union.

I found out in advance from other students that one of the questions Roz would ask is, "Do you have a foreign student friend?" Not having one, fortunately I spotted what appeared to be a foreign student coming out of the World Literature class I had just come out of just 10 minutes before my appointment with Roz. In haste I introduced myself and asked him for his name and which country he was from. He said, "Aziz Abdul Nabi*and I'm from Baghdad, Iraq." Then boldly I told him of the weekend retreat I was going to that coming weekend on the Oregon Coast which was sponsored by InterVarsity Christian Fellowship.

Then I asked him "would you like to join me and the group?" Quickly he responded "yes." After exchanging names and phone numbers for follow-up, I crossed the street and went into the Erb Memorial Student Union where Roz was awaiting me. When she came to that question I had been waiting for, "Do you have an international student friend?" I was so relieved that I could reply in the affirmative. I proudly added, "In fact he is going to join me and our IV group for the weekend conference in which you are the speaker." I thought much like a young collegian would back in those days, "Wow, that just gave me some brownie points with the IVCF leadership."

I am happy to report that at the retreat whenever there was a speaker, Aziz was busily taking notes in Arabic. When asked why he was doing that he replied, "To send to my family back home." As the weekend ended and we were back in Eugene, I asked Aziz if he would like to join me for the Sunday evening church service at the First Baptist Church. Again, Aziz's immediate response was "yes." By Aziz's quick "yes" replies it showed me how hungry international students are for friendship with Americans. I was certain then, as I still am, that most American students on a U.S. college campus would not be so quick to accept an invitation from a total stranger to join him or her for a weekend at a religious retreat when the stranger was of a different religion and culture who used words not always understood, and looked a little different.

From then on, Aziz would periodically join me for the weekly InterVarsity meetings and at times for meals at the Christian men's fraternity-type house where I was living on campus. We became very close friends. He was very moved at the viewing of the movie, "Quo Vadis," one that had a Christian theme which we attended together on a Friday evening. After the movie was over Aziz told me that he did not realize that Christians went through such terrible persecutions.

After graduating from Oregon and finishing medical school Aziz returned to Iraq where he became the personal physician to Abdul Karem Kassem, the political leader who staged a *coup* in Iraq leading the opposition to the ruling power. Fearing for his life before the attempted *coup d' etat* Aziz was able to escape Iraq with his wife and child and return to the states where he later became a cardiologist in Schenectady, New York.

D'Ann and I hosted Aziz and his wife Anna Marie in our Houston home and years later visited them in their Schenectady, N.Y. home for a weekend after I had retired. I was able once again to openly witness to Aziz. Although he never made a decision to receive Christ as his Savior he told me that his relatives back in Iraq were pressuring him to become a devout Muslim by going on a *hajj* to Mecca, the holiest city for Muslims, which he said he could not do. We kept in touch throughout his life and one thing we could do is discuss each other's faith in an atmosphere of mutual respect and acceptance. Although he had married Anna Marie, a Catholic lady from Belgium, and never went on a hajj to Mecca like good Muslims do at least once during their lifetime, I never found out whether he had made a commitment to follow Christ before Aziz died. It was always my prayer and heartfelt conviction that he would make that decision. I lost a dear friend whom I would like to see in heaven some day.

*Aziz Abdul Nabi – now deceased

My calling to International Student Ministry (ISM)

As a new student at Fuller Seminary I was considering options for missionary service when like a flash out of the blue the question popped in my mind **"Who is ministering to international students like my University of Oregon good friend, Aziz? They are the brightest and best. They have the promise of becoming future world leaders, people of influence, affluence, and movers and shakers of their own countries. If won to Christ they could become much more effective missionaries to people in their own respective countries at no expense to mission boards here in America.** Right then and there, I made a commitment to work with international students as a ministry. I made appointments with visiting chapel missionary speakers to discuss international student missions. All said it was a good idea but that their mission organization did not have an outreach to international students. This led me to think that I was the first to come up with the idea of ministry to international students until another seminary student told me about a relatively new organization, International Students Incorporated (ISI) whose leader was Bob Finley. My brother Harry also told me about his InterVarsity colleague Paul Little who was located in New York City and was in charge of IVCF's outreach to international students.

During my second year of seminary, D'Ann and I were married. I was so glad to find that she too could see the need for ministry to international students. This ministry soon became "a calling" to her as well. As it has turned out, for the rest of our lives ministry to international students became a team effort.

What Steps Did We Take to Implement that Vision?

In our determination to be in contact with area international students, mostly from nearby Pasadena City College, my wife D'Ann and I found that we could attend a Sunday afternoon tea with international students at the YMCA in Pasadena. When Linda our first child was born, that didn't stop us. We just took our baby daughter in a stroller to the "Y" each Sunday afternoon. In fact we found Linda was an "ice breaker" for us in not only befriending international students, but also the leadership involved. It wasn't long before the student leaders were asking D'Ann and me to be chaperones on a Thanksgiving Weekend retreat at some rustic overnight facilities on top of Mt. Wilson. The students received permission from the college official in charge for us to be chaperones. Since the students wanted D'Ann and me to bring some of our American friends, we invited some friends from Fuller Seminary to join us. So D'Ann and our baby daughter slept with the gals in one dormitory room and I slept with the guys in another large room.

Before the Christmas break we were able to persuade some of these students to sign up for the InterVarsity Christian Fellowship sponsored "Christmas House Party" at Lake Tahoe. A controversy broke out one evening at the House Party while Paul Fromer, the IV speaker, was talking about the Day of Passion and crucifixion of Jesus. Joseph, a student from Israel disagreed vehemently with the speaker's interpretation. Since this aroused so much interest in the study of the Bible, the students from Pasadena City College wanted to continue this study and discussion once we arrived back in Pasadena. While still at the IV House Party, Hanna, a student leader from Gaza, upon reading the third chapter of the Gospel of John wanted to know the meaning of being "born again" and upon hearing the interpretation said that he too wanted to be born again. At that moment I led him in a prayer to receive Christ as his Savior. Meanwhile, much effort was made by the conference leadership to calm the student from Israel. Since his car had a big problem, he had to stay until the end. Meanwhile, the conference leadership went to great extremes to help him and his wife get the necessary repairs.

After returning to Pasadena, among the students who attended each Friday evening's Bible study and dessert in our home, were the President of the International Student Association and the President of the International Relations Club. The Bible study was led by InterVarsity's Paul Fromer who had befriended some students himself at Lake Tahoe's InterVarsity Conference. We found out that through this study of the scriptures students were attracted to the life of Jesus. To illustrate, two brothers from Damascus, Syria, Samir and Monir, made commitments to follow Christ.

Returning Home with students from Damascus, Syria

Having received an invitation to visit the home of Samir and Monir in Damascus, Syria, D'Ann and I decided to join them in their return home in June, 1957. I had just graduated from Fuller Seminary when my brother Norman bought me a 16 mm movie camera to film this trip. We felt it important to film the two international students returning to their home country as committed Christians. Aboard the ship on our way to Beirut we enjoyed having Bible study together each day. In Damascus, the father, being the General Motors dealer in Damascus, met us in his bright shiny new Chevrolet.

- While visiting Samir and Monir's family in the July heat of Damascus, these Syrian Christian brothers took us to a missionary compound as I mentioned before where we visited with two women missionaries. They told D'Ann and me that **they would never have met people of this high class if we had not brought them to their missionary compound.** Among our activities we went with their friends to a mountain retreat, Bloudan, where we enjoyed sitting out on the restaurant patio in the coolness of the higher elevation. On the return to Damascus we stopped off at the home of our Syrian friends' relatives. **At the end of our stay with the family, D'Ann and I were impressed with the fact that** <u>these brothers, in returning to Syria,</u>

- *were able to speak fluent Arabic without spending a day studying the language*
- *mixed well with family and friends, indicating that no time had to be spent studying the culture of the Syrian people*
- *were in an established and prestigious family with a network of people who respected and trusted them and with whom they could easily interact. Further,*
- *they needed no visa to enter the country because they were native citizens, and*
- *they did not have to raise financial support to live in Syria. For them, they were simply "returning home."*
- *They did not need a work visa*
- *They could share their faith, be involved in a church, and cooperate with missionaries, all in perfect Arabic and in culturally sensitive ways.*

So many missionaries have told us through the years that returned students like Samir and Monir, are much more effective in reaching their own people with the "good news" than foreigners going to their same countries as missionaries.

Following seminary graduation and the summer abroad, D'Ann and I taught school for five years during which time we earnestly sought the Lord's guidance as to which path to follow in entering full-time ministry to international students. Still involved in volunteer ministry to international students mainly through InterVarsity, we took a close look at InterVarsity and International Students Inc. Two Conservative Baptist Church pastors had agreed to help us financially but they wanted us to work through a parachurch organization. D'Ann and I had met with Bob Finley, the then President of ISI in Washington, D.C. in mid-June of 1957 en route to Europe and the Middle East after graduating from Fuller. In asking Bob about being assigned specifically to ISI's open position at the University Presbyterian Church in Seattle, we were told that we would have to submit ourselves to ISI first with no commitments as to where we might be placed.

Bob explained that in joining the ISI staff, it was like joining the army. ISI would make the decision as to where we would be placed. Not feeling comfortable with that option, we decided not to pursue it further. However, a few years later Bob Finley did try to recruit me to be in charge of ISI's ministry in the Los Angeles area. By then I was looking at other possibilities. ISI's Hal Guffey, during a stop-over at our home in California, encouraged me to pursue the foreign student advising career if that's where I thought the Lord was leading me.

Through the years we have cooperated with ISI staff and have tried to provide assistance whenever possible. ISI has recognized that help by granting me the "Foreign Student Advisor of the Year" award in 1991 and the two of us ISI's "Excellence in Service to International Students" annual award to a volunteer (or in our case "volunteers") in June 2006 at their annual staff conference in Seattle).

We have also been strong supporters of InterVarsity through the years as has already been indicated. As an IVCF staff member himself my brother Harry was successful in getting D'Ann and me involved in helping with the International Student House Parties at Lake Tahoe in 1955 and 1956. Also as was indicated earlier we had a good meeting with Paul Little, one of InterVarsity's original staff in charge of international student ministry, who lived in New York City in 1957. At the end it was the decision to follow the Lord's leading into becoming the university's administrative director of the office that was in charge of the institution's services to its international students that won out. From my perspective it couldn't have been a better fit.

34

Chapter

CONCLUSION

Identifying, Recruiting, Training and Equipping Christian International Students for Missions Work in their Home Countries Just Makes "Common Sense"

WE ALL REMEMBER OUR mom or dad telling us to just "use common sense" when making decisions. When it comes to who to support to do foreign missions work, there are many of us who strongly believe it makes good common sense to support church staff or Christian parachurch organization staff who work with international students. Why? They are the ones who help recruit and train Christian international students become the most ideal missionaries upon return to their homelands for the following reasons:

1. Two years of foreign language and culture training – not needed

International students learn their native language starting with birth. Therefore there's no need to spend time studying the dominant language of that country's population for 2 years. Students simply return home as fluent speakers of the dominant native language of their people. No foreign accent either. For you who are on the phone trying to understand foreign computer techs, international airline representatives, or in ordering flowers when speaking to a representative from abroad, you know exactly what I am talking about. But if the international students are Christians, they have certain advantages in communicating the gospel to others in their own countries. Christian international students return to the very countries where they learned to speak their language and understand the culture and customs of their people from birth. Therefore, there is no need to spend a couple of years in an intensive course of study to learn about their own country's language, customs and culture.

2. **International returnees are at home with family and friends who form their support base.**

International students have the advantage of a family home to which to return. They have the emotional and, if needed, the financial support too of family, relatives and friends.

3. **International student returnees are often from families of influence in their own countries.**

Returning home to a family of influence either through government, business, education, field of science or engineering, world of finance, or other profession, international students have built-in connections to begin working themselves into positions of influence themselves. Properly trained Christian returnees have the opportunity to exert their influence for Christ. Just refer to the chart in this book which shows the large number who have returned to become world leaders.

4. **Acceptability factor: international student returnees blend into their own communities.**

Since international students are often from families of influence, leadership, and wealth, they have a higher degree of acceptance than the foreigners who have come to their countries as missionaries out to convert them.

5. **Being citizens of their respective countries is an advantage.**

No passport and visa problems for students <u>returning to home country.</u>

An international student with a valid **passport** from his country of citizenship does not need to apply for a passport to re-enter his own country. Nor does the student need to apply for a **visa** or an extension of stay as do non-citizens. Therefore, there is no "red tape" involved. They are back to being citizens again instead of being looked on as "foreigners" when studying abroad, and as foreign missionaries who come to their country.

6. **When internationals return home they do not experience "culture shock" or homesickness to the degree many missionaries do when living abroad.**

Since the international student is returning home there is no homesickness involved. The family upon receiving the missing member of their family back home no longer sheds tears of sadness but rather tears of joy.

7. **No furloughs needed by Christian internationals who return to their country of birth.**

Once Christian international students have returned home there is no need for furloughs as is the case for missionaries. Missionaries from the USA for example, need to return to the United States on furlough every so many years in order to meet with their supporters, take care of family needs, and to take a break. I know of missionaries who returned to the states twice a year in order to take care of specific needs. Just the opposite is the case of Christian international student returnees. They are already at home in their countries of origin. They can continue their ministries without any serious interruption of time.

8. **Returnees can provide leadership to struggling church back home.**

Some can serve as pastors. An example which is cited in chapter 8 is the Yan Fook Church in Hong Kong in which returned student Patrick So became pastor when the church only had 100 members. Through the years he developed that small church into a mega-church that now has two branch campuses which all together totals 10,000 members, and a Bible institute/seminary to train "budding" pastors. Serving as his Sunday School Superintendent is another returnee who also received his bachelors degree in the U.S. at the University of Houston.

9. **Returning Christian international students properly trained are the most effective "missionaries" to home country in this dangerous world.**

American Christians have a target on their back in some regions of the world. First, because they are Americans. For example, I heard from a friend whose American son-in-law is a U.S. Marine in Saudi Arabia. His job is to train the military in Saudi Arabia. To work there he had to let his hair grow long, grow a beard, and have no markings on him of the U.S. Marine Corps. Without belaboring the obvious, one can see that the closer one looks like others in the country, the easier it is to gain acceptance. For the most part, that's the way Christian international students appear in their return home. Second, because of those who are identifiable as professional missionaries out to convert the people of a predominately different religious persuasion, their lives are at risk in some countries. For example, there are still stories in the news of Christians who are captured, imprisoned, tortured and/or killed because of the visibility of their involvement as Christians in those countries. The ideal is for Christian international students, clothed with spiritual maturity and Biblically well-equipped, to return to their respective countries, and perform the kind of ministry that is needed. Since they can speak the language fluently and without accent plus understand the culture, they can blend more easily into the societal environment. This way they can become more effective witnesses for Christ to their family, friends, neighbors, professional associates, and members of the broader community.

As Sam Tin, former international student and influential Christian businessman in Hong Kong once said, "**We Hong Kongers are in 'much better position than the foreigners' to work with the three-self churches.**"[42] Reason for Christian Hong Kong Citizens greater influence for Christ: "**Chinese government is sensitive to foreign influence with respect to religious beliefs.**" (Email from Sam Tin to Dr. Jack Burke, 8/28/2014)

When we consider such Asian countries as Thailand and Japan, I think it is quite widely known that the percentage of Christians is low despite relatively open access by missionaries from Western countries for 150 years in the case of Japan and even longer in the history of Thailand. In an article that addresses "Why So Few Christians in Japan?" It is noted that less than one percent of Japan's population is Christian even though Christianity was introduced to the country over 150 years ago.[43]

A reason given by noted authority, Dr. Minoru Okuyama, director of the Missionary Training Center in Japan, is that "Japanese people value human relationships more than truth and principle." During his presentation at the Tokyo 2010 Global Missions Consultations, Dr. Okuyama, a former Buddhist and Shintoist himself, continued by stating that it is "Because they are afraid of disturbing human relationships of their families or neighborhood even though they know that Christianity is the best. . .Thus, Japanese make much of human relationships more than the truth. Consequently we can say that as for Japanese, one of the most important things is harmony; in Japanese 'Wa'." He added, "Those who harm the harmony are bad, whether they are right or not has been beside the question."[44]

With the priority being given to the importance of "human relationships and harmony" it shouldn't take a rocket scientist to figure out that returning Christian Japanese students would have a distinct advantage over any other method of Christian outreach. It would be much easier for Japanese Christian students returning to Japan to know how best to develop good human relationships. Also, to create harmony it takes an in- depth knowledge of Japanese culture, which Japanese Christian returning students most certainly have.

In an article on **"The Difficulty of Evangelizing in Thailand,"** [45]Brian Stiller raised the question, "Why is that after over 183 years of evangelical missionary work, an investment of thousands of lives and millions upon millions of dollars, out of a total population of 65 million there are only 370,000 evangelical Christians, one half of one percent?" One of the reasons he gave was that the foreign mission boards held on to the controls of leadership within their foreign mission boards." Brian went on to say there is now "optimism and hope for discipleship and church growth." He cited a key reason given for their current optimism. According to Dr. Winacha Kowae, founder of the Assemblies of God and chairman of the Evangelical Fellowship of Thailand (EFT), today . . . the Thai church is

<u>not run by foreigners.</u>"[46] [author underlined] It has been multiple centuries since the Europeans first introduced Christianity in Thailand. It looks like the missionaries from the West were not able to penetrate Thailand's culture with the Gospel. So now they are concentrating on the Thai Christians themselves.[47] **That fits perfectly into one of the purposes of this book. That is to prepare the Christian students from countries like Thailand to be witnesses for Christ upon their return home.**

10. **International students returning home as actively involved Christians help defuse the prevailing thought in Asia that Christianity is a Western Religion.**

According to Y.P. Yohannan, Asian missionary and statesman, "Western missionaries seldom are effective today in reaching Asians and establishing local churches in the villages of Asia. Unlike the Western missionary, the national missionary can preach, teach and evangelize without being blocked by most of the barriers that confront Westerners."[48]

11. **It's cost effective: international student returnees are not dependent upon churches and mission agencies in North America or any other country, except for their homeland, for financial support.**

When we look at the cost involved for a Christian international student to return to his/her country of origin it is relatively minor. The cost of air travel is most often covered by the student himself or his/her family. For those comparative few who are fortunate enough to be government or privately sponsored, then the sponsoring agency covers the cost for airfare. Upon graduation, once the student arrives in his homeland, then the costs are borne by the student himself or his/her family until the student finds employment.

Further, Christian international students are not required to do deputation work in North America to raise funds for their financial support. There are few exceptions, one being Lily Lam from Hong Kong who had become a Christian when she was attending the University of Houston. Before graduation she signed up with Campus Crusade for Christ to be on staff when she returned home to Hong Kong. I helped her raise funds by introducing her to Dr. John Bisagno, the then Sr. Pastor of Houston's First Baptist Church. He in turn provided an opportunity for her to make a brief presentation on a Sunday evening. At the end of the service Brother John gave the audience an opportunity to respond financially which they did ever so generously. Christian international student returnees do not need long-term support of a North American church or Foreign Missions Board. By contrast it is expensive for mission boards to equip and support a missionary to go to another country. Additionally, there is the expense of missions' organization staff who are needed to provide logistical support for missionaries on the field.

12. **The reverse is sometimes the case once the Christian international student becomes established economically in his/her profession back home.**

Former Christian international students who are well-off financially are known to contribute to the support of international student ministry staff who mentored them spiritually when they were attending a university in the states.

13. **Upon <u>retirement</u>, Christian international students who returned home need no support from country abroad in which they received their education.**

The traditional foreign missionary often has a pension fund set up by the supporting church and/or missions organization. This fund will provide some of the needed support once the missionary retires. However, the Christian international student who is engaged in missions in his own country finds support upon retirement from personal savings, the government, a company pension fund, and/or family resources. I have often heard that the social security resource for the support of aging parents in some Asian countries is the family. That's where it helps to have large families. Like a multiple choice test, it could also be "all the above."

14. **The process of identifying, recruiting, training, equipping Christian international students for the return to their homelands should begin soon after their arrival in America or other host country.**

15. **Follow-up is extremely important.**

There are a number of training programs. When Jesus said "The harvest is plentiful but the laborers are few" (Matt. 9:37), it still holds true today. None of us can afford to say that the way to do foreign missions should be restricted to <u>only</u> returned Christian international students or <u>only</u> traditional foreign missionaries. As was discussed in an earlier chapter, "There's room for both." You can see that there's still need for the traditional foreign missionary approach to reach the world for Christ. Yet, considering that this is a dangerous world, that Christian international students with proper training are better qualified and are available in larger numbers than ever, it makes more sense to do our best at supporting programs designed to recruit and train Christian international students for ministry in their own homelands. If a choice has to be made, trained and equipped Christian international students returning home is the most effective choice rather than to concentrate on sending American missionaries or other missionaries from the West to the Christian student returnees' countries.

35

Introduction to Survey of ACMI Members Engaged in International Student Ministry (ISM)

A SURVEY WAS SENT to members of ACMI engaged in ISM, requesting basic ISM information be returned using the following format. Those who returned the completed survey form are listed according to the following categories:

- Churches
- Denomination
- Parachurch Organizations
  1. General
  2. Ethnic/language
  3. Country Specific

The survey questions were:

*<u>Name of your organization and contact information</u>

* Who do you minister to?

*. What is your mode of ministry?

* What are your services?

* Recruitment information, both international students with whom you minister and personnel to work with your organization

* Other

Knowledge of churches with paid staff was received independent of the survey.

FOR **UPDATES** GO TO WEBSITE OR E-MAIL ADDRESS OF ORGANIZATIONS LISTED

Chapter

EXAMPLES OF CHURCHES WITH PAID ISM STAFF AND OTHER CHURCHES

Churches with Paid ISM Staff Responding to 2012 ACMI Survey (Information is limited*)		
Briarwood Presbyterian Church	Birmingham, AL 35243	UAB, Samford
First Evangelical Free Church	Fullerton, CA 92835	Cal State Fullerton and area
Lakeview Baptist Church	Auburn, AL36830	Auburn Univ. area
Park Street Church (Focus)	Boston, MA 02108	Harvard, MIT. & Boston area
Tenth Presbyterian Church (TIF)	Philadelphia, PA 19103	Penn, Temple, Drexel, etc.
Truro Anglican Church	Fairfax, VA 22030	DC campuses
Westminster International Friends North Avenue Presbyterian Church	Atlanta, GA	Atlanta campuses

(Email sent from Beau Miller to Jack Burke – 2/26/2014, taken from listing of churches compiled while serving on ACMI's Board, including use of ACMI records)

*Name of your organization and contact information

Briarwood International Outreach (a ministry of **Briarwood Presbyterian Church***)
Contact: BIO Office: bio@briarwood.org or 225-776-5404.

* **Who do you minister to?** All international students and scholars
* **What is your mode of ministry?** Bible studies (groups and one-on-one), Sunday School, Church
* **What are your services?** Shopping trips, sight-seeing trips, airport rides, ESL, Friendship Partners, and hospitality meals.
* **Recruitment information, both international students with whom you minister and personnel to work with your organization:** Recruiting students and scholars through various events, especially welcome picnic and beach trip to Florida in the beginning of fall semester, and trip to US Space and Rocket Center in the beginning of spring semester. Others through shopping trips, sightseeing trips, Friendship Partners program, ESL classes, and hospitality meals.
Recruiting Christian Americans as volunteers through church (Sunday school groups, missions conference, advertisement).
(Email - Jacob Jasin to Jack Burke – 3/26/2012 Orig, 2/9/18 Rev)

*Name of your organization and contact information

Internationals Outreach (IO), a ministry of Tenth Presbyterian Church
1701 Delancey Street, Philadelphia, PA 19103. 215-735-7688; www.tif.tenth.org; Rev. Enrique Leal, Minister of Internationals

*Who do you minister to? All internationals
*What is your mode of ministry? We have a variety of avenues for ministry. On Sundays we have a worship service for internationals. Attendance ranges from the mid-50s to 70. Earlier in the morning we offer an English class using the Bible as text. Once a month we have a potluck luncheon at the church after the morning worship service for

the internationals. Some American volunteers attend as well. On Friday evenings we have conversational English classes in the church in which a volunteer meets with usually 1-3 students to teach English the first hour and after a refreshment break teaches the Bible and English the last 45 minutes. Often this is the first place we meet many new students. We also have several Bible study groups that meet during the week for both evangelism and discipleship. Often these are a key to seeing internationals come to Christ. Each spring we have a retreat outside of the city on a weekend with a speaker sharing on some Christian topic. We offer some outings throughout the year. During Thanksgiving we match internationals with host families in the church for hospitality at a meal. We have a Christmas celebration and a Lunar New Year celebration every year. A few families in the church also house internationals in their home as renters.

*What are your services? See above.

*Recruitment information, both international students with whom you minister and personnel to work with your organization: Recruitment of internationals to come to our ministry events is largely through word of mouth. Many come through one international inviting their friend who is an international. A few people find us through our website. Sometimes internationals will come into the church because they see the church walking by and attend a worship service and then meet someone involved with IO.

*Other: Every year we have one to two seminary student interns working with our ministry.

(Email - Bruce McDowell to Jack Burke – 4/03/2012 Orig,; 2/13/18 Rev by Enrique Leal)

*Name of your organization and contact information

Westminster International Friends
The organization is a partnership between the North Avenue Presbyterian Church and the Westminster Christian Fellowship (campus student ministry at Georgia Tech). Contacts: Neale and Carol Hightower

[mailto:nealeh1@bellsouth.net] home number 404 378 5763. Our website is www.wifriends.org. The site is primarily pictures of our various events and we keep it "intentionally secular."

Who do you minister to? Our focus is on mainland Chinese students and scholars (and their families), but we welcome everyone.

What is your mode of ministry? Relational Evangelism: We build trust relationships with people we meet and we share the Gospel through these relationships – teaching and regular contact.

What are your services? Weekly Bible "discussions", trips, furniture for apartments, practical assistance (how do I?), airport pickup/welcome/temporary housing, and English Second Language classes. As more scholars bring their children, we offer ESL for these children as well during the worship time on Sundays. We offer opportunity for parents to observe Christian worship services on Sunday and provide an "ESL" style class during the Sunday School hour to help them understand what's going on in the worship and what we mean when we do it. In addition, we host a welcoming dinner in mid-August (beginning of the semester) and a Christmas party (end of fall semester).

Recruitment information, both international students with whom you minister and personnel to work with your organization: American families are recruited and trained in North Avenue church and some other Atlanta area churches who share our mission and direction. The church and its staff are very supportive of this ministry and encourage people to be involved. Chinese student contact is through a large welcoming effort at the beginning of fall semester. Most of our student contact is through referral from the existing student base. When a new scholar arrives, for example, an existing scholar who is part of our program brings his friend. We have some limited contact with Chinese students and scholars at Emory University, CDC and Georgia State University though we are not active on those campuses. Regular workers (all volunteer) are recruited primarily from North Avenue Church. Around 30 people are regularly involved with the program. A larger number of families host students during the year.

Other: Our financial resources come from North Avenue church and Westminster Christian Fellowship. We have use of the church facilities and buses for trips, etc. and the WCF building on campus for meetings when needed. The church building is also available to us for events, but is not as convenient as the WCF (on campus) building which works well for smaller group meetings during the week.

(Email - Neale Hightower to Jack Burke – 3/20/2012 Orig,; 2/9/18 Rev)

*I received information that there are other churches that might have ISM paid staff too. (Email sent from Beau Miller to Jack Burke – 2/26/2014)

Other Churches <u>Responding</u> to 2012 ACMI Survey

Houston's First Baptist Church (HFBC)
International Student Friendship Ministry (ISFM).
Contact: Marie Downing, Volunteer ISFM Director, <u>downings@flash.</u>
<u>net</u>, 713-956-6052,
<u>https://houstonsfirst.org/the-loop/opportunity/international-student-</u>
<u>friendship-ministry</u>

*Who do you minister to? ISFM ministers to the University of Houston international students who request an American friend through the UH Friendship Program.

*What is your mode of operation? ISFM provides a means whereby University of Houston Students and HFBC members are brought together in a meaningful cross-cultural relationship. HFBC members wishing to befriend an international student are matched with an international student(s) after completing the required orientation.

*What are your services? Friendship families and singles are required to be in contact with their student(s) and meet at least once a month, provide opportunities to observe and join in mutual inquiry into cultural and religious differences, to be an American and Christian ambassador of goodwill, respond to program surveys, share the gospel in a non-proselyting manner and pray for their student(s). In addition, some friendship partners volunteer for the UH Friendship airport student pick-up and assist with the UH Friendship Program student check-in. The HFBC International Friendship Ministry was formed by Jack and D'Ann Burke in the early 70's and through God's grace the ministry continues to minister to international students. The HFBC Missions office under the leadership of William Taylor, Missions Pastor, provides for needed materials, meeting and gathering facilities and monetary and spiritual support. HFBC provides friendship partners for approximately 25% of the students participating in the UH Friendship Program.

* Recruitment information, both international students with whom you minister and personnel to work with your organization:

- HFBC friendship families and singles are recruited through various means including but not limited to brochures, bulletin announcements and making announcements in Bible study classes.

- After an initial communication with the ISFM director, the friendship family/singles are required to complete the required orientation and complete an application. The University of Houston manages the program requirements for the students.
- The family/single are then matched with a student(s) and are free to begin their friendship. Follow-up emails and surveys are sent by the UH to ensure that the connection between student and friendship family/single is continuing and functioning well.
- HFBC host at least one Houston-wide gathering (Fun Night) so students and friendship partners can mingle among others participating in the ministry.

(Personally delivered, Marie Downing to Dr. Jack Burke, 5/29/15 Orig, 2/10/18 Rev)

37

Chapter

DENOMINATIONS WITH ISM AFFILIATED ORGANIZATIONS

(Those responding to ACMI Survey – updated 2018 – listed alphabetically)

*Name of your organization and contact information:

RUF International (RUF)
RUF-I is the ISM division of Reformed University Fellowship of the Presbyterian Church in America. The PCA's ISM was founded as "International Students Christian Fellowship" (ISCF) in 1983 by Ms. Jean Lappin, a former MTW medical missionary. From 2008 — 2014, Rev. J. Al LaCour served as RUF's International Coordinator. Contact information: RUF National Office: 1700 North Brown Rd. Suite 104, Lawrenceville, GA 30043. Telephone: (678) 825-1070. www.ruf.org/about/ruf-international

* **Who do you minister to?** RUF-I serves international students from all nations. RUF-I ministries are chartered as Registered Student Organizations (RSO) by local universities. RUF-I Campus Ministers,

ordained and sent by PCA churches, recruit and lead teams of church members, Interns, career Staff, and Missionaries.

 * **What is your mode of ministry?** RUF-I partners with, supporting Christians and local churches. On-campus, RUF-I Campus Ministers serve as chaplains to international students. Off-campus, RUF-I Campus Ministers "equip the saints" (Ephesians 4:12) to offer Biblical hospitality, and so to "welcome the nations."

 * **What are your services?** RUF-I Campus Ministers develop local ministry programs, in partnership with churches, to fulfill RUF-I's three missions:

1. WELCOME students from all nations, offering Biblical hospitality through gospel deeds. *For example, holidays (Thanksgiving, Spring Festival, etc.), excursions, airport pickups, temporary hosting, English conversation partners, and friendship families.*
2. EXPLORE the gospel with internationals, through gospel words. *For example, Dinner and Bible Discussion programs with Christian table hosts, small groups, and one-on-one relationships.*
3. EQUIP servant-leaders for God's kingdom in their home nations. *For example, when internationals become followers of Christ, RUF-I Campus Ministers train them in Biblical discipleship and servant-leadership before students return to their home nations.*

 * **Recruitment information, both international students with whom you minister, and personnel to work with your organization:** RUF-I Campus Ministry Locator at www.ruf.org/ministries

1. STUDENTS: RUF-I Campus Ministries are on numerous American campuses. International students can connect to a specific Campus Minister through RUF's website at www.ruf.org/ministries
2. MINISTRY TEAM MEMBERS: Church members and pastors should contact a local RUF-I Campus Minister to get involved in a cost-effective, "global-local" mission field. College and Seminary graduates, or Missionaries interested in RUF-I employment, should apply at http://ruf.org/internships/apply or http://ruf.org/contact

*Other: RUF-I believes that, while some Christians are gifted and called to serve as foreign missionaries, all Christians are commanded to practice Biblical hospitality. RUF International Investigative Bible Studies and other resource materials are available through the RUF-I home page: www.ruf.org/about/ruf-internationa(Email - Al LaCour to Dr. Jack Burke – 3/20/2012 Orig,; 2/8/18 Rev)

*Name of your organization and contact information:

ISM Inc is a Recognized Service Organization (RSO) of **The Lutheran Church—Missouri Synod (LCMS)**
PO Box 22, Stevens Point, WI 54481; website: http://www.isminc.org/ email: isminc@isminc.org tel: 715-677-4877.

   *Who do you minister to? All international students, scholars and their families
   *What is your mode of ministry? ISM, Inc. (International Student Ministry, Inc.) is designed to offer contacts and resources for individuals and groups working among the university and college international student communities. We are a Christian-based organization with a desire to offer those "at our doorstep" friendship, hospitality and the Gospel message.
   *What are your services? We currently serve 90 LCMS ISM sites with ideas, funding for Christian resources and personal contacts. We offer two yearly conferences: **In-Depth Bible Seminar** for international students and **Equipping Conference for Directors and Volunteers.** We publish a bi-monthly prayer newsletter, *The Doorstep*, sent to approximately 10,000 praying partners.
   *Recruitment information: Both international students with whom you minister and personnel to work with your organization. The national organization, ISM, Inc., has a volunteer working board of directors and a part-time salaried communications director. The 90 ISM sites are locally supported by a congregation, area ISM society or through an LCMS district. Each site operates by itself and determines its administration, area of impact and implementation of its working plans and vision.
   *Other: (Email from Carl Selle to Jack Burke – 3/19/2014 Orig,; Confirmed -Attachment to email from Karol Selle to Dr. Jack Burke, 7/17/2018)

Jack D. Burke, Ph.D. M.Div.

*Name of your organization and contact information:

National XAi (Chi Alpha International) Chi Alpha Campus Ministries
1445 N. Boonville Ave
Springfield, MO 65802
PHONE
417.862.2781 ext: 1425
Fax: 417.865.9947

The National Chi Alpha International Student Director is Severin Lwali, a former international student from Kenya.

Who do you minister to? Chi Alpha is on 316 campuses with an estimated 27,000+ students involved. Approximately 55% of our groups report intentional ministry to international students, and 80% of our groups have at least one international student involved in our spirit empowered diverse community of prayer, worship, fellowship, discipleship and mission.

What is your mode of ministry? Chi Alpha exists to reconcile students to Christ, equipping them through Spirit-filled communities of prayer, worship, fellowship, discipleship and mission to transform the university, the marketplace, and the world. Our vision for reaching international students is to see all our groups engaged in moving international students from friendship to leadership as each one of us loves, serves, proclaims Christ to and disciples international students. Our goal is to move 100,000 international students from friendship to leadership (discipleship) in the next 10 years.

What are your services?

National Chi Alpha provides specific training, resources, and support for Chi Alpha campus missionaries to mobilize staff and students alike (including international students) to engage international students on their specific campuses.

National Chi Alpha yearly hosts "All Nations," an international student leadership conference. This catalytic conference is at the heart of moving international students from friendship to leadership. The conference helps international students embrace who they are in Christ and embrace the role they play in the kingdom of God through the example and permission offered to them during the conference. Students are empowered, trained and empowered to impact their current context as ambassadors for Christ so that they can impact the world later when they go to the marketplace or the world. Key features of All Nations, are international speakers, international student testimonies, workshops relevant to international students, and "tribe times"/small groups led by international students to connect with each other around the topic of what Jesus is doing in their lives as internationals. There are also powerful worship times, with international students and international staff leading the worship times.

To better train and resource our staff and students to move international students, we have a training called Discover The Nations. Four of eight Chi Alpha areas offer "Discover the Nations," a cross-cultural training conference for campus leaders, campus missionaries in training, staff, to help them be effective in international student ministry in their specific contexts. Several Chi Alpha areas also have specific outreach events for international students. Local outreach and discipleship varies across chartered groups.

In each of our 8 areas Chi Alpha has XAi Area Reps who serve as the Ambassadors for international students to Chi Alpha staff and students in an area as well as the local church. Their leadership and relationship with our campus leaders in an area help Chi Alpha be more effective.

The National Chi Alpha International Student Director is Severin Lwali.

(Email sent from John Schutte, XAi Program Coordinator, Chi Alpha Campus Ministries to Dr. Jack Burke, 6/21/2018, for Severin Lwali, international student program director).

*Name of your organization and contact information:

Chi Alpha Christian Fellowship
Linda Seiler
Chi Alpha Director
Purdue University
www.xapurdue.com
765.543.5292

*Who do you minister to? American & international students (probably about 60% American and 40% internationals at this point)
*What is your mode of ministry? student-to-student
*What are your services?

- Conversation partners
- Small group inductive Bible studies
- Large group worship gatherings
- Weekend retreats, social trips

Int'l Thanksgiving Dinner (the Saturday before Thanksgiving)—this is always our largest turnout as internationals are interested in experiencing American culture."Ignite the Nations" worship service (missions service where we have groups of students from each ethnicity dress in their traditional attire and lead songs in their first language. For example, Asians, Africans, Latinos, etc.) One year we had an Indian (former Hindu) share about her supernatural conversion to Christianity as a result of campus ministry influence in her life.

*Recruitment information, both international students with whom you minister and personnel to work with your organization:

- Int'l welcome BBQ in August (in conjunction with ISS office at Purdue)
- Info tables during first week of school
- Students inviting students to regular events
- We have a great relationship with the 4 local Assemblies of God churches who
- provide host families and other resources
- We recruit all over Indiana through the AG youth groups and so forth. We pray in the staff we need, and God provides in amazing ways over the past 11 years (we started in 2007).

*Other: National Chi Alpha International Student Director is Severin Lwali

(Email from Linda Seiler to Dr. Jack Burke - 3/28/2012 Orig., Rev. 6/21/2018)

*Name of your organization and contact information:

Baptist Student Union - Warrensburg, Missouri; some activities are in conjunction with the Navigators on campus.

> ***Who do you minister to?**
> All international students and scholars
> ***What is your mode of ministry?**
> "Student to student" "friendship family" "Bible studies" "holiday home stays" "staff to student relationship" etc.
> ***What are your services?**
> Weekly dinners provided by several churches, camping trips, weekly discussion groups, Bible studies, holiday home stays, rides to local churches and ministry experiences. Students recently went to Joplin, Mo over spring break to help with the tornado clean up.
> ***Recruitment information both international students with whom you minister and personnel to work with your organization:**
> Students are notified through e-mails, flyers, group meetings, and through friends of upcoming activities. Local churches are contacted to help with meals during the year and at new orientation times. One local church recently helped to put siding on the BSU and helped to decorate the interior.
> ***Other:** I know of the work of these organizations, but am not directly involved with the planning of all of these events. As faculty, I have contact with both students and the campus organizations, and I have taken part in some of the activities.
> (Email from Mary Winters, Instructor, IEP, University of Central Missouri. to Dr. Jack Burke – 4/01/2012) (Confirm: 8/9/2018)

Chapter

ISM PARACHURCH ORGANIZATIONS

(<u>Responses</u> to 2012 Survey of ACMI membership,
Updated 2018, listed alphabetically)

ALONG WITH GOVERNMENT ORGANIZATIONS (both US and foreign) and universities, **parachurch organizations** show the greatest interest in international students. Although interest in ISM among churches is growing, it still has a long way to go to catch up with the strong interest parachurch organizations have demonstrated through many years of ministry to international students. I think the lack of interest shown by many churches in international student ministry has been the chief cause for the flourishing of tax-exempt 501(c)3 organizations that focus on ministry to international students. It is my fervent prayer and strong desire that <u>all</u> church leadership through the reading of this book will at last catch the vision.

The list is divided into three groups of parachurch organizations that responded to my original ACMI Survey in 2012 and has recently been updated.

1. Parachurch organizations for all international students
2. Parachurch organizations that focus on language/ethnic groups.

3. Parachurch organizations that focus on those from a particular country.

*Name of your organization and contact information:

(Presented in alphabetical order)

Bridges International
PO Box 500073, Austin TX 78729; Phone: 512-250-5046
Web: bridgesinternational.com

*Who do you minister to?** All international students and scholars

*What is your mode of ministry?** Our mode of ministry is wide-ranging—because we are ministering to students from various cultures and because our staff and volunteers are operating in various campus settings. Most any approach or activity that would honor God and would appeal to international students is being done somewhere by our 360 staff and hundreds of volunteers.

*What are your services?** Our staff and volunteers offer help in four major arenas—"Service" (practical help that ranges from airport pickups to English instruction); "Social" (opportunities for internationals to enjoy interaction with fellow international students, with American students and with other Americans); "Spiritual" (individual, small group and large group activities that allow non-Christians to explore the gospel and/or help Christians to grow in faith) and through "Student Leadership" (developing the next generation of global leaders)

For those who are already Christians or who place faith in Jesus, we offer small group Bible studies and one-to-one opportunities for discipleship. We also offer large conferences to promote the spiritual development of non-Christians and Christians ("Vision 2017" involved 1213 delegates from 83 nations). And we sponsor 8-10 special projects each summer—some designed to meet the needs of non-Christians for friendship and exploration of the gospel; others designed to help Christians grow in faith and develop ministry skills.

*Recruitment information, both international students with whom you minister and personnel to work with your organization:** Our conferences and projects provide ideal settings in which to recruit Christian international students for internships or staff positions. Likewise, we recruit American students through dialogue at our conferences. And, of course, our leaders recruit prospective laborers on a year-around basis. We are strongly convicted by the truth of Jesus' words as found in Matthew 9:37, 38.

*Other: We have a strong burden to mobilize Christian internationals to participate in ministry to other internationals. Many will humbly defer to American Christians who are older or more experienced in ministry, yet we want to urge these internationals to take on spiritual leadership whenever they are able. We are concerned that if they do not lead during the formative years of their Christian experience—which is often during their time in America—then they will probably not lead after their return to various home nations. And, of course, our ultimate goal is to raise up godly Christian leaders in nations across the globe.

(Email from Bill Horlacher for Trae Vacek to Dr. Jack Burke – 3/26/2012 Orig,; 2/8/18 Rev by Trae Vacek)

*Name of your organization and contact information

Campus Ambassadors, an arm of Missions Door
We use the term Campus Ambassadors International to distinguish the international ministry from other campus work http://www.campus ambassadors.com/

*Who do you minister to? We minister to all international students and scholars, but emphases may vary according to location.

*What is your mode of ministry? Operating from a philosophy of friendship evangelism, we engage in any activity that will give us opportunities to meet and converse with students. These include, but are not limited to, weekly gatherings, participating in orientation on campus, hikes and camping trips, visits to local attractions, investigative and discipleship Bible studies, classes in English as a Second Language, summer picnics, conversation partner program, and holiday events.

*What are your services? These vary by campus: Homestay programs, Furniture giveaway at the beginning of the school year, Airport pickups, Tax workshops.

*Recruitment information, both international students with whom you minister and personnel to work with your organization:

International students: Presenting the opportunities at Orientation, website, postings on campus. The greatest recruitment tool is word of mouth from previous students. Students who return home often tell their friends about the gatherings so that they are primed to come as soon as they arrive at the airport.

Volunteers: Actively recruiting volunteers from local Bible colleges and seminaries, local church mission conferences. Volunteers will often recruit their friends or other church members. Approaching those who have returned from foreign mission service. (Email from Carmen Bryant to Dr. Jack Burke – 4/02/2012 Orig,; 2/8/18 Rev)

*Name of your organization and contact information

The Cultural Discovery Group

The Cultural Discovery Group is a group of community volunteers assisting the international students and scholars at the University of Missouri-Kansas City (Kansas City, MO, USA). Our organization has been working with students for approximately 25 years. For further information, you may contact Roger Lantz at rdlantz@hotmail.com, or call 816-333-5483.

*Who do you minister to? We provide services and activities for all international students and scholars. UMKC's largest student groups are from India and China. There has been an increasing number of students from Saudi Arabia in recent years, as well as from Vietnam and Bangladesh.

*What is your mode of ministry? Identifying and providing those services that are most needed by students, services needed both upon their initial arrival and as they settle into life in the university and in Kansas City. It is our desire that those services then become a bridge to ongoing and deeper relationships with students.

*What are your services? We partner with another organization, International Students Incorporated (ISI), to provide monthly shopping trips to a discount store and to ethnic stores on Saturday mornings. Because UMKC is located in the urban core of the city, students without personal transportation can find it difficult to purchase all the groceries, clothing, and day-to-day items they need nearby, particularly ethnic foods from their countries. Many stores that students would like to shop at are located in the suburbs, and public transportation can be limited to those areas of the city from the university. In the fall, we also assist students to find suitable winter clothing at stores that sell coats, hats and gloves. These shopping trips serve as a way to meet the physical needs students have for food and clothing, but also serves as a very natural way to meet students, engage in conversations to find out more about their cultures and their lives, through which we seek to develop friendships over time.

*Recruitment information: Our community volunteers are from Graceway (formerly Kansas City Baptist Temple). We provide training for our volunteers in international student ministry.

*Other: **We have worked hard over the years to build and maintain a good relationship with the International Students Affairs Office (ISAO) and the Applied Language Institute (ALI), which provides ESL instruction for students.** [Author added bold type] Having a healthy working relationship with the administrators in these offices has been invaluable. Providing our volunteers with training has helped to preserve a good relationship with these administrators.

(Email from Roger Lantz to Dr. Jack Burke – 3/31/2012 Orig,; 2/14/18 Rev)

*Name of your organization and contact information

Global Friends
Ministry of ISI and the Christian and Missionary Alliance. However, we work with any life-giving church or individual interested in ISM. Please contact Julie Arant at 402.301.4951 or juliearant@hotmail.com

*Who do you minister to? We minister to all international students and scholars in the Omaha area.
*What is your mode of ministry?

- Weekly Friday Night Gathering with a meal, music and 4 tracks: English, Leadership, Bible Learning and Bible Discovery.
- Conversation Partners
- Monthly Large Access Events
- Conferences, Retreats and Training Seminars
- Airport pick-up; furniture give-away; apartment finding; temporary homestays, and welcome picnics.

*What are your services? Same as above.

*Recruitment information, both international students with whom you minister and personnel to work with your organization:

- For recruiting students - we are an official recognized campus organization whereby we are able to promote our large access events to attract students.
- For recruiting volunteers – through church college groups, Sunday School classes, prayer base participants.

(Email from Julie Arant to Dr. Jack Burke –4/02/2012 Orig., 10/22/2014 Rev, 2/14/18 Confirmed)

*Name of your organization and contact information

Helping International Students (HIS)
1801 Anderson Avenue, Manhattan, KS 66502; 785-537-3988
If you need to get in touch with this ministry email Terry Cole, terry@ hismanhattan.org or Katie Palani, katie@hismanhattan.org; info@hisman hattan.org; www.hismanhattan.org

*Who do you minister to? We minister to all international students, scholars and their families who are living in Manhattan, Kansas.
*What is your mode of ministry? Student to student, friendship family, Bible studies, conversational and reading English partners, welcome events, service opportunities (shopping shuttle, bike giveaway, furniture, etc)
*What are your services?

- American/international friendship partners
- Conversational and reading English partners
- pre-semester/holiday homestay opportunities
- welcome events at the beginning of each semester
- annual friendship banquet, furniture giveaway, shopping shuttle
- bike giveaway, Bible studies, Bibles in multiple languages
- The JESUS Film showings

*Recruitment information, both international students with whom you minister and personnel to work with your organization: American friends are recruited through more than 30 partner churches and campus ministries in Manhattan, Kansas and the surrounding area. Students are invited to sign up for our programs during welcome events and other events/service activities during the year. Students also sign up through our website and by word of mouth recruitment.

(Email from Melisssa Rupp for Steve Graber to Jack Burke – 4/02/2012 Orig,; 2/8/18 Rev by Katie Palani for Terry Cole; Confirmation email from Melissa Rupp Harstine to Michelle Postrano, copy to Dr. Jack Burke 7/2/18)

*Name of your organization and contact information

InterFACE Ministries
PO Box 450816, Atlanta GA, 31145-0816, office:770-934-7797 www.iface.org
iFace began in 1983 and incorporated in 1990 as an innovative, cross-country, hospitality and trip ministry that included conversations about Christianity.

*Who do you minister to?** InterFACE (aka iFace) partners with churches and other ministries across the country with creative and relevant strategies to reach international students and scholars, and other temporary visitors in the US.

*What is your mode of ministry?** "face to face friendships", "hospitality" "Bible studies," "Christian conferences around the holidays," "trips," "ELS" All of the above.

*What are your services?** As a personal face to international friendships, iFace staff create their own local ministries that usually revolve around hospitality and welcoming "the stranger in our midst." Many staff use their homes, apartments and churches to partner with churches and Christian volunteers to invite students/scholars for parties, dinners, conferences, Wal-Mart shuttles, furniture giveaways, English classes, etc.

*Recruitment information, both international students with whom you minister and personnel to work with your organization:** We recruit American families and volunteers trained by iFace staff. Most students learn about iFace through their "oikos" (Greek,οἶκος, meaning household or network) and sign up for our programs at new student orientations on campuses, or visit our website, www.iface.org. We do not recruit people to become staff. They find us and apply for a position if they desire.

*Other:** Some staff specialize in church planting, Muslim ministry, overseas orphans and/or abused children and relief projects overseas. We also emphasize preparing the next generation of ISM workers by initially training them when they are high school juniors and seniors.

(Email from Bill Perry for Bob Culver to Dr. Jack Burke – 3/20/2012 Orig,; 2/8/18 Rev by Bob Culver)

*Name of your organization and contact information

International Campus Connections
Ellen Coble, Director & Founder of *International Campus Connections*internatcampusconnections@gmail.com
http://www.intlcampusconnections.com
Is a ministry of connecting international students from the *University of North Carolina Charlotte* campus to *Stonebridge Church Community* through socials, trips, church activities, and Bible Discussions. We pray that through these activities and friendships with those from the church, that these students will learn what the Bible says about Jesus Christ, and will come to faith in God, experiencing his saving grace. We know that some of the students will have never read a Bible, and some will come from unreached people groups. We pray that some will go back to their countries as new Christians sharing their faith in their own language and culture. "Connections" is also a ministry of training volunteers so that they might learn ministry skills and develop friendships with international students. It was founded by Ellen Coble ten years ago in Charlotte, North Carolina.

Who do you minister to? To any of the 2000 plus international students and scholars at *University of NC Charlotte.* The majority who have attended our activities over the last 8 years are Indian graduate students, Chinese researchers and faculty, as well as numerous graduate and undergraduate students from Taiwan, Korea, Iran, Viet Nam, Iran, Ecuador, Pakistan, Spain, etc
What is your mode of ministry?

- Friendship Partners, dinners, Game Nights, Bible Discussions, ESL Bible classes, visits in homes, invitations to church services and activities, weekend retreats including speakers, Tennis Group, etc
- Retreats and conferences with other organizations*: Discovery Weekend* with *InterVarsity* and *Bridges International* from

universities of NC, <u>Urbana Missions Conferences</u>, and an overnight with *St. Matthews Episcopal Church* (50 members), who hosted us in their homes and on their farms including kayaking, fishing, dancing, and a hayride as well as rides in a private plane !

• Events celebrating holidays: Thanksgiving & Christmas dinners with families in their homes, Valentine's dinner and program, St. Patrick's Day program, Chinese New Year celebration at a Chinese church, and Christmas Celebrations including Christmas dinner, music, and Christmas play (story from Luke 2).

*What are your services? Cultural outings, sight-seeing, help obtaining free furniture and mattresses, orientation to the city and to American culture, rides to stores and to the airport, trips to the beach or to the mountains, re-entry help, ESL classes, English conversation practice, informal counseling, "Electives" which could be a class in guitar, cooking, tennis, or job searching, and visits to museums, concerts, and sports events.

*Recruitment information on international students with whom we minister: Each August on campus, we have a free Welcome Dinner & program with Lisa Chinn as speaker. At the dinner, students give their email addresses if interested, and we then invite them to activities and encourage them to bring their friends. We also give out information on events on campus at the information fair as we are "an official *UNC Charlotte Student Organization*" with officers and a constitution.

*Recruitment information on personnel to work with your organization: Volunteers are recruited through *Stonebridge Church Community* and a few other churches. *Reformed Theological Seminary* advertises an "internship" in campus ministry with us. This year a graduate of RTS and his wife are working with us on the recommendation of the mission agency of his denomination to gain cross-cultural experience as they prepare to go on the mission field. Since I've been on the Task Force for the *Perspectives on the World Movement* classes for many years, I always offer the opportunity for getting to know an international student to the members of the class, as that helps meets requirements for the course and the ministry gives them an excellent way to apply what they're learning in the course.

Our bi-monthly *Prayer and Planning* meeting, which I lead, is attended by the core team. Usually the team is made up of members from four or more different nationalities!

*Other:
(Email from Ellen Coble to Dr. Jack Burke – 4/06/2012 Orig,; 2/14/18
(7/03/2018 Rev.)

*Name of your organization and contact information

International Friends Meet
Paula Parker, Director Contact: internationalfriendsmeet@gmail.com
Website: internationalfriendsmeet.org

*Who do you minister to? International Friends Meet was founded
in 2013 to serve and encourage churches who want to start, or grow, their
own ministry to international students.

*What is your mode of ministry? Prayer, a strong team of volunteers,
and God-given opportunities.

*What are your services? Providing resources, consulting, and
networking events to equip the Church for local, cross-cultural outreach
and effective discipleship among international students. We work in
partnership and cooperation with many other ISMs.

*Recruitment information, both international students with whom
you minister and personnel to work with your organization:
Ministry partners and people to serve come as a result of relationships,
invitations, vision casting, training, customized job descriptions,
communication, ongoing support, and prayer always.

*Other: InterGen Global Forum is an annual gathering of church
leaders and volunteers, ISMers, and Christian administrators working with
international students at colleges and universities. Visit intergenglobalforum.
link for details.

(Email from Paula Parker to Dr. Jack Burke 3/19/12 Orig,; 1/1/16 Rev,
2/15/18 Rev)

*Name of your organization and contact information

International Friendships, Inc.
In my present position as the Executive Director of IFI since 1998. Contact
information: **Richard Mendola,** Executive Director
International Friendships, Inc., 2500 N. High Street, Suite 200, Columbus,
OH 43202, Phone: 614-294-2434 ext 205

www.ifiusa.org (student website); www.ifipartners.org (volunteer/donor website)

*Who do you minister to? Our campus ministries serve all international students, scholars and their families. IFI serves on 27 campuses in 20 locations in 9 states. IFI ministers overseas by partnering with returned international students.

*What is your mode of ministry? To partner with and serve area churches and individual Christians by providing cross-cultural training, resources, and opportunities to befriend international students. To develop a ministry team of international and American laborers whose purpose it is to minister directly to the spiritual needs of internationals.

- To see Christians who have been involved with us go into other cross-cultural ministries both here and abroad.
- To publicize **announcements** of meetings which clearly and ethically state there will be opportunities for international students to learn about Christianity and how people become Christians. This may be done through one-on-one relationships, small group Bible studies, and special outreach events.
- To provide practical help to international students fulfilling Deuteronomy 10:18.
- To train and resource Christian internationals to prepare for effective service and ongoing ministries among the nations of the world, especially in the 10/40 window.

*What are your services? IFI campus ministers design and implement programs and services to fulfill our mission: We (IFI staff, volunteers, donors and churches) serve (outreach events, meet practical needs and evangelistic and discipleship Bible studies) internationals and partner with them (disciple and impart vision of reaching out to family and friends) to make Christmas known among the nations.

- Year-round airport pickup for new students
- Weekly Bible studies, both evangelistic and discipleship
- Donated furniture for students who request it
- Children's ministry at our largest Bible study
- Weekly English Conversation Partners
- Quarterly English Conversation Club

- Potlucks & picnics at various times throughout the year
- Monthly Friendship Partners
- Garage Sale Shopping before fall semester
- Holiday Hosting (Thanksgiving, Christmas, and Easter)
- Housing (Short Term or Long Term)
- Bimonthly International Moms Group (IMG)
- Weekly International Wives Group (IWG)
- Trips to famous and beautiful places in the U.S. (Washington, D.C., Niagara Falls, Smokey Mountains, Grand Canyon, etc.)

*Recruitment information, both international students with whom you minister and personnel to work with your organization:

Recruiting international students: IFI campus ministers seek practical and spiritual ways to serve the needs of internationals and their families. Practical ways of serving students are included in number 4. By serving students in practical ways, trusting relationships are built and lead to one-on-one evangelism and discipleship, weekly evangelistic and discipleship Bible studies and other evangelistic and discipleship events, such as Christmas programs or interning with IFI for one year.

*Other: IFI has developed a one year internship program to provide the means necessary for Christian international students to prepare themselves to return home as effective witnesses for Jesus with a clear vision of God's calling on their lives and ready to stand strong in the midst of persecution. The IFI internship program combines classroom instruction, personal mentoring, and training in ministry.

- Recruiting ministry team members: IFI ministry teams are comprised of both IFI campus ministry staff and volunteers from local churches who are recruited and trained with the skills necessary to relate to international students. Volunteer opportunities are the same as the practical and spiritual services mentioned above. Www.ifipartners.org/careers gives more opportunities for staff involvement. Www.ifipartners.org/volunteers gives information about volunteer opportunities
- IFI has developed a one year internship program to provide the means necessary for Christian international students to prepare themselves to return home as effective witnesses for Jesus with a clear vision of God's calling on their lives and ready to stand

strong in the midst of persecution. The IFI internship program combines classroom instruction, personal mentoring, and training in ministry. This program is called ISEED (International Students as Equipped and Empowered Disciples). You can learn more about ISEED at www.ifipartners.org/iseed/

- IFI has developed ethnic specific ministries. 1.) The Chinese Fellowship provides Chinese Christian undergraduates an opportunity to worship, fellowship and study the Bible in their own language to prepare them for their return home as an effective witness. 2.) A contextualized ministry among Hindus. 3.) A team of people committed to sharing their lives and the gospel among Muslims.

(Email – Rich Mendola to Dr. Jack Burke – 8/08/2014 Orig,; (2/13/18 Rev)

*Name of your organization and contact information

International Ministries at Penn State
Our website with contact info. is: www.impsu.org. (Source: Bill Saxton)
Below is the corrected new information statement.

*Name of your organization and contact information:

Our international student ministry team at Penn State team includes staff of Campus Crusade's Bridges, the Coalition for Christian Outreach, Reformed University Fellowship, China Outreach Ministries, and the Navigators' international student ministry. We all work together on some of the welcome events and other big events during the year such as a 'Garage Give away' and a Chinese New Year party.

Contacts:

Chris Cunningham (Bridges)- cpc10@psu.edu; (814) 880-0134
Kirk Zuercher (COM)- kzuercher512@gmail.com; (814) 769-6193
Ken Layton (Navs-I)- kjl7@psu.edu; (814) 404-9747
Walt Johnston (CCO/ICF)- walt1636@gmail.com; (814) 404-8116
Richard Smith (RUF-I)- richard.smith@ruf.org; (229) 894-9167
(Source: Bill Saxton)

*Who do you minister to? all international students and scholars

*What is your mode of ministry? Each organization provides a blend of outreach events and services, trips and special experiences, small group fellowship, individual and group Bible studies

*What are your services? various Welcome Events, weekly home fellowship groups with dinner and Bible study/program

*Recruitment information, both international students with whom you minister and personnel to work with your organization: Over the years we have had a number of interns with us from Bridges and from COM. Generally they are here for 1-2 years. We have not been successful at recruiting staff from the international students with whom we minister, in large part due to the support-raising issue, family expectations, and visa complications.

*Other: ICF website - www.impsu.org

(Email from Bill Saxton to Dr. Jack Burke – 3/19/2012; Update 7/02/2018)

* Name of your organization and contact information

International Student Christian Association (ISCA)
kevin.smith@iscanwa.net
Tel 479.601.1750; US Postal address: 89 Duncan Ave., Fayetteville AR 72701

*Who do you minister to? We minister to all international students and scholars at the University of Arkansas

*What is your mode of ministry?

a.   ISCA is a student led ministry.
b.   Campus ministers and community volunteers provide support and guidance to our student leaders.
c.   ISCA also has a housing ministry for international students in our two ministry houses.
d.   Campus wide Christian international events such as Christmas Fest, Easter Festival, speakers and international concerts.

*What are your services?

a. Leadership development and discipleship through housing Bible studies, on campus Bible studies, and our weekly Bible study meeting at the ISCA house.
b. Cultural exchange through our Friday Culture Night weekly meeting to discuss cultural issues and our participation in programs sponsored by the office of International Students and Scholars on campus (Conversation groups, Friendship families, trips . . .)
c. **Hospitality services** through our yearly "Free Yard Sale" for new international students, shopping trips, road trips . . .ISCA also seeks to partner with other cultural organizations in any way that we can partner with them such as co-sponsoring events and providing physical support for events.
d. **Campus wide Christian international events** such as Christmas Fest, Easter Festival, speakers and international concerts.

*Recruitment information, both international students with whom you minister and personnel to work with your organization:

a. Students are recruited primarily through friends inviting friends. We do advertise at any campus event we are invited to join in.
b. ISCA has paid campus ministers (positions currently available) and Volunteer leaders who run our housing ministry. Inquiries can be sent to Kevin.smith@iscanwa.net or mailed to 89 Duncan Ave, Fayetteville AR, 72701;

(Email from Kevin Smith, Director ISCA, to Dr. Jack Burke - 3/30/2012; Update 6/29/2018)

* Name of your organization and contact information

International Students, Inc. (ISI)
www.isionline.org
PO Box C, Colorado Springs, CO 80901
Phone: 719.576.2700; Email: Team@isionline.org
Student Mobile APP: "iStudents" available for iPhone, iPad, Android and Windows

Who do you minister to? All International Students

What is your mode of ministry? Friendship Evangelism, Friday Night Fellowships, Bible Studies, Disciple-making Initiatives, ESL Training, Student Events (Retreats, etc), Outbound Student and Returnee Support/Follow Up, Organic Church Planting,

What are your services? See #3. Additionally, ISI provides: Airport Pick-ups, Homestays, Friendship and Conversation Partners

Assistance with acclimating to the American culture including Walmart trips, meals with an American family during special holidays, etc.

Recruitment information, both international students with whom you minister and personnel to work with your organization: Staff, Ministry Representatives, Friendship Partners and Volunteers – ISI actively recruits US nationals including young college graduates, returning missionaries, second career individuals, lay volunteers and selective current and former international students to serve with ISI.

International Students – ISI actively seeks to introduce international students to our ministry via a host of avenues including one-on-one friendships, ESL training, Friday night fellowships, student events PLUS web and social media based approaches including through ISI's iStudents mobile app, international student websites, Facebook, Twitter, etc.

*Other:

ISI's Mission, Vision and Core Values

Mission:

International Students, Inc., exists to share Christ's love with international students and to equip them for effective service in cooperation with the local church and others.

Vision:

To see every international student befriended, led to a personal relationship with Jesus Christ, and discipled for His service—to impact every nation with the Gospel of Jesus Christ.

<u>Core Values:</u>

In everything we do, we will conduct ourselves in keeping with Biblical principles through:

Christ-Centered	Serving others, applying Biblical principles, standards and practices as an organization and as individuals.
Concentration	Designing our student-centered ministry programs in response to the needs of international students and their families, treating every student with dignity, compassion and sensitivity.
Complete-Cycle	A full-cycle evangelism approach, ministering to students so they come to a knowledge of salvation in Christ, and are equipped to reproduce the life of Christ in others.
Churches	A dependency on churches as we accomplish our objectives through the mobilization of the people of God.
Consistency	Creating a ministry culture with local flexibility with which all ISI constituents can identify on a national basis through the use of common distinctives and operating procedures.

(Email from ISI's Executive Team for Dr. Doug Shaw to Dr. Jack Burke – 5/21/2014 orig., confirmed 6/22/2018)

* Name of your organization and contact information

International Village Ministries (IVM)

Exists to increase communication across ethnic cultures for the sake of the Gospel. Details on this ministry can be found on the web link at www. International-Village.org International student ministry is one of the four major components (other three are preach/teach the Word of God, ministry among global business professionals/owners, and literacy evangelism www.WhereStrangersCross.org). IVM is a parachurch organization, non-denominational, which allows us to work with all churches / ministries nearby local campuses. It is incorporated and 501(c)3 certified. John Long, Pastor & Founder, 4105 Dornoch Lane, Norman, OK 73072; Direct: (405) 618-8882; Email: John@WhereStrangersCross.org

*Who do you minister to?

We minister to all international students and scholars desiring to learn English and/or more about the Bible.

*What is your mode of ministry?

You could say "student to student," "friendship family," "Bible studies," "Christian conferences around the holidays," "trips," "re-entry," etc.

All of the above.

*What are your services?

Through the Tulsa International Baptist Church (reaching out to the University of Tulsa) we offer a weekly English Corner on campus, friendship families, short term housing upon arrival (mostly in members' homes), community tours, fall and spring parties, and an ongoing "$1 furniture fest" giveaway program.

Through the Norman Chinese Fellowship (reaching out to the University of Oklahoma) we have a Friday Bible study, local outings (for a day), overnight trips (Branson, MO or Dallas, TX), English tutoring on Sunday mornings, discipleship groups, conferences, etc. We have many student-turned-career leaders serving here.

*Recruitment information, both international students with whom you minister and personnel to work with your organization:

American families are recruited and trained in local churches who co-labor with IVM. Students are invited to sign up for the programs during new student orientations on local campuses. We have a very strong relationship with most Chinese students/scholars (who in turn always invite the new students to visit the churches).

*Other: The majority of the services provided come from members of the two churches named above. Another church (Trinity Chinese Baptist Church, reaching out to the Oklahoma City University) will soon join us in various ways. I am tent-maker working about 10 to 20 hours per week to manage these ministries. if you have any questions. (Email - John Long to Dr. Jack Burke - 3/28/2012 Orig,; 2/13/18 Rev)

* Name of your organization and contact information

InterVarsity International Student Ministry (ISM)
P.O. Box 7895, Madison, WI 53707-7895 608-274-9001 ism.intervarsity.org

*Who do you minister to? International students, scholars, and faculty at US campuses
*What is your mode of ministry?
ISM seeks to:

a. Meet, serve, and connect international students to life on campus and in the US through a welcoming campus community
b. Introduce international students to Jesus in respectful and sensitive ways through genuine friendship, Bible studies, discussion of life issues, special events and conferences
c. Partner with Christian international students to grow in following Jesus, in developing leadership skills, and in serving God where God leads.
d. Draw American students and faculty into real relationships with international students and scholars for mutual encouragement and growth.

*What are your services? In response to God's love to us, we extend that love with and to international students through practical services which may include any or all of the following depending on the type of ministry, its history and maturity. It is a core value to partner with internationals themselves in doing this ministry:

1. *Opportunities for students, staff, and the community to give to International students:*
    a. <u>Welcoming services:</u> from airport pick-ups, rides to Wal-Mart, short-term stays with hosts while awaiting campus housing, helping with settling in, furniture giveaways, cross-cultural orientation, etc.
    b. <u>Language:</u> We offer English conversation partners and social events that give ample opportunities to practice English.
    c. <u>Social:</u> We offer a welcoming community that they call "home." Here they find a safe and nurturing place to find friends and be a friend to others. Groups offer fun trips and cultural experiences such as hay rides, apple picking, park visits, and city tours. Students can visit families during holidays such as Christmas, Thanksgiving, and Easter
    d. <u>Spiritual:</u> They are exposed to God's Word through regular small group Bible studies, campus events, camps and conferences. Other spiritual issues are addressed in personal conversations, group meetings, and conferences. They also grow in understanding what Christians believe and do by being a part of the Christian community on campus.
    e. <u>Reentry:</u> are met through personal counseling, seminars offered at events and conferences, and resources such as workbooks and devotional guides. UrbanaStudent Missions Conferences also provide great opportunities to consider the reentry issues.

2. *Opportunities for International students and scholars to serve and give*
    a. We invite international students to opportunities to serve others on campus, in the community, and outside the community.
    b. They have opportunities to live and share the Gospel with others on campus and at other events.
    c. International students and scholars give shape to the ministry by praying, leading, discipling, and partnering through their various gifts and joys.

*Recruitment information:

- Through our campus groups – InterVarsity staff and Christian students see the vision and receive a call to work with international students
- Through the community volunteers – they have seen the work and apply for a full-time position as InterVarsity ISM staff
- Through Urbana Student Missions Conferences - the vision for God's mission in the world is clearly given; ISM has a booth to talk to interested students and participants
- Through returned missionaries and InterVarsity staff who work overseas
- Through the web – we advertise our job opportunities (ism. intervarsity.org) and interested persons send our office an ISM Interest Form.

*Other: InterVarsity's vision is to see students and faculty transformed, campuses renewed, and world changers developed.

*Through ISM, we seek to engage international students and faculty with the Gospel in respectful, loving, culturally-sensitive, and intellectually appropriate ways. Through ISM, we contribute to the renewing of the campuses by adding a welcoming and hospitable atmosphere to campus life and relating to campus officials with God-honoring attitudes and actions. Through ISM, we work at developing godly traits, leadership skills, and Kingdom vision among our international students so that they will leave the campus as world changers.

*We are also committed to providing quality resources to people working with international students. Our website and InterVarsity Store are commonly visited for the hundreds of resources we offer. We have a transition and reentry series of publications that serves a wider ministry population, including overseas organizations. We also lead the way in having the largest Christian international student missions conference as a track within InterVarsity's larger Urbana Student Mission Conferences. Being one of the founding members of ACMI (Association of Christians Ministering among Internationals), InterVarsity has continued an active role in the organization by sending members, board members, speakers, and workshop presenters for its annual conference.

(Email from Lisa Espineli Chinn to Dr. Jack Burke 4/27/2012 Orig,; 2/13/18 Rev by Marc Papai)

* Name of your organization and contact information

The Navigators, International Student Ministry
Contact Karen Taniguchi, The Navigators International Student Ministry Administrator
PO Box 6000 Colorado Springs, CO 80919; email: ism@navigators.org phone: 800-530-8282

Who do you minister to? All international students and visiting scholars
What is your mode of ministry? You could say "student to student," "friendship family," "Bible studies," "Christian conferences around the holidays," "trips," "re-entry," etc. All of the above
What are your services? Friendship partner, monthly community tours, fall and spring parties, and an ongoing furniture giveaway program. Varies on location but primarily through weekly Bible study, monthly student events, overnight trips, annual international student conferences, one-on-one discipleship, yard sales, friendship partner programs, airport pickup.
Recruitment information, both international students with whom you minister and personnel to work with your organization: Varies on location but students are usually invited to sign up for programs and activities during annual welcome picnics, university student orientation on local campuses, etc. American families and volunteers are recruited for friendship partner programs and often go through orientation in local churches.
Other: Several staff try to stay connected with alumni via personal visits in home countries, Skype, email.
(Email - Karen Taniguchi to Dr.Jack Burke - 3/23/2012 Orig,; 2/14/18 Rev)

* Name of your organization and contact information

Overseas Students Mission (OSM)
Street address: 257 Bob Finley Way, Charlottesville, VA 22903, Mailing address: P.O. Box 6511, Charlottesville, VA 22906, Cell phone: 434-227-0811, *Bill Bray, President*

*Who do you minister to? International students on university and Bible School/Seminary campuses

*What is your mode of ministry? We support and assist the traditional evangelical efforts such as student to student and Friendship Family or Friendship Partner and international host programs as well as outreaches to international students and short-term workers in training programs here but are ultimately interested in finding "chosen vessels" whom the Holy Spirit is sending back as native missionaries to all nations.

*What are your services? We provide training, mentoring, support-raising and administrative services in the USA such as communications, collecting, receipting and transmitting funds to missionaries when they go home.

*Recruitment information, both international students with whom you minister and personnel to work with your organization: All applications to serve should be sent to Overseas Students Mission, Office of the President, at the address below. We currently play a low-profile support role but are eager to find and support young leadership to revitalize and expand ISMs in general and missionary sending in particular.

*Other: We are especially interested in finding new missionaries to the 3000 unreached people groups or nations where Americans are forbidden to openly do missions. We were founded by Dr. Bob Finley in 1953 and reorganized in 1974 in co-operation with Christian Aid Mission.

(Email from Bill Bray to Dr. Jack Burke – 4/02/2012 Orig, 2/8/18 Rev)

* Name of your organization and contact information

Wilberforce Academy
PO BOX 130551, ST PAUL MN 55113 www.wilberforceacademy.org
651-402-2600,
Dr. Robert Osburn

*Who do you minister to? All international students and scholars, as well as American students

*What is your mode of ministry? Leadership development centered around the vision of training students to courageously, creatively, intelligently, and skillfully apply a Christian worldview to the challenges back home and in the workplace.

*What are your services? Development of curricula, personalized mentoring, specialized conferences, workshops, and retreats.

*Recruitment information, both international students with whom you minister and personnel to work with your organization: We are looking for students and volunteers who want to take students beyond basic discipleship to a more advanced level of Christian faithfulness where in order to leverage the future of our societies and workplaces for the Kingdom of God.

*Other: We are <u>not</u> a college or campus, and only work collaboratively with other organizations and ministries.

(Email from Robert Osburn to Jack Burke - 3/24/2012 Orig, (2/8/18 Confirmed)

39

Chapter

Examples of Parachurch Ministries by Language/Ethnicity

(ACMI Survey, updated 2018, in alphabetical order)

*Name of your organization and contact information:

Ambassadors for Christ, Inc.
David Chow, President
Dr. Yeou-Cherng Bor, Executive Director
Anita Martin, Distribution Manager21 Ambassador Dr
Tel. 717-687-8564
Paradise, PA 17562
www.afcinc.org
afc@afcinc.org

2. Who do you minister to?

We are focused on ministry to Chinese students.

3. What is your mode of ministry?

Assist students with personal needs (furniture, shopping, and others), student to student, Bible studies, special evangelistic meetings, bring to Chinese churches, trips, Christian conferences (evangelistic, discipleship, and challenge for missions), re-entry.

4. What are your services?

With both full-time staff and associate staff, primarily Chinese staff, but also non-Chinese, we minister in direct outreach to Chinese students presently on about 60 campuses in North America, but also with some outreach to students in the United Kingdom and Continental Europe, and in China, including ministry to returnees.

There are other supporting ministries within AFC. A prime one is the Chinese Resource Ministry which distributes strategic resources for our own campus outreaches and for scores of others, both in the United State and over 30 other countries around the world, including many for reaching students in China. It distributes presently about 120,000 pieces a year, including some strategic projects for students in China.

Other supporting ministries are Seminars and conferences, including Gospel Camps, Discipleship Training retreats, Chinese Missions Conferences, and Family Conferences. These are not exclusive for students, but do have a strong emphasis for students.

Ambassador Magazine, published bi-monthly, and AFC Bookstore are still other supporting ministries to AFC and the Chinese Churches in North America.

5. Recruitment information, both international students with whom you minister and personnel to work with your organization:

On various campuses, staff work with others, especially Chinese churches. Local students are discipled and trained as leaders to help conduct outreach.

Publicity of the ministry and thus recruitment is made especially through Chinese churches, including publications, such as Ambassador Magazine.

A great number of volunteers are recruited for the supporting ministries of conferences and outreach through the resources distributed.

Originally written by Jim Brubaker former Director (4/01/2012) and updated by Anita Martin (8/20/18) to Dr. Jack Burke

*Name of your organization and contact information

China Outreach Ministries (COM)
555 Gettysburg Pike, A200, Mechanicsburg, PA 17019; 717-591-3500;
com@chinaoutreach.net; www.chinaoutreach.org

COM has two staff whose primary responsibility is mobilizing people to serve in the ministry. The largest number of new staff are recruited by existing staff from their cadre of volunteers. COM's leaders share its vision at missions conferences, annual fund raising dinners, and local church events. As people hear about COM's ministry, they contact mobilization directors who coach them through the process of joining the staff. COM's mission is to give Christ to China's future leaders.

*Who do you minister to? COM reaches out to Chinese students and scholars at American universities, focusing on graduate students and visiting scholars. Staff members serve at more than 50 campuses throughout the US.

*What is your mode of ministry? COM staff members help meet the practical, social and emotional needs of Chinese scholars. As we meet these needs, we build friendships. These friendships open opportunities to share Christ. When scholars come to Christ, we disciple them, connect them with the church and help them prepare to return to China.

*What services do you provide? For students and scholars, COM provides airport pickups, assistance in finding housing, furniture give aways, welcome and fellowship dinners, holiday celebrations, tours, English classes, Bible studies, discipleship training, and retreats and conferences. It also offers volunteer opportunities for community churches and individuals.

*Recruitment information, both international students with whom you minister and personnel to work with your organization: Students and scholars are contacted through referrals from informal networks, word of mouth, and our promotional efforts. Many participants come by the invitation of Chinese students and scholars involved in COM programs. Special events, such as welcome picnics, furniture give always, holiday celebrations, and other activities are advertised on campus. Staff request contact information from those who attend to build a data base. Students and scholars are sent emails about upcoming opportunities.

COM has two staff whose primary responsibility is mobilizing people to serve in the ministry. The largest number of new staff are recruited by existing staff from their cadre of volunteers. COM's leaders share its vision at missions conferences, annual fund raising dinners, and local church events. As people hear about COM's ministry, they contact mobilization directors who coach them through the process of joining the staff.

Volunteers are recruited from local churches. Staff speak in church services or small groups and share opportunities to be involved in cross-cultural ministry in their own communities.

(Email from Don Hines for Glen Osborn to Dr/ Jack Burke – 3/26/2012 Orig, 2/14/18 Rev by Daniel Su)

*Name of your organization and contact information

FollowOne International Inc.
Helps Christ followers and congregations connect with Jesus' mission to lost and hurting people in the most strategic places in the world. One of FollowOne's most effective ministries is our work that equips churches to connect Chinese scholars with Christ and His mission.
James Loftin, President – followone.org

*Who do you minister to? In our ISM strategy, we encourage churches to focus on Mainland Chinese scholars, but depending on the city/campus situation this approach may be modified.

*What is your mode of ministry?

Church-based Local churches provide the volunteers, often in partnership with parachurch ministries. **Trained Workers** Effectiveness of volunteers relates to thorough and ongoing training. **Culture-specific** Ministries that focus on a specific culture/country are the most effective. **Multifaceted** Scholars experience the love of Christ through a variety of approaches. **Relational** The heart of the ministry is the formation of authentic friendships. **Discipleship-oriented** Help scholars follow Jesus in such a way that the world is blessed. **Indigenous Leadership** Many aspects of discipling are most effective in the convert's heart language. **Long-term** As converted students move, FollowOne lines up local Christians to provide encouragement.

*What are your services? We train and equip churches and families to offer transformative hospitality to Chinese scholars. We provide resources for English/Bible classes, training for Friendship Family programs, connections for returning/relocating scholars, creative ideas for outreach and more.

Recruitment information, both international students with whom you minister and personnel to work with your organization:

American families are recruited and trained in local churches. We provide language and ideas to help churches recruit. We help churches explore various avenues for meeting Chinese scholars including English corners, Family matching programs, connecting with the CSSA or other Christian ministries.

*Other: FollowOne International has a broad array of programs to help churches engage more strategically and effectively in mission. International Student Ministry is just one of these strategies. Local ministries create their own program name - the FollowOne name is not used and we have a few security concerns as we do have ministry projects inside China. Because of the location of our office, our staff have spearheaded a ministry to the Chinese scholars at the University of Central Florida for the past 10 years. Families from more than a dozen churches have participated over the years. Through long-term relationships with the UCF CSSA, local Chinese churches and Chinese student leaders, we have had the opportunity to share the Gospel with hundreds of scholars. Some of these scholars are now back in China sharing with others. In the summer of 2012 we will be passing primary responsibility of the UCF ministry to new Bridges staff members. (Email from Laura Messina, Director of China Programs, FollowOne International, to Dr. Jack Burke, 3/29/2012 Orig, 2/11/18 Rev)

*Name of your organization and contact information

Horizons International
Georges Houssney, P O Box 18478, Boulder CO 030880 georges@ horizonsinternational.org

*Who do you minister to? We minister to all international students and scholars **with an emphasis on Muslims**.

*What is your mode of ministry? You could say "student to student," "friendship family," "Bible studies," "Christian conferences around the holidays," "trips," "re-entry," etc. All of the above and more.

What are your services? We have a housing facility for 50 students who rent rooms at our headquarters. We have I-house activities such as dinners, music, talent shows, Bible studies, one on one witness and discipleship. We also invite nonresidents to participate in our weekly dinners where we have lectures and discussions on spiritual and scientific topics. Outside the facility we sponsor trips, excursions, field days, conferences and social events. Our friendship partner program matches students with Christians from churches in the community. We also have conversational English groups.

Recruitment information, both international students with whom you minister and personnel to work with your organization:

Our ministry is in 10 cities serving 15 campuses in 8 states. Each location has a different approach although the standard practice is to recruit from churches and Campus ministries.

Other: To order my book and for information on training, visit: http:// engagingislam.org

(Email from Georges Houssney to Dr. Jack Burke – 3/29/2012 Orig, 3/2/18 Rev)

*Name of your organization and contact information

Japanese Christian Fellowship Network (JCFN)
Mailing Address: P.O. Box 17982, Irvine, CA 92623-7982
Phone: 949-424-7535 E-mail: ushq@jcfn.org Webpage: www.jcfn.org

*What are your services?

- Follow Up ministries of those who move back to Japan or go to other parts of the world.
- WIT Leadership training camp (Whatever It Takes) during summer
- Equipper conference to prepare returnees and those who 'send' them and 'receive them during 12/27-1/1 (off on Urbana year)
- Training student ministries (leadership training, ministry consultation)
- Networking with Japanese speaking churches to provide resources and leadership training

- Empowering and provide resources to English speaking churches to do ESL ministries and also to do follow up of those who return.
- Provide resources such as Bibles, Bible study materials and other Christian literatures
- In Japan, we do small group ministries to receive returnees
- Train small group leaders
- Regional meetings for returnees
- Global Returnees Conference to receive and disciple returnees

*What is your mode of ministry?

- Training Student to Student ministries (Seattle, Chicago, Los Angeles areas)
- Networking and partnering with Japanese speaking churches around the world
- Empowering ESL ministries (English speaking churches) reaching out to Japanese businessmen's wives

*Recruitment information, both international students with whom you minister and also personnel to work with your organization:

- Interns for summer/winter. Need to be able to speak Japanese (preferably read and write as well.)
- Full-time field staff
- Full/part time/volunteer finance and/or administrative staff

(Email from Setsu Shimizu, North America Director, to Dr. Jack Burke – 11/12/2014 Orig, 2/13/18 Rev)

40

Chapter

EXAMPLES OF ISM PARACHURCH ORGANIZATIONS BY COUNTRY

(Those <u>Responding</u> to 2012 Survey, countries listed alphabetically)

AUSTRALIA

<u>*Name of your organization and contact information</u>

AFES = Australian Fellowship of Evangelical Students (We are like InterVarsity USA). Within AFES our ISM section is called FOCUS (Fellowship of Overseas Christian University Students). Our FOCUS website is <u>http://www.afes.org.au/focus</u>
Matthew Meek, AFES FOCUS (ISM) Director, <u>mmeek@uow.edu.au</u>
(m) +61-400-270-424; Skype: matthewjmeek

*Who do you minister to? We minister to all international students and scholars (Christian and non-Christian, any race, any religion).
Currently (as of January 2018) China, India & South-East Asian countries provide the largest source of our international students.

*What is your mode of ministry? Public meetings, small group (multi-lingual) Bible studies, personal discipleship with both staff & students ministering to students, social outings, dinners, sports, Christian teaching & training conferences, welcome & re-entry seminars etc.

*What are your services? Introducing international students to Jesus as King through God's Word & friendship. We also help out informally in many loving, practical ways of caring for international students.

*Recruitment information, both international students with whom you minister and personnel to work with your organization:

- We 'recruit' or better said 'encourage' local (Australian) students and mature Christian people to help with our ministry.
- We encourage international students to minister to other international students.
- We run a 1-2 year ministry training course (MTS) for apprentices considering ministering cross-culturally in the future.
- We employ staff (many if not all theologically trained) to serve & minister to the international students.

*Other: I and a number of our FOCUS staff are with ACMI-Link to provide help for international students coming to Australia.

(Email - Matthew Meek to Dr/ Jack Burke– 3/30/2012 Orig, 2/10/18 Rev)

CANADA

*Name of your organization and contact information

International Student Ministries Canada
Founded by ISI in 1984, we are located in 23 cities across Canada. Our national office is located in Three Hills - e-mail - info@ismc.ca; website - www.ismc.ca; phone - 403-443-5676; address - Box 1205, Three Hills, AB T0M 2A0

*Who you minister to: We minister to all international students and scholars.

*What is your mode of ministry: Student to student, friendship family, Bible studies, trips, ESL groups, re-entry

*What are your services: We offer a friendship partner program, airport pick up, community tours, seasonal activities - camping, golfing, etc, and an ongoing furniture giveaway program. Through the International Christian Fellowship/FOCUS clubs we have weekly Bible studies, regular activities/ outings (day trips and overnight trips) weekly English Conversation clubs on campus, discipleship groups, weekend retreats, student internships.

*Recruitment information, both international students with whom you minister and personnel to work with your organization: Staff workers are recruited mainly from existing ministries where they first serve as volunteers. Volunteers are recruited from local churches. Students are recruited through official clubs on campus as well as through other students. Several students involved in leadership of FOCUS club have become associate staff.

*Other: Also noteworthy is

- Our growing Friends For Dinner campaigns where we link students and families for Thanksgiving, Christmas or Easter Dinner depending on the season. This program is rapidly catching on in cities across Canada.
- Our concentrated effort in developing leadership programs as a value added benefit for students, staff and volunteers.
- Our increased multi-level partnerships locally, nationally and internationally with fellow international student ministries, churches and returnee networks

(Email Paul Workentine to Dr. Jack Burke, 4/2/2012 Orig, 2/13/18 Rev by Twylla Plett for Dr. Yaw Perbi)

*Name of your organization and contact information

English Corner at University of British Columbia
My name is Suzanne Perry and I have led the ISM at the University of British Columbia since 2006, primarily under the banner of "English Corner." We don't have an official name for this organization, but are part of the Baptist Student Ministry Network (BSMN) at UBC. Address: 304-2233 Allison Road, Vancouver, BC V6T1T7 Canada. My title is Baptist Chaplain and International Student Minister; University of British Columbia (UBC), Vancouver, BC Canada. [Note: The BSMN is currently comprised of 2

church plants (Origin Church and UVillage Korean Church), a registered student club (Born For More Baptist Student Ministry), and the English Corner ministry described below.]

*Who do you minister to? All international students (undergraduates and graduate students) and visiting scholars, as well as faculty, staff, and post doctoral researchers. Also often spouses and children of students living or working on campus, and occasionally immigrant neighbours.

*What is your mode of ministry? English Corner conversation group, Bible studies, local sightseeing and social outings, potluck meals, large holiday events, and one-to-one pastoral care. I belong to the UBC Chaplains Association, and am able to introduce myself as being available to students who are seeking God, and to international students who are trying to adjust to life in Canada. This seems to open many doors, and has led to a variety of ministry shapes. It is our perpetual hope to plant and water seeds of the Gospel in the lives of students, seeds that will sprout and eventually bear fruit. We see this work as highly strategic, especially among temporary visitors from closed countries.

*What are your services? I lead a weekly English Corner on campus to encounter newly-arrived people and help them develop strategies to reduce the impact of culture shock in their lives. This includes practicing English, learning about the local culture, and making friends. I try to follow up individually with relationships formed in this group, whenever possible, walking through whatever doors the Lord opens. If and when students are curious about Christianity, I lead an exploratory Bible study for beginners. I also organize social events/outings and plan holiday dinners/parties as outreach events. Desiring to keep in step with the Spirit, I try to watch for other opportunities to emerge, like conversation groups, meeting practical needs (furniture hand-me-downs, grocery shopping trips, etc.), or other affinity groups that may gather around different interests from year to year. For example, one year we ran a series of cooking classes that was very popular; another year the ladies wanted to gather and drink tea together; another year several were interested in painting. Building relationships amidst these affinity groups, personal conversations naturally go deeper, including opportunities to have personal and heartfelt discussions about Jesus. If people are interested in attending a church, I assist them in finding a suitable congregation. I also live in an apartment very near campus to have a ministry of presence and to better identify with the campus community in an incar national way.

*Recruitment information, both international students with whom you minister and personnel to work with your organization:

Students are primarily contacted through English Corner, which is publicized on campus via posters, fliers, and at booths during orientation and Clubs Days. My details are also listed on the Chaplaincy website. Over the years, many students who have grown to trust us and have referred their classmates, roommates, or other new contacts. Students from the Born For More (Baptist Student Ministry) and Origin Church are sometimes keen to participate in outreach to internationals, and other staff members from our Baptist network have occasionally joined us for the holiday events. As for recruiting personnel, we sometimes host mission teams and visitors interested in the ministry, and the invitation is then extended for interns or co-workers to join me in the work. One year we had a full-time intern. There was a semester when I needed to be away to attend to family matters, and the Lord provided two local volunteers who assumed responsibility for the weekly English Corner meeting, and a church planter's wife stepped in to lead the weekly Bible study during my absence.

*Other: This is a support-raising position with the denomination lending official endorsement and encouragement but no financial backing. Although in years past there has been denominational finances provided for traditional student ministers and even ISM personnel on our campus, it is the current trend to fund predominately church planting efforts on campuses in Canada. I depend on the Lord to provide 100% of my salary and ministry budget for this cross-cultural outreach work. (Email - Suzanne Perry to Dr. Jack Burke – 4/07/2012 Orig; 2/14/18 Rev).

*Name of your organization and contact information:

*An English Survey of the Bible for Chinese Students
The course is a 14 week survey of the Bible, beginning in Genesis. Each week we stop at a new event and ask what God wants to say to us. There are 8 classes in the Old Testament and 6 in the New Testament held at Grace Chinese Alliance Church, 405 Marie Ann, Montreal, Quebec at 10AM to 12:30 on Saturdays. Lunch is served at the conclusion to the class. Teacher/Contact: Joseph Cherng: josephcherng@gmail.com

*What are your services? Family groups for fellowship in Chinese – an especially important follow-up for those who believe in the 14 week course.

Job Seminar

Parenting Seminars

Special luncheons and some social events in the summer

*Recruitment information:

Chinese newspaper advertising

On a Chinese website for events in Montreal

Word of mouth – personal invitation

WeChat

*Other: These courses have been offered for many years. We finance, plus some of our "helpers" (new believers from the course) the purchase of bilingual Bibles for all participants. We also get a lot of literature from Ambassadors for Christ. The purpose of the courses is to help them improve in their English, learn the basis of Western culture, to know the message of the Bible and to know God. Most become believers and are nurtured by our "helpers" in the Family Groups that they offer in their homes.

The course that we offer is an intensive 2 hour course which begins in Genesis to the death and resurrection of Jesus. We've had students believe by the time we get to Genesis chapter 3!

We are also linked with a Chinese Alliance Church which helps to nurture these new students and gives them opportunities to serve. Presently, some are serving as elders in the church.

(Email - Ted and Margaret Kass to Dr. Jack Burke – 3/28/2012 Orig, 2/12/18 Rev)

INDIA

*Name of your organization and contact information

International Students Friendship India and Komensky Consultancy for Inter-culture Training

Affiliated with Interserve

Emmanuel F. Benjamin, Executive Director and Mercy Emmanuel, Director, International Students services

Address: **Res.: B- 703, Shan Ganga, Salisbury Park, Pune -411 037, M.S. India**

Res: 91 20 24266993 Mobile -91-9421013939
E-Mail: findemmanuel@gmail.com / isskomensky@gmail.com
Skype: emmanuel.f.benjamin Website: www.komensky.biz

*Who do you minister to? We minister to all international students in India with special focus on students from Muslim Countries.

*What is your mode of ministry? Student to student, Nature camps, International students cultural programs, national days, sports events, special lectures, Bible studies, Discussion groups etc./ Volunteer orientations/training, casting vision in Churches.

*What are your services? Counseling, Events (sp. National days, guided tours, nature programs) English coaching, services like, accommodation, Hospital services, transport, admission, UN related services etc. Apart from these annual camps, retreats, welcome parties, farewell parties, Fresher's orientations, sp. Meeting with girls.

*Recruitment information, both international students with whom you minister and personnel to work with your organization:
We depend on volunteers and do not have paid workers so far. Few international students do help on a voluntary basis.

Other: (International students friendship) We are committed for International student's ministry in India to reach out over 3,000,000 students from nearly 200 Countries. Right now we are strong and concentrating in 2 major Cities of India. The City of our base Pune has over 30,000 students from over 100 Countries. We host many students from Iran, Afghanistan and Middle East. India attracts many Muslims students from Muslim nations and also African students.

(Email from Frederick Benjamin to Dr. Jack Burke – 3/20/2014 Orig, 2/10/18 Rev)

JAPAN

*Name of your organization and contact information

International Students Incorporated ISI is partnering with TEAM, a church planting mission agency that has had missionaries in Japan for 125 years.

*Who do you minister to? My wife [Carolyn] and I [Dan Brannen] are in Japan to raise the awareness and cast the vision among Japanese Christians of reaching international students who are living and studying in Japan. The most probable early adopters are Japanese who themselves have studied abroad [and became] international returnees.

*What is your mode of ministry? You could call me a missions mobilizer. Since the mid-eighties international student ministries have been popping up all around the world. Some have become national organizations with multiple staff and volunteers. This is our dream for Japan—to see the flame of the Holy Spirit spread this vision from the northern island of Hokkaido to the southern islands of Kyushu and Okinawa.

*Other: We are praying and believing that someday people from nations all around the world will say, "I found Jesus while I was studying in Japan." We are praying for Japanese Christians who will come forward, called by the Holy Spirit, to take leadership of this ministry in Japan. Just yesterday we heard the good news that William Wen from San Diego was granted his missionary visa to Japan and will be leaving soon to go back and lead the international student ministry (ICF) in Tokyo.

(Email from Dan Brannen to Dr. Jack Burke – 3/18/2012 Orig, 2/11/18 Rev)

New Zealand

*Name of your organization and contact information

Email: office@ism.org.nz
Website: http://www.ismnz.org.nz/
Facebook: https://www.facebook.com/groups/24941859628/
Box 6082, Palmerston North 4445
Tel 0064 63570762, Mb 0064 276033562; <terry@ism.org.nz>

*Who do you minister among? ISMNZ ministers amongst the 130,000 plus international students in New Zealand. These are drawn from over 160 nations and renew their numbers approximately every three years. Usually there are in excess of 40k graduating any one year. The 160 nations are primarily drawn from Asia, but with significant representation from South & Latin America, North America and Europe plus Africa and the Middle East Over 80 % of international students who come to study in New Zealand return home after study with a small percentage staying on for work experience and then returning home. This is easily understood as NZs total population is 4.3 million so 130+K is a very high proportion of population and with concentrations in education destinations the diversity of international students is very apparent

* **What is your mode of ministry?** Outreach disciplemaking and preparation for return home with follow up through ISM NZ staff and origin country connections. ISMNZ is missionally intentional and very focussed in depth discipling of those who respond in outreach - Out reach is largely through friendship through existing students, community friends and staff embedded in education providers. Many ISMNZ staff are international specialised chaplains to and in education providers and as such enjoy some freedoms of operation and frequently are introduced to new international students by the staff in education providers where they serve. In addition some programmes from church and Christian student group connections also yield fruit. Some groups of ISM NZ connected students form clubs within campuses. Individual staff develop means that fits the context for their ministry so there are varied programmes many of which have connection with the education provider eg community engagement, ESL, pastoral care initiatives etc.

For ISM NZ staff the mode is to function as catalysts to a team of volunteers and to ensure in depth discipling and preparation for post academic transition (largely re-entry) plus the responsibility to follow through with returnees and those who stay on to ensure productive placement in the context of mission and the body of Christ either in NZ or in origin countries and occasionally a third country.

* **What are your services?** The services ISMNZ provides are reflected in our approved aims namely:

OBJECTS OF THE SOCIETY

a) To introduce International Students and Migrants to the person of Jesus Christ, mentoring and training them to become lifelong followers and influencers, making positive contributions to societies throughout the world.

b) To assist in the pastoral care of international students and migrants

c) To provide pastoral care workers and chaplains for international students and migrants

- To initiate and manage projects and research of benefit to: international student sojourn, re-entry, and post-academic transition;
- export education
- pastoral care best practice and international student adjustment for living and academic success;
- recent migrants, particularly those enrolled in education and settlement.

d) To provide supervised biblical, cultural and cross-cultural training and leadership development for international students, migrants and New Zealand nationals interested in furthering their education around the area of Christian living and ministry service.

ISMNZ provides a range of services designed to meet the above outcomes. These include forms of Christian ministry outreach, discipling. leadership training and capacity building. Research, professional development training, internships. leadership training, staff and volunteer development as well as training for other organisations and ministries such as churches, missions groups and theological and Bible training providers.

*Recruitment Information, both International Students with whom you minister and personnel to work with your organization.**

Recruitment information is provided on our website for potential; staff there is a portal for initiating entry. Missions and Missions interlink NZ especially advertise vacancies for staff opportunities. All staff are either bi-vocational or in faith workers. Sponsorship can be by a variety of avenues

Recruitment of international students is through the above mentioned activity and through our embedded staff within education providers

(Email from Terry McGrath to Dr. Jack Burke, 1/14/18) National Director, International Student Ministries of NZ

UNITED KINGDOM

Name of your organization and contact information

Friends International
We exist to see international students transformed by the good news of Jesus, so that they fully engage with the mission of the Church in the world. Alan Tower, National Director of Friends International www.friendsinternational.uk; info@friendsinternational.uk; +44-1920-46006

Who do you minister to? We support and minister to international students in the UK, no matter what country they are originally from, or what educational institute they are studying at in the UK. In the academic year 2015-16 there were over 435,000 international students attending UK universities. There are a further estimated 600,000 students coming to UK language schools to learn English every year.

What is your mode of ministry? We do this primarily by envisioning and equipping local churches. The focus is on holistic care and friendship evangelism, facilitated by international student cafés, international Bible studies, trips away, as well as individual discipleship.

What are your services? For churches and volunteers we provide training and resources that they can harness to equip and strengthen their outreach. For international students we are directly involved in organising trips away, hosting programmes (especially at Christmas), and also a meet and greet service at Heathrow Airport, London. Amongst our materials for students there is a booklet and mobile phone app that introduces students to life in the UK, and also a work-book that helps them with their return home.

Recruitment information, both international students with whom you minister and personnel to work in your organization: We employ some 60 staff members across the UK to serve and minister to the international students they meet, but also to encourage and equip the local churches to do so. We actively engage with the international student community, both through face-to-face meetings and online & printed publicity, to make them aware of our presence, services and to introduce them to our resources and staff members. We also run a voluntary programme called

The Reach Programme. This allows recent graduates to dedicate a year or two to befriending and reaching out to international students.

*Other: We also seek to support the development of international student ministry in mainland Europe through resourcing and training mainly through the IFES network and with Intonations. There are many opportunities for development here as so many international students in Europe pursue their studies in English.

(Email - Jack Bentley for Dave Pepper to Dr. Jack Burke 3/23/2015 Orig, 2/13/18 Rev for Alan Tower)

41

Chapter

ISM Global Developments via the Lausanne Movement

*Leiton Chinn, Lausanne Catalyst for ISM; Director,
Lausanne ISM Global Leadership Forum: Charlotte'17;
Former Lausanne Senior Associate for ISM*

<u>The Lausanne Movement:</u> The Lausanne Movement is an outgrowth of the initial gathering of 2,300 evangelical leaders from more than 150 countries in Lausanne, Switzerland, in 1974, for the *International Congress on World Evangelization*. The catalyst for the event was Billy Graham. A continuation committee formed the Lausanne Committee for World Evangelization which has evolved into the Lausanne "movement", which continues to be a **network of evangelical leaders from 200 nations who pray, plan, partner, communicate, and work together in strategic alliances.** Lausanne hosts global and regional consultations, conferences, and forums for its goal of global evangelization. **As a member of the Lausanne International Leadership team I have the opportunity to be an advocate, consultant, coordinator, and convener for the worldwide advancement of ISM** as part of Lausanne's vision for calling the whole

Church to take the whole gospel to the whole world. For more information about its structures, resources, and events, see **www.lausanne.org**.

Proposal for ISM to be on the Agenda for the Lausanne 2004 Forum: In 2001 while I was serving as the president of ACMI, I received a survey from the Lausanne Senior Associate for Research, requesting recommendations for strategic kinds of ministries that could be considered as an Issue topic for the upcoming global Lausanne Forum to be held in Thailand. Up to that time, ministry among International Students had never been on the program agenda of global or regional events. My proposal that ministry among "Diaspora" peoples and International Students was accepted, and in 2003 I was asked to be the Convener for the Issue Group on ISM, which would also be combined with an Issue Group on Diaspora ministry. The ISM Group was comprised of 33 people from nearly 15 countries, and together with the Diaspora Group, we compiled the <u>Lausanne Occasional Paper # 55</u>: *Diasporas and International Students: The New People Next Door*, which is freely downloadable from the Lausanne website, under Documents.

Establishment of the Lausanne ISM Special Interest Committee: While still serving as ACMI president in 2007, I [Leiton Chinn]was invited to join the Lausanne International Leaders Conference in Budapest where the International Student Ministries Special Interest Committee was inaugurated, and I was asked to serve as its Chair. An initial goal was to establish a global network of ISM leaders, and I invited ISM leaders from New Zealand, South Africa, Japan, Singapore, India, Australia, Korea, Poland, and England to consider being part of the SIC. As president of the US/Canadian Association of Christians Ministering among Internationals, I represented North America on the SIC. From among the ISM SIC I appointed Richard Weston, the former national director of Friends International (U.K) to be a coordinator for networking ISMs in Europe, and Terry McGrath, the founding director of ISM New Zealand, to serve (with his board's approval) as a regional coordinator for the Asia-Pacific region.

Lausanne Regional ISM Leaders Consultations: Another goal of the ISM SIC was to host regional ISM Leaders consultations in 2009 as part of the preparation for the 3rd Lausanne worldwide congress, *Lausanne III: Cape Town 2010*. Each regional consultation was to identify and address ISM issues that were relevant to each regions contexts. Up to now, only three regions of the world have developed multiple ministries dedicated to ISM: North America; Europe; and the Asia-Pacific region. North America has been having an annual, regional ACMI conference for 30 years. Europe has had sporadic regional or national ISM staff conferences for perhaps 40 years, hosted by the International Fellowship of Evangelical Students (IFES) and/or Friends International.

Richard Weston directed the 2009 Lausanne Greater Europe Regional ISM Leaders Consultation that was held in Amsterdam, Holland. About 30 participants came from nearly 15 countries. An IFES group of participants from Poland later convened a European IFES ISM consultation in 2010 in Poland.

The Asia-Pacific region had not had a regional ISM Leaders consultation until the 2009 Lausanne Asia-Pacific Regional ISM Leaders Consultation was held in Singapore, under the leadership of Terry McGrath. About 60 ISM leaders and workers from over 15 countries participated. An Asia-Pacific ISM Leaders Forum is being considered for 2013.

Regional ISM Dialogue Sessions at Lausanne III: Cape Town 2010:
Several of the ISM leaders who participated in the 2009 regional consultations were asked to report on the ISM movement in their countries at the Cape Town 2010 congress, which had 4,000 evangelical leaders. The presentations were part of 4 Dialogue Sessions (seminars) on ISM in Europe, Asia-Pacific, North America, and South Africa.

ISM Included in Revised Version of the *Cape Town Commitment*:
One of the more significant and tangible fruits of the Lausanne III Congress was the publication of the *Cape Town Commitment*, a combination of the affirmation of our evangelical faith and 33 calls to action as a blueprint for world evangelization for the next decade. In reading the original printed version, I noticed that there was no mention of international students. That omission was brought to the attention of the editor of the publication, and now the updated version includes *"'diaspora' is used here to mean people who have relocated from their lands of birth for whatever reason. Some relocate permanently, and others, like three million international students and scholars, temporarily"*, and, we *encourage Christians in host nations which have immigrant communities and international students and scholars of other religious backgrounds to bear counter-cultural witness to the love of Christ.*

Reorganization: Chairs of Special Interest Committees become Lausanne Senior Associates:
In 2012 the position or title of "Chair" of Special Interest Committees was replaced by Senior Associate, and the use of "SIC"s were discontinued.

Thus, I am now the Lausanne Senior Associate for ISM, and I'm in the process of converting the former SIC into an ISM Global Leadership Network. Some of the functions of the Senior Associate for ISM will include: advocating for the Cape Town Commitment and its calls to action in relation to ISM; coordinating a global team of ISM leaders/advisors; encouraging emerging younger leaders in ISM (and mentoring 1-2); stimulating biblical and strategic reflection, discussion, and action for ISM; convening ISM international meetings in consultation with other Lausanne leaders; engaging in periodic conference/skype calls with ISM leaders; and meeting at least bi-annually with other Steering Committee members of the ISM Global Leadership Network

42

Chapter

Ministry to International Students in the US: A Periphery Movement Heading for the Center

Katie J. Rawson, Ph.D., D.Min, 1987

Introduction of Dr. Katie Rawson by author, Dr. Jack Burke

THERE IS SOME VERY good historical data written on the development of the International Student Ministries movement which includes early ISM's like ISI and InterVarsity. ACMI was unique because it was an association for ISMs and individuals to join. Rather than replicate the work of scholars and practitioners like InterVarsity's Dr. Katie Rawson, I have selected her well-documented work that she did as a doctoral student at Fuller Seminary for this presentation. Although I cannot find any updates to her research, you will find out about those who cast the vision, who developed the organizational structure for staff and volunteers to implement the vision, and what the message is of those who see this as a dynamic, strategic, yet common-sense approach to the Great Commission in today's world.

Ministry to International Students in the US

Dedicated to my sisters and brothers in the Association of Christian Ministries to Internationals:[renamed Association of Christians Ministering among Internationals]

"And let us not lose heart in doing good, for in due time we shall reap a harvest if we do not "Rawson paraphrase of NASB" version of Gal. 6:9) grow weary" (Dr. Katie Rawson 9/24/28 email explanation of source to Dr. Jack Burke: This was Many thanks to Everett Boyce, Jack Burke, Leiton Chinn, Arthur Everett, Maurine Georgiades, Ned Hale, Bette McGee, Mesghina Medhin and Robert Taussig for answering my questionnaire, granting interviews and sharing much helpful information.

A Precursor Movement: The Committee on Friendly Relations Among Foreign Students

Among the 251 men at the Mount Hermon conference that launched the Student Volunteer Movement was a small group of internationals. One meeting toward the end of the conference centered on the needs of foreign students in the U.S., and each overseas student present made a brief speech on the situation of students from his country. It must have been at this meeting that seeds were planted in the mind of Cornell student John R. Mott. Later on Mott visited many countries around the world on behalf of the YMCA and the World Student Christian Federation, met foreign students in many of them, and became increasingly aware of their special needs (Thompson 1982, 18-20).

After the Boxer Rebellion the U.S. government decided to return much of the indemnity money to China to finance the education of Chinese students in America. This resulted in a ten-fold increase in the number of Chinese students here between 1895 and 1911. Mott and others organized an independent service agency to Chinese students in 1909. But Mott had an even larger vision. In 1911, with the help of Cleveland Dodge, chairman of the International Committee of the YMCA, Mott presented the needs of foreign students to Andrew Carnegie. With pledges from Carnegie, Dodge and others, Mott was able to launch the Committee on Friendly Relations Among Foreign Students (the CFR) (Thompson, 22-24). The need for such an agency had been growing steadily during the 25 years since Mt.

Hermon. The influx of Chinese students provided a special impetus for action when key people met together in 1911.

The CFR put students of the same nationality in contact with each other through publications and summer conferences. And it made efforts to help students in financial need because of wars in their homelands. The committee organized a port-of-entry service to meet students at the boat, enlisted faculty to aid students on various campuses, and organized a home hospitality program and summer camps for mixed nationality groups. The CFR also assisted various nationality associations, some of which were Christian associations (Thompson, 25-44).

In reading Mary Thompson's history of the CFR (now called International Student Service), it is difficult to discern the role played by religion in the Committee's activities. Much of the CFR's work was done through campus Y's. International Y directors and missionaries were asked to advise CFR officials of students planning to come to the US. The first survey of foreign student needs in the US, (Wheeler, King and Davidson, 1925), which was commissioned by the CFR, was described later as having "strongly religious overtones" and as being concerned with the students' zeal for mission after re-entry to the home country (Du Bois 1956, 8-9). In 1925, the CFR appears to have had religious concerns. Since one of the CFR's main activities was the aid of student Christian associations, it seems reasonable to assume that the religious content of CFR activities evolved in a way similar to that of the Student Volunteer Movement as described by Howard (1970,90-95).

In 1918 - thirty years before the organization of the National Association for Foreign Student Advisors (now Affairs) (NAFSA) - the CFR was calling for the appointment of foreign student advisors on college campuses. When NAFSA was finally born, CFR leaders provided some of its first leadership (Thompson, 42-43,99-103). In the interim, the CFR had played a major role in improving the circumstances of foreign students in the US. Thus an organization begun by an evangelical (CFR) fed into the most effective secular professional association serving internationals today, NAFSA. Over the years, many members and leaders of NAFSA's Community Section (COMSEC) have been Christians of various persuasions. The CFR was renamed International Student Services and still functions today, although there is no longer any religious content to its activities.

Bob Finley and the Post-War Context: A New Mission Structure for an Exploding Field

The years following World War II saw a dramatic rise in the number of foreign students in the US, from 9,643 in 1930 to 33,647 in 1953 (Du Bois,3). This was also the era of the "third burst" of Protestant missions, an age in which 150 American foreign mission agencies appeared (Chinn 1979,1). Chronicling the rise of several evangelical youth movements during that period, Bruce Shelley notes that the evangelical resurgence sparked by Billy Graham resulted in several efforts to contextualize the faith for the youth culture of the day (1986,58-59). From the staff of one of these new groups Youth for Christ International, came many new mission agencies: the Billy Graham Evangelical Association, World Vision, Greater Europe Mission, Trans World Radio, Overseas Crusades, and International Students, Inc. (ISI) (Shelley,52). Thus the first mission structure devoted to evangelizing foreign students in the US came at a time of general renewal among evangelicals. The mission field itself had also grown significantly: both spiritual and missiological conditions were right.

The key person in the founding of ISI, Bob Finley, worked for Youth for Christ for a while and went to China in 1948 as a staff member of the International Fellowship of Evangelical Students (IFES). Finley had had a burden for ministry to international students before leaving the US. In China he observed Chinese people propagating communism after returning from studies in the USSR. His vision for ministering to international students in the US was nurtured by a visit from Navigator founder Dawson Trotman in 1949.

After being expelled from China along with other missionaries Finley ministered in the Far East for Billy Graham. Trotman met him a second time in 1951 in Tokyo and urged him to act on his vision for foreign student ministry. So in 1951, Finley began the Fellowship of Overseas College and University Students (FOCUS), later to become ISI (Chinn,1-2;Everett 198711-2).

Finley's first partner was Carroll Lindman, a recent graduate of Moody Bible Institute. Lindman began work at the University of Southern California with the cooperation of the Navigators and the newly-established Campus Crusade for Christ. Finley started the ministry in Berkeley, with the help of two Navigator staff (Chinn,3).

Soon the young mission structure began to exert an influence on at least one congregational structure. Dr. Donald Grey Barnhouse, pastor of Tenth Presbyterian Church, Philadelphia, invited FOCUS to start an outreach there. So Finley and FOCUS headquarters moved to Philadelphia in 1952, while Lindman took over the work at Berkeley. Max Kershaw joined the team to begin a ministry in Chicago. Early FOCUS strategy was to link internationals with Christian host families provided by local churches. The cooperation of mission structures and congregational structures was essential to ministry success. In 1953 FOCUS became ISI and moved its headquarters to Washington, D.C.

Through the years, ISI has developed a two-pronged attack: some staff concentrate on outreach themselves while others work with churches. Their new Operation Friendship program links several congregations in a given locale. Based on a very successful model in Dallas, Operation Friendship trains church people to become "Friendship Partners." ISI desires to see a similar program in fifteen cities by 1990 (ISI 1986). ISI is also seeking to recruit 500 new staff during the next five years. Having grown 137% in the last three years to a total of 337 staff, ISI believes that 500 new staff is an achievable goal (Boyce 1987a).

A central part of the vision of Bob Finley and ISI is certainly a missiological breakthrough, the realization that centripetal mission did not end in Old Testament times. The first few chapters of Acts are replete with stories of persons becoming Christians while visiting or residing in foreign lands. Yet much of the church appears to be blind to this biblical precedent for centripetal mission.

In 1975 ISI staff Mark Hanna wrote a pamphlet entitled "The Great Blind Spot in Missions Today." Even in 1987, though great strides have been made, foreign students are still an often overlooked mission field. But ISI's presence at ACMC and other, similar meetings has begun to turn the tide. In international student work, the mission structure has served as a goad and model to the congregational structure.

Other Groups Discover the Field

The Southern Baptist Sunday School Board appointed Jane R. Beane as the first Associate Director for International Student Ministry in 1955. Acquainted with Bob Finley and the work of ISI, Beane organized host families from churches and utilized American Baptist students to befriend internationals. Beane also held training seminars for state Baptist Student Unions and started regional retreats for internationals.

After several different directors in the 60's and 70's, Nell Magee became ISM consultant for the Southern Baptists in 1979. Today there is a ministry to students on 371 campuses. Around 3000 internationals are involved in 30 state conferences each year. Two significant Southern Baptist strengths are programs for wives and pre-school children and excellent literature for Americans desiring to minister to internationals. The existences of a sodality, National Student Ministries, and key people as ISM directors have kept ISM before Southern Baptist congregations. Magee is noteworthy because she has been active in the leadership of NAFSA's Community Section, bringing an evangelical presence into a secular (and sometimes hostile) organization.

When Inter-Varsity first reached the US, ministry to internationals was its fourth goal (Hale 1987b). But this ministry really gained steam in the early '50's. David Adeney, forced out of China like Bob Finley, encouraged staff to reach out to internationals while serving as IVCF Missions Director. At this time IVCF's "houseparties" (week-long Christmas and New Year conferences emphasizing friendship evangelism) came into being. They have multiplied and today are held even during Urbana years.

In 1958 Paul Little created a National Department of International Student Ministry (ISM) within Inter-Varsity. Little developed a network of volunteers across the country, many of whom were IVCF alumni. As with ISI, IVCF volunteers met students at planes, assisted them with lodging and tried to link them with Christians at their final destinations. When Little moved over to become an evangelism specialist in 1964, IVCF's official ISM was dissolved. So little growth occurred until 1981 when Fuller grad Ned Hale was appointed ISM director.

The years since 1981 have seen a veritable explosion of ISM within IVCF, due in part to Hale's leadership. Information diffusion has also played a key role in encouraging ISM in Inter-Varsity. Hale encouraged the production of the multimedia FRIENDS: Ministry Among International Students, which premiered at Urbana '84. Hale was also instrumental in the publication of Lawson Lau's The World at Your Doorstep by Inter-Varsity Press, an Urbana '84 book-of-the-day.

Periodic newsletters sent to an increasingly large volunteer network and yearly meetings for staff interested in ISM have also facilitated diffusion of information. The result has been an increase in the number of international students involved in IVCF chapters from 200 in 1982 to over 1100 in 1986. ISM within IVCF is a sodality within a sodality. The existence of the separate department has facilitated ISM growth throughout the movement.

Leadership of ISM in IVCF has often gone to women staff or women volunteers, perhaps more so than in any of the other parachurch organizations. Student leadership has also been key. In several places IVCF has international chapters or international students on the executive committees of regular chapters. This use of the giftedness of all members of the Body may be another reason ISM has grown so rapidly in IVCF.

Although Carroll Lindman of ISI had contributed to Bill Bright's vision for ISM, it was not until 1968-69 that a formal ISM department was organized in Campus Crusade for Christ. Frank Obien, author of the ISM handbook <u>Building Bridges of Love,</u> was the first director. The number of staff involved grew from 37 in 1970-71 to around 60 in 77-78 (Chinn 1979,10).

The ISM campus staff position within CCC was dissolved in 1978. The purpose in doing so was to shift ISM responsibility to regular staff. However the same thing appears to have happened in Crusade that happened in Inter-Varsity while there was no ISM department. Informal ISM work has continued, but there has been no visible growth spurt. In 1987 CCC is seeking to give the ISM coordinator responsibility to a senior administrator someone within the existing leadership who can be an ISM advocate (Foote 1987).

Although Dawson Trotman had had a deciding influence on Bob Finley, the Navigators were the last of the three major campus ministries to appoint a full-time ISM staff. The first Nav ISM specialist (appointed in 1977) was Nate Mirza, an Iranian who had become a Christian as a student through IVCF. Ten years later there are six staff couples doing full-time ISM work. The Navigators have a yearly International Student Conference at Glen Eyrie. In 1985 they began an International Bible Institute to train internationals who then serve as leaders at the Conference. As in IVCF and CCC, Nav ISM has been hampered by the lack of a national ISM department. Some Nav ISM specialists have been meeting in unofficial strategy sessions. One of their 1987 goals is an enabling organizational structure (Tuel 1987).

ISM workers in all three parachurch organizations are periphery groups. Because Ned Hale heads an official department, IVCF ISM is a little nearer the center of power. But Hale himself referred to ISM as a "skunk works" within IVCF at a specialist gathering in 1985. Just as ISM in general is a periphery movement on the foreign missions scene, ISM groups within the three major evangelical student organizations remain far from the centers of decision-making. But all three specialist groups are attempting to exert a leavening influence in their organizations.

Additional denominations have begun to discover the field. Mainline Presbyterians began Christmas International Houses in 1964. There is now a nation-wide network of sites where local Presbyterian and other churches band together to host international students at Christmas.

Sometimes evangelical Christians serve in secular community organizations and have opportunities to share their faith with students as they develop personal relationships with them. One example is the Columbia (South Carolina) Council for Internationals, a secular group that is largely run by Christians. Southern Baptist Mary Rogerson has been active in this group and also in NAFSA's community section.

Another innovative form of ministry for evangelicals is to become part of the university foreign student office. Fuller grad Jack Burke saw this potential, got a Ph.D. in Educational Psychology with minor in comparative/international education after Fuller, and is now Director Emeritus of the International Student and Scholar Services Office at the University of Houston. Burke and his replacement upon retirement, Anita Gaines, have mentored many evangelicals interested in foreign student advising, helping them get experience and placement through an internship established by his office. Although usually unable to do direct evangelism themselves, Christians in secular foreign student offices are able to put internationals in contact with Christians in the community.

A number of local church ministries to international students have emerged since the 1950's. Some have had a connection to ISI; others have been totally independent. Structures vary considerably, but the local church ministry is generally a sodality within a modality. One example of a mission structure effectively involving a large proportion of the congregational structure is Helping International Students (HIS), organized by Robert and Mary Taussig within Grace Baptist Church, Manhattan, and Kansas in 1978. Half of the HIS volunteers are Grace Baptist members; the other half are recruited from other churches and student parachurch groups (Lau 1982). Churches that get involved with international students generally report an increased interest in missions among their members. In a personal letter to me, Taussig wrote: We began ISM in our church (a congregation of

400) in 1977. In 6 years we saw 15 young people leave the church with a call to go into foreign missions. Before we averaged 1 per year. Most of these were involved in ISM and testify that by working with I's [internationals] on a personal friendship basis they were encouraged - given confidence - and alerted to missions - which led to their commitment to give their lives to the Lord as missionaries. All of the above are either now on the field or in the process of going. Our mission budget increased -nearly doubled. Part of this was the sensitization of congregation, pastors and elders to the need to do more to "let the whole world know". Maurine and George Georgiades, founders of FOIL, also report a revitalization of the missions program in their local church, Sierra Madre (CA) Congregational, since the introduction of ISM. Another model links local Christians from various denominations together in outreach to internationals. Some examples are International Friendships Columbus, Ohio, and the Madison Wisconsin community group that is connected to Inter-Varsity. It is my observation that those ministries that utilize both students and community people are the most effective. The international student needs friends on campus and substitute families off campus.

One final model is the banding together of Christian internationals to serve and evangelize their non-Christian peers. Sometimes these internationals involve Americans in their efforts. T.E. and Indhira Koshy founded International Friendship Evangelism in Syracuse, New York. Koshy now leads an international church patterned after the assemblies of Bakht Singh. Various associations linking Christian students of the same nationality living all over the US have also sprung up, with evangelism usually being one of their goals. In 1984, Ned Hale was able to identify African, Iranian and Ethiopian fellowships.

The ministry organized by the international students at Talbot Theological Seminary is a particularly interesting model. In 1983 Mesghina Medhin, an Ethiopian pastor who had been a Campus Crusade missionary to Kenya, arrived at Talbot for study. Frustrated because he had no ministry and few friends, Medhin gathered his fellow international students together to minister to the non-Christian internationals in the four universities surrounding Biola in 1984. **When Billy Graham mentioned the importance of international students during his 1985 Anaheim crusade, local churches became alerted to this mission field at home.** (Bold type by book author) The Biola and Talbot students were then able to involve Granada Heights Friends Church in their ministry. The Americans provide the food and arrangements for various functions, but the internationals take the lead in evangelizing. At Christmas the Americans give money so that international Christian families can invite non-Christians into their homes for holiday meals. A multicultural committee within the church - composed of missionaries and international students -oversees the ministry. Medhin reports that 85% of the students attending ministry functions are non-Christians. And the international students at Biola now have a ministry and an involvement with American Christians Medhin 1987).

The various ministries described here illustrate many of the dynamics we have already seen at work in ISM history. Usually a key person, responding to a particular contextual need, has organized some kind of mission structure that has later involved one or more congregational structures. Information diffusion has sometimes played a role in the founding of new groups. Lay people, women and students have held significant leadership positions. Training has most often been through experience or short seminars. The relationship between mission and renewal appears to be a circular one. International student ministry often sparks revived "foreign missions" interest. The variety and appropriateness of the structures that have surfaced testify to the creativity of the Holy Spirit.

The Association of Christian Ministries to Internationals: Diffusion in Full Blossom (renamed Association of Christians Ministering Among Internationals) ACMI

By 1980 information diffusion had already played a key role in the growth of ISM in the United States. But there existed no national network linking the various ministries. Sensing the need for communication among the groups, Jack Burke and Nate Mirza had a vision for a consultation of ISM workers. When Burke shared his vision with ISI president Hal Guffey the consultation idea got off the ground. In December 1980, Burke, Mirza, Ned Hale and Max Kershaw and Arthur Everett of ISI met at ISI's Star Ranch to plan a consultation for Memorial Day weekend, 1981.

This first consultation drew 102 people representing around 30 churches and organizations involved in ISM. At a post-conference meeting on Memorial Day, around 25 people discussed the need for an ongoing association to continue the networking begun during the consultation. A committee of ten was appointed to meet in Kansas City in July to organize the association, with consultation director Arthur Everett as chairman.

Ned Hale was designated to represent InterVarsity at the Kansas City meeting, but Hale asked me to attend instead. So I joined Everett, Burke, Mirza, Taussig, Daniel Bice of Campus Crusade, Joseph Sabounji of Park Street Church, Boston, and two other women, Magee and Rogerson, for three days of intense work. The presence and assistance of the Holy Spirit were evident throughout the meetings. It seems remarkable that a group representing such methodologically diverse ministries was able to produce an organizational blueprint, statement of purpose, basis of faith, ethical guidelines for members, and membership categories and qualifications, all within the space of three days. Commenting on the association's beginnings in a letter to me in 1987, Everett remarked that all the conditions were right in 1981. Organizations which a few years earlier would have been afraid of such a group saw the need to cooperate by 1981.

We appointed a committee of three, Everett, Burke and Taussig, to incorporate the new Association of Christian Ministries to Internationals (ACMI). At the first ACMI conference, held at Wheaton College in 1982, some association leaders felt that ACMI needed a full-time staff member. So in September of that year Arthur Everett became Executive Director of ACMI.

Since 1982, ACMI (which is open to Canadians) has sponsored six annual North American conferences at various locations in the US, drawing between 90 - 135 persons each time. Perhaps the most helpful service of ACMI is the networking opportunities it offers. The ACMI mailing list includes every known evangelical ministry to internationals. In 1987 ACMI is responding to 6 - 8 calls per month from individuals or churches just getting involved in ISM.

Almost immediately after the organization was founded, local and regional networking increased considerably. There are five local associations permitted to use the ACMI name, Denver, Fresno, Los Angeles, Seattle, and Washington, D.C.; and other, more loosely-knit groups have been formed. A Western Regional Conference was held in Pasadena in 1985. Using ACMI contacts, I was able to involve Southern Baptists, ISI staff and independent groups in an IVCF ISM conference I directed in Atlanta that same year.

High points in ACMI history include the appointment of Denver ISM worker Julia Castle-Wright as Associate Director in 1985 and the organization of the InterLink Program in 1986. The brainchild of Fuller alumnus and ACMI board member Leiton Chinn, InterLink seeks to provide fellowship for Christian internationals coming to study in North America and assist Christian internationals - some of whom may have been converted here - during their period of re-entry to the home country. The computer system will also be used to help ISM workers to follow up on internationals who move from one location to another. Dorothy Everett was appointed InterLink Director in 1986, thus becoming the third ACMI staff member.

In June 1986 Arthur Everett presented the InterLink concept to the 240 delegates of the World Evangelical Fellowship General Assembly in Singapore. Several individuals committed themselves to representing their countries in the InterLink program at the WEF meeting. Thus the CFR's early international networking vision is now being tackled by ACMI, with the help of modern technology.

One additional contribution of ACMI is the development of a Master's Program in International Ministries. Largely the work of Julia Castle-Wright, the program is in the process of approval by Denver Seminary. ACMI plans to propose similar programs to other seminaries in the future.

The history of ACMI to date illustrates the powerful results of widespread information diffusion. But having participated in ACMI from the outset, as a board member and frequent seminar leader, I think that there has been something more than just information diffusion. In a quote on the ACMI promotional brochure Ralph Winter calls the association "evangelical cooperation at its best." I must agree with Winter. Although there have been tensions at times, the association has maintained a remarkable degree of unity. This unity and the fruit that ACMI has already borne must be attributed to the Holy Spirit.

The Influence of ISM on World Mission: A Little-Known Story

What are the tangible results of ministry to internationals? (**Bold type segments to end of chapter added by book author.**) **The ISI vision has always been to make disciples in North America who will become disciple-makers upon re-entry to their home countries.** One early example that God does use this strategy in the 20th century is Bakht Singh of India. [featured in chapter 8] Impressed by the lives of Canadian Christians he met on board ship and by the peace and joy of a man he encountered while living at the Winnipeg YMCA, Singh became a Christian in 1929 through some deeply emotional, if not supernatural, experiences (Smith

1959,33-36). Singh has established around 600 indigenous churches and is known as India's foremost evangelist and Bible teacher (ISI,1983). What has happened since Bakht Singh was converted? ISI can provide names and stories of many lesser-known but very significant returnees. Some have become full-time Christian workers; others are tentmaker witnesses to fellow professionals (ISI 1983; 1986). In a recent letter to me, ISI vice-president Everett Boyce said that the number of returnees becoming active witnesses to co-workers and neighbors particularly impressed him. A few examples from ISI's "Returnee Christian Involvement Report" (1986) demonstrate the effectiveness of ISI strategy:) Dr. and Mrs. Joseph Luhukay helped start a prayer group for faculty at the University of Indonesia, Jakarta. Masaki Kakitani established the first Christian counseling service in Japan. Adam Biela leads an evangelical Bible study in the Catholic church in Poland. Charee Dhanyvong works in a missionary hospital serving refugees and lepers in Thailand. The other organizations have not kept as systematic records of returnees as ISI, but conversations with colleagues assure me that they could add other faithful Christian returnees to the list.

From a missiological perspective, it is significant that some of these persons are returning to countries that are not open to official missionaries. For example, ten of the persons who have become Christians during my seven years of ministry in Raleigh, N.C. have been mainland Chinese. Even those who did not become Christians warmly welcomed and tried to help two volunteer workers in our ministry who later went to teach English in China. Two who did become Christians have relatives in influential government positions (the Shanghai city council and the Chinese Cabinet). Witnessing has certainly happened in some family groups; one scholar writes that his son has become a Christian. My colleagues report similar results with mainland Chinese all over the country.

Leading internationals to faith and training them while in the USA through one-to-one discipling and participation in fellowship groups and special conferences is in reality an innovative method of leadership selection and training. Most of these returnees are not seminary-trained, but many have had experience witnessing to non-Christian peers on campus. So witnessing to co-workers is easier once they are established in jobs at home. The 1986 ISI returnee report listed a significant number of persons sharing with fellow faculty members and others starting Bible studies at home or work. Evidently, experience and training in the US is serving these individuals well. It has been frequently noted by ISM promoters that - unlike the North American missionary - such returnees have no language and fewer cultural problems when returning home.

But what influence has ISM had on the Americans involved in it? [Bold type and underlining added by book author.}Renewal, foreign student work and overseas missions interest seem to be mutually stimulating. The example of the Taussigs' church has already been cited. Leiton Chinn reports that his church, Truro Episcopal in Fairfax, Virginia, has had its missions program revitalized by ISM. In response to my question regarding the relationship of ISM and foreign missions interest, ISI vice president Everett Boyce wrote:

I could write a book on the examples you requested. ... One of the outstanding examples I know of regarding a church that credits international student ministry with stimulating their interest in missions, and really turning the church "on" is Northwest Bible Church in Dallas. Pastor Jim Rose is really excited about ISM (Boyce,1987).

Some church missions committees have even chosen to require ISM or some other kind of cross-cultural ministry of all persons approaching them for support for long-term missions involvement.

Ned Hale stated that ISM and overseas mission interest have been mutually enhancing in IVCF (Hale,1987b). During the early history of the IVCF ministry in Raleigh, N.C., ISM greatly strengthened a rather small Inter-Varsity chapter (McGee,1986). In my seven years in Raleigh, I have seen at least twenty-four Americans committed to ministry overseas trained through their involvement in ISM. Some of them have gone or are going as tentmakers. I have been aware that my brief seminars and weekly studies might be the only cross-cultural training they receive. Preparing Americans for ministry overseas through ISM here is another innovative and extremely practical kind of leadership selection and training. In Raleigh, participation in a multicultural international IVCF chapter (a bridging fellowship or "bicultural bridge" cf. Hiebert 1983) has trained both American and Christian international leaders for cross-cultural ministry.

It would appear then that ISM is not only a powerful way to revitalize a missions program; it is also an effective means of recruiting, directing and training cross-cultural witnesses. (Some of the students I worked with had a general interest in missions but discovered through ISM a call to a specific country.)

Ripening Harvests and the Need for Laborers

From a missiological point of view, ministry to international students in the US in the past twenty years has been at least to some extent - a story of harvests quickly ripe and quickly gone. International economic and political conditions have brought large numbers of certain groups here and then rather quickly stopped the flow. In some cases students have only been here for months. Jack Burke reports that 90 Libyan students were at the University of Houston for three months in 1978 and were ministered to by Christians during that time (Burke 1987b). During the 1970's US foreign student enrollment increased rapidly due to an influx of students from OPEC countries. By 1986, the number of students from OPEC countries had dropped considerably.

The new significant mission field is among South and East Asian students, particularly mainland Chinese. The PRC had the largest percentage increase of students between 1985 and 1986 - 38.4 percent, a total of 13,980 students alone (Institute of International Education 1986). This number does not include scholars. My colleagues around the country report great receptivity among the Chinese, but they are a volatile harvest. Events in China can easily spread fear among them, making them unwilling to attend activities sponsored by Christians. I have watched the fear level rise and fall during my years of ministry.

Faced with what we consider to be missiologically significant harvest fields (because of the closed countries represented and the potential for ministry on return), we in ISM often experience considerable frustration with the low visibility and lack of support we generally have among evangelicals. At a consultation of ACMI leaders held in January of this year Jack Burke told the rather poignant story of Tom and Diane Lawrence, two ISM workers who had a fruitful ministry in Houston. As long as they were in Houston, financial support was a nagging problem. When they decided to minister in China and then Hong Kong, the funds came in. But they discovered that students with whom they had had open doors in Houston were too busy and too affluent to listen to them in Hong Kong. They had actually been more effective at home, but support comes easier while they are overseas.

The church has begun to recognize the importance of evangelizing the growing minorities in the US. Refugees and immigrants have attracted a great deal of attention. A <u>Christianity Today</u> cover story in July, 1985 highlighted this mission field "next door and down the street" (Bjork 1985). In a companion article, EFMA director Wade Coggins pointed out that ethnic churches in the US could "bridge" the gospel back home. Writing in Missiology in 1982, Mortimer Arias pointed out the neglected potential of centripetal mission. But most of this attention has been directed to permanent residents. **In spite of the fact that students are generally destined to become leaders in their countries, most evangelicals have largely ignored the significance of reaching them.**) We in ISM feel like a periphery movement, and that in spite of the fact that great progress has been made since Bob Finley started ISI.

Most of the major theses concerning mission developed in MH520 are clearly visible in ISM history. At a time of general evangelical renewal Bob Finley started the mission structure that has served as a stimulus to congregational and other mission structures. Other key people have started ISM in their organizations, but the existence of a sodality within the organizations has proved necessary for ISM to continue in vigor. Lay people, women and students trained through experience, apprenticeship and short seminars have provided much leadership. Information diffusion, particularly through ACMI, has benefited both new and more experienced workers. All of this activity revolved around the rediscovery of centripetal mission at a time of increasing numbers of foreign students.

ISM is growing rapidly, as evidenced by the number of contacts from newcomers to the field received by ACMI. We have a particularly ripe harvest at the moment: the PRC students. Yet we are a periphery movement still needing the attention of the evangelical mainstream. At the January consultation, Burke suggested that we seek the help of evangelical opinion leaders. Since our mission field is so important and so volatile, we desire to move quickly from the periphery nearer to the centers of power.

Bibliography

(All undocumented information comes from personal acquaintance with the people mentioned or involvement in the events described.)

Arias, Mortimer 1982 "Centripetal Mission or Evangelization by Hospitality," Missiology 10(1): 69-81.

Bjork, Don 1985 "Foreign Missions: Next Door and Down the Street." Christianity Today 29(10):17-21.

Boyce, Everett 1987a International Students, Inc. Report to Jan. 1987 ACMI consultation. 1987b Personal letter to author, 11, 1987.

Burke, Jack 1987a Address to ACMI consultation on NAFSA/ISM Cooperation, Jan. 31, 1987. 1987b Memorandum to author, Feb. 18, 1987.

Chinn, Leiton E. 1979 "Historical Development of the International Student Ministry Movement in the USA; 1987 Telephone conversation with author, Mar. 15, 1987.

Coggins, Wade, 1985 "Getting the World View." Christianity Today 29(10):21.

Du Bois, Cora, 1956 Foreign Students and Higher Education in the United States. Washington, D.C.:American Council on Education.

Everett, Arthur 1987a "The Historical Growth and Development of International Student Ministries in North America to Date." [presented to ACMI consultation]. 1987b Personal letter to author, March 14, 1987. 1987c Telephone conversation with author, April 8, 1987.

Foote, G.P. 1987, "Campus Crusade for Christ National Ministry Report" [to ACMI consultation]

Georgiades,Maurine, 1987 Personal conversation with author, March, 1987.

Hale, Ned,1987a, IVCF Organization Report for ACMI consultation.1987b author, Feb. 12, 1987.1987c Telephone conversation with author, Mar. 19, 1987.

Hanna Mark. "The Great Blindspot in Missions Today" [1975], Colorado Springs: ISI Hiebert Paul G. 1983 "The Bicultural Bridge." In Anthropological Insights for Missionaries. Pp.227-253. Grand Rapids. Baker.

Howard, David 1970 Student Power in World Evangelism. Downers Grove, Il InterVarsity Press.

Institute of International Education, 1986 "Number of Students from People's Republic of China Enrolled in U.S. Colleges and Universities Increases Nearly 40 Percent." [IIE News Release for Oct. 21, 1986].

International Students Inc. 1983 Doorways. [Special anniversary issue].

1986 Returnee Christian Involvement Report.

Lau, Lawson, 1982, "Why Foreign Students Usually Hate the United States... And What One Couple Decided to Do About It." Christianity Today 26: (May 21) :30-31.

McGee,Bette, 1986, Personal conversation with author, Dec. 18,1986.

Medhin, Mesghina G., 1987 Telephone conversation with author, Mar. 19, 1987.

Shelley, Bruce, 1986, "The Rise of Evangelical Youth Movements." <u>Fides Hetistoria</u>18(1)45-63.

Smith, Daniel, 1959, <u>Bakht Singh of India</u>. Washington, D.C. [now Colorado Springs] International Students Press.

Taussig, Robert, 1986, Personal letter to author, Feb. 10, 1987.

Thompson, Mary A., Ed.,1982, Unofficial Ambassadors: <u>The Story of International Student Service.</u>

New York:International Student Service.

Tuel, Gene 1987, "The Navigators - ISM: Report to ACMI Consultation."

Wheeler, W.R. H.H.King and A.B.Davidson, Eds., 1925, The <u>Foreign Student in America</u>. New York: Associated Press.

43

Chapter

AUTHOR'S CREDENTIALS and MAJOR CONTRIBUTIONS TO INTERNATIONAL STUDENT MINISTRIES

Jack D. Burke, Ph.D., M.Div., M.S.

President, International Student Ministries Assistance, Inc (ISMA)

Director Emeritus,* International Student and Scholar Services, University of Houston

Founder, NAFSA Christian Specific Interest Group (SIG); NAFSA Honorary Life Member

Co-Founder, Association of Christians Ministering among Internationals (original title: Association of Christian Ministries to Internationals); ACMI Honorary Life Member

Under God's guidance, Dr. Jack Burke's <u>major contributions</u> to International Student Ministries were to:

1. Build a strong base of support at the University of Houston gaining a national reputation for its outstanding services to international students.

Why not? This was D'Ann's and my ministry. We were doing our work as unto the Lord. The multiple awards received from the International Student Organization and various nationality associations attested to the high quality work our office was known for. I was accorded the honor of being "chief guest" for numerous nationality group programs and dinners and received the "Outstanding Staff Advisor of the Year" award from the University in 1994. In recognition of our office's international contribution to the City of Houston (through our Friendship Family Program), Houston's Mayor Fred Hofheinz named April 29, 1976 as "Dr. Jack D. Burke Day" in Houston. Again, the Mayor's Office in April 1987 named a day in D'Ann's honor for her outstanding contribution as a volunteer to the city through our office's Friendship Family Program which she developed. She also received the University's "Volunteer of the Year" award in May 1994 from the University President, Dr. James Pickering, at a downtown hotel luncheon for corporate executives and distinguished alumni. At my retirement banquet on March 15, 1994 there were two emcees, one being the University president and the other being the Vice President for Student Affairs. Our office sponsored banquets honoring friendship families brought not only great respect to our office, but also favorable recognition to the University itself. In 1987, the V.P. for Student Affairs said that our banquet was the best thing that happened in our Student Affairs Division that year. More than 500 attended the last banquet in 1992. At my retirement banquet in 1994, planned by Anita Gaines, my successor, with the aid of a university committee, raised nearly $25,000 for a Jack and D'Ann Burke Scholarship fund given in perpetuity to needy international students. The amount has grown through the years. With the help of Jerry Naylor I was able to organize the Faculty-Staff Christian Fellowship at the University of Houston. Along with its spiritual benefits it helped to build a strong base of support with Christian faculty and administrators for my office.

2. Pioneer the way for Christians to become university Foreign Student Advisors (FSA) or directors of International Student and Scholar Services Offices, as a ministry.

Many Christians sought the opportunity of serving an **FSA internship** in international student advising at the University of Houston, where I served as Director from 1968 until my retirement in 1994. Approximately 25 have worked in professional positions in the ISSS Office or, at the conclusion of their internship, have gone to work for other university international offices throughout the U.S. Eleven have served or are currently serving as deans or directors.

3. **Initiate the first conference (consultation) for Christians working with international students nationally to meet together.**

In the spring of 1980 D'Ann and I submitted a four-page proposal for such a conference to Hal Guffey, President of International Students Inc. After setting up an appointment with Hal for June, we drove to Colorado Springs from Houston to meet with him and his executive staff to discuss the proposal. Hal told us that Nate Mirza had also expressed interest in such a conference. This was followed by another appointment in December 1980 to meet with the ISI leadership and several heads of leading international student ministry organizations, again at the ISI headquarters, to gain support for the proposal and to help organize such a conference. The decision was made to plan the conference for Memorial Day weekend, 1981. An ISI executive, Art Everett, was placed in charge of the conference planning (referred to as a Consultation at the time), which brought together more than 100 to Star Ranch, the headquarters at that time of International Students, Inc. (ISI), in Colorado Springs, Colorado Memorial Day weekend 1981. At the end of the Consultation a small group of us met to discuss how we might continue this movement. We decided to meet in the Kansas City area that summer at the invitation of Dr. Bob Taussig.

4. **Serve as co-founder of ACMI**

Ten of us who attended the Consultation met at a site selected by Dr. Bob Taussig in August 1980 in the Kansas City area, where we organized an Association of Christian Ministries to Internationals (ACMI). Art Everett, Bob and I were given the charge to be the Executive Committee. Bob and I asked Art Everett to become ACMI's first Executive Director. Art accepted, resigned from ISI and appointed my wife D'Ann Burke as Treasurer. As a volunteer her work was overseen by Travis Pittman, a Christian CPA in Houston.

5. **Lead the way, together with my wife D'Ann's capable assistance and leadership, to develop a strong university-based friendship family program.**

D'Ann became the first volunteer director of the University of Houston's Friendship Family Program, in which international students were assigned to friendship families or single adults who would host the students in their homes. Christian and non-Christian leaders alike, concerned for the welfare of international students, have found that church families are by far the easiest and most dedicated people to recruit to become friendship families.

Biennial banquets with attendances of up to and above 500 to honor friendship families brought the support and acclaim of the University administrative leadership, the Houston civic leadership, the Christian community involved in the friendship family program, and both International Student Organization and alumni leaders. In D'Ann's honor an award was established in April 1987 at the University called the "D'Ann Burke Award for Excellence in Service, University of Houston International Hospitality Program, April 11, 1987". Our friendship family program at the University of Houston has been cited as a "model" by many in NAFSA: Association of International Educators, the professional organization for the nation's international educators. The success of the University's Friendship Family Program was a cornerstone for the reasons D'Ann and I received NAFSA's top award nationally for involving the community in our work with international students, that is, the "Hugh M. Jenkins *Award for Excellence in Community Programming*."

6. Founder of the NAFSA: Association of International Educators Christian Specific Interest Group (SIG).

What started out in 1969 as a time of Bible reading and prayer with my room-mate and office Assistant Director, Jerry Naylor, at NAFSA conferences, gradually developed through the years into the formation of a specific interest group of Christians. My first attempt to gain NAFSA's recognition of our group was in 1998. I had submitted a proposal and petition of almost 80 signatures but the Board tabled the proposal and froze further attempts by organizations to gain Board approvals until 2000. With the encouragement of Rose Mary Valencia, a NAFSA officer and member of our group, Anita Gaines, my successor as Director of ISSS at the University of Houston, and Michael Brzezinski, Purdue's Dean of International Programs (and former U. of H. FSA Intern/Counselor), I submitted a more sophisticated version of the proposal in 2000 with 112 signatures of international educators representing all professional sections and regions of NAFSA. The Board approved it in an 8 to 4 vote. After serving the three year probationary period for new SIGS, the NAFSA Board unanimously approved our continuation of our group's focusing on religious beliefs and faith issues.

7. Initiate and organize a strong Christian base of support within NAFSA: Association of International Educators

D'Ann and I both were elected chairs of the national NAFSA Community Section, but 20 years apart. I was chair in 1970, and D'Ann in 1990. I served on the NAFSA Board of Directors, and held various elected and appointed leadership positions within NAFSA during my career from 1963 to 1994. D'Ann became the first volunteer director of the University based friendship family program. In recognition of our work within NAFSA, D'Ann and I were recipients of the following national and regional awards:

(1) "The Hugh M. Jenkins Award for Excellence in Community Programming" (top national award for community leadership in working with international students), in 2004.

(2) The <u>NAFSA Life Membership was presented to each of us in</u> 1994 (Life Membership Award is regarded as the highest award NAFSA offers, usually awarded to former NAFSA presidents.)

(3) In 2004, in a celebration marking the 50th anniversary of NAFSA's Region III (Texas, Oklahoma, Louisiana, and Arkansas), 10 awards were presented to those who were regarded as the <u>most influential over the past 50 years in "Shaping Region III With Outstanding Service: Inspiring Us to Follow Your Excellent Standards for International Education</u>." D'Ann and I were each recipients of this award.(4) I <u>received Region III's top annual award, "Citation for Extraordinary Service in International Education</u>" in 1993. (D'Ann and I have been active conference presenters as panel chairs and workshop/session presenters, and have both <u>served as NAFSA appointed paid consultants to help other universities.</u>)

8. With the help of Chris Troupis, a highly esteemed Christian attorney who voluntarily helped D'Ann and me to:

*   <u>establish a 501(c)3 non-profit, tax-deductible organization titled "International Student Ministries Assistance, Inc."</u> <u>(ISMA</u>) I serve as President and Chair of a board consisting of five members. D'Ann is Treasurer. ISMA's main objective is to make it possible for international students to attend Christian conferences for international students. A priority is to prepare Christian international students for their return home as effective ambassadors for Jesus Christ.

9. **Author of the book, <u>Paradigm Shift: Why International Students Are So Strategic to Global Missions</u>** which is best described as a "Case for International Student Ministry."

This book is unique. To date ISM has not received the support of churches like it should. My fervent hope and prayerful desire is that this book will help change the tide. It helped to have the unique background of 60+ years of combined experience, 30 years at the university level and 30+ years as an ISM volunteer. Started as the university Director of the Office of International Services at the private ivy league University of Pennsylvania and then throughout most of my career until retirement again serving as the office director, this time for the state supported University of Houston's International Student and Scholar Services Office. Of the 60+ years, 30+ years was spent before and after my career as a university's director in charge of serving the special needs of its international students by volunteering to initiate and serve as

- co-founder of ACMI
- founder of the NAFSA Christian SIG
- develop a non-profit to support ISMs, International Student Ministries Assistance
- author of Paradigm Shift: Why International Students Are So Strategic To Global Missions.

*Emeritus title conferred to Dr. Jack Burke by University of Houston President, Dr. James Pickering, in a memorandum following my retirement banquet, April 15, 1994.

AUTHOR'S RESUME (Brief Version)

JACK D. BURKE, Ph.D., M.Div., M.S.

Education B.A.. University of Oregon; M.Div. Fuller Theological Seminary; M.S. followed by one year Foreign Student Advisor Internship; and Ph.D., both latter degrees - University of Southern California.

Positions and Accomplishments: Director of International Services Office at University of Pennsylvania and Director of International Student and Scholar Services at University of Houston; retired in 1994, a career spanning 30 years. Volunteered to help international student ministry organizations and individuals, a total also of 30+ years, before and after working for universities.

- Author of chapters for books (one being for Ivy League's University of Pennsylvania Press on international students); Master's Degree Project: Handbook for Foreign Student Counselors (165 pages); Ph.D. Dissertation: "Predictive Validity of English Language

Screening Instruments for Foreign Students Entering the University of Southern California;"
- Author of <u>Paradigm Shift: Why International Students Are So Strategic to Global Missions</u>

University of Houston Awards and Honors :

- $25,000 endowment set up at University of Houston for "Jack and D'Ann Burke Scholarship" announced at Jack's retirement banquet. (Amount has increased through the years)
- University of Houston's "Staff Advisor of the Year" (1993-94)
- Plaques and Awards from University of Houston's President and V.P. for Student Affairs
- Received multiple International Student Organization and nationality organizations awards for "outstanding leadership;"
- U. of H. Asian Alumni Association award for "outstanding dedication and contribution to all international students" presented at University of Houston International Alumni Association dinner. (2005)
- Received award from University of Houston administration for 25 years of service as Director of International Student and Scholar Services.

Honors and Awards from NAFSA: Association of International Educators

- (Honorary) Life Member upon retirement
- "Founder and First Coordinator." NAFSA Christian Specific Interest Group (SIG)
- Hugh Jenkins Award "for excellence in Community Programming." (top annual national award for involving community in providing hospitality and involvement with international students)
- Elected Region 9 Chair 1965 (when NAFSA had a Region IX, the regions have changed)
- In 1993 received top annual award at NAFSA Region 3 annual conference (TX, OK, LA, AR).
- Received NAFSA Region 3 award for being "one of Region 3's 10 most influential International Educators in past 50 years."

- NAFSA Region III Best Presentation Award at Regional Conference
- Appointed NAFSA Consultant

Awards from Christian organizations

- (Honorary) ACMI Life Member
- Jack and D'Ann Burke received two top national awards from International Students Inc. (early 1990's and 2005) and one from Bridges International. (2012). The latter is presented annually in perpetuity to a non-Bridges volunteer for "leadership and passion."
- North American Mission Board (Southern Baptists) presented Dr. Jack Burke at 25th anniversary of ACMI for serving as co-founder of ACMI.

Other Awards

- EDUCARE FELLOWSHIP (The top graduate level fellowship presented by University of Southern California's School of Education) – 2 consecutive years 1966–67)
- Mayor of Houston proclaimed April 29, 1976 as Dr. Jack D. Burke Day in Houston.
- Received Fulbright-Hays Award to tour German universities in January 1980.
- Received invitation to be one of 12 selected twice to tour Taiwan's higher education institutions; also one of 12 selected by the PRC (China) and NAFSA to tour China's higher education institutions; received "Honorary Professor" Award presented by President Dr. Li Jianlin, China's Three Gorges University, following my speaking engagement there in 2010.
- Only one to receive Houston higher education leaders award from Houston's Immigration and Naturalization Service (INS District Director at Immigration & Naturalization Service presented award at July 4, 1976 ceremony celebrating 200th year birthday of our country).

ADDENDUM

Resources Available for International Student Ministry

Submitted by Ned Hale, Former InterVarsity ISM Director. Former ACMI Staff Workshop Presentation With Co-presenters **Ned Hale (ACMI Staff) and Brian Hart (InterVarsity Staff)** at ACMI National Conference, May-June 2012, Houston, Texas

This handout is **not** a comprehensive list. It is more like <u>an update of some of the best and currently available ISM resources</u> both of earlier and recent years.

Table of Contents/topics:

Finding Bibles in Many Languages

Bible Study Guide Books
Conversing/Teaching in English as a Second Language ("ESL"):
Prayer:
Demographics:
Identifying International Student Ministry locations:
International Student Ministry Descriptions:
Bibliographies, Books and booklets on ISM:
Publications on religions and regions of the world:
Various Visual and Electronic Media:

Finding Bibles in Many Languages:

Brian Hart of InterVarsity ISM says: "At www.intervarsity.org/ism/article/5342 I've added a link: Where to Find Bibles, Tracts, Christian Audio and Video Materials in Other Languages. Wycliffe Associates UK created a new site that is geared precisely to help students find Bibles in non-English languages. http://worldbibles.org lists downloadable, online, and print-Bible sources in 4,000 languages (and whether each Bible is free or costs money). In the Spring 2010 Leiton Chinn also wrote: "Millions of people are on the move to new countries. Do you know someone who has moved away from their home language area? It is often difficult to find Bibles in those other languages. The *"World Bibles"* site can help you. It lists over 14,500 places on the internet where you can find Bibles (many downloads free). This site includes Bible sources in Braille, video, audio and mobile phone formats." **Another good starting point for finding Bibles and related resources in a range of languages, including the English Bible is:** www.biblegateway.com/passage/?search=Genesis%201&version=NIV **(New International Version).**

Japanese scriptures: In November 2011 Don E. Regier (Word of Life Press Ministries - WLPM) in Japan, at Dan Brannen's (ISI) suggestion, wrote to Carmen Bryant in ACMI asking her to share some news with the ACMI network re ministering to Japanese in North America. WLPM was developing the *JAPANESE-ENGLISH BILINGUAL BIBLE* (Bairingaru Seisho). ISI members...helped convince the WLPM editors that there really was a market for the Bilingual Bible with the NIV and the Shinkaiyaku translations. In 2006 WLPM began shipping the Bilingual Bible to the US. ISI members spread the word among many involved in ministering to Japanese so they could easily be gotten without the necessity of ordering from Japan. If you type "Japanese Bibles" in the search slot of www.Amazon.com and/or www.christianbook.com there several of WLPM's titles.

Delores Wirz, a missionary in Japan, has also developed Bible studies that are bilingual, with the English part having multiple choice questions. These can be ordered from her mission's website: www.asianaccess.org/opportunities/ebc-main.html New Life Ministries in Pomona, CA (Phone: 717-738-0582 or 909-620-4255) may still carry this material A full listing of her titles is given at the following and can also be ordered directly from Japan: www1.biz.biglobe.ne.jp/~clcfb/Biling.English%20Texts.htm

Chinese New Testaments: Jim Brubaker says: "the CNV/NIV bilingual New Testament is available from AFC. They will be called CNV in the future (Chinese New Version) so as not to be confused with the English NCV - New Century Version. The popular butterfly-cover NT's are for ministry use only, but are the older Chinese Union Version along with the NIV in English. Request via a note to: mclit@afcinc.org or by calling 888-999-7959. Similarly an introduction to the *New Testament Contemporary Chinese Version* published (in 2010) by Chinese Bible International Society (CBI), which spent 16 years to translating Bible directly from the original text. [The OT is scheduled to come to the market in 2014].

See: www.asianbookone.com (type "new testament contemporary" in Quick Find slot).

Bible Study Guide Books:

Paul and Peggy Schlieker say: "There are very few resources designed for people who don't have a "Christian" background. (Virtually all published studies assume either personal faith or some degree of familiarity with biblical concepts). To fill this need, we wrote "*Bible Basics*" and "*What's Missing Inside You?*" *Bible Basics* lays a foundation for future Bible studies and is designed to be a natural "on-ramp" for *What's Missing Inside You?* Both books do not assume that the reader is a Christian or is even familiar with the Bible. We have successfully used both of these workbooks with internationals, business professionals and students. "See: www.christianbiblebasics.com/aboutus.aspx

Passport to the Bible (1999 IV Press, 118 page paperback) is one of the very best of these guidebooks which is particularly helpful to international student "seekers" as well as young Christians. Six ISM workers spent two years developing these 24 Bible studies incl. leaders' guidelines covering crucial passages from Genesis to the New Testament Gospels. It is in its second printing now and available from IV Press! See: www.intervarsity.org/ism/article/105

The ACMI website, www.acmi-net.net [since changed to members@ ascmai.memberclicks.net], has a number of excellent Bible study guides by Tom Sirinides (ACMI Board member and former InterVarsity ISM staff). [(Author added, now Assoc. Director of International Student Services at New York University.] To access them you have to be a member of ACMI, then use the member-password to access the "Private" side of the site. Bruce McDowell has also authored a series of Bible studies (available online) on the message of the Gospel for Muslims. See: www.tenth.org/index.php?id=206 It is in English, and also translated (further down) into Turkish.

A simply brilliant publication, _the St. Francis magazine_, celebrated the life (at the death) of missionary Vivienne Stacey at: www.stfrancismagazine.info/ja/content/blogcategory/35/49 Included on this web page is a list with links to many of her publications on Muslim outreach, including (at the bottom) some excellent _cross-cultural Bible study guides_ for use with intls. In dialogue with Muslims one of the main matters of discussion is the Trinity. A way to help Muslims begin to understand the concept is found in the article (on A-I) "The Unique Oneness of God" at www.answering-islam.org/authors/dawud/oneness.html

Conversing/Teaching in English as a Second Language ("ESL"):

Craig and Shirley Colbert emailed the ACMI e-network in March 2012 suggesting a 3-series (12 lessons in each) curriculum for teaching English as a Second Language (TESL), including materials for those not trained in TESL. They have also taught a seminar at ACMI conferences on a program they do with children, called "Passport to School." The following have series samples:www.efca.org/reachglobal/reachglobal-ministries/efca-connect/resources/outreach-english-class

Julie Arant has recently put together a _"Discussion Topics for Internationals"_ booklet with 48 topics. **The questions range from the light-hearted and gradually go deeper for meaningful sharing. Provides guidelines for use of the discussion-question format.** See website for the list of 48 and to order: www.multilanguage.com/esl/ESLDisT.htm

Heidi Chew writes: "(try) _doing inductive bible study_ with high beginning (or) low intermediate students _using the NIRV_ (New Intl Readers Version - written at a fourth grade English level); as we go thru the process of observation, questions, interpretation and application, we allow a time for vocab. questions at the beginning; but generally, the text is so easy to understand, there are few questions. You can print passages at www.Biblegateway.com ; there is a drop down menu that allows you to choose which translation you want to use."

The HOPE ESL software curriculum is now ready for use in ESL teaching environments. Using audio and video from The HOPE film (www.thehopeproject.com) an effective ESL ministry tool has been created. Students will be able to work through the vast amount of content on this interactive CD-ROM at their own pace. Additionally, it can be copied and distributed without charge.

Prayer:

There are a host of mission organizations and churches as well as ISM ministries who give prayer concerns from around the world, primarily through mailings or internet postings. Most of us use prayer letters on specific ISM concerns to generate specific targeted prayer for internationals. The internationals themselves, of course, come from a context outside North America which is of deep concern to most of them. So it is helpful for us to be familiar with prayer concerns about the areas from which some of our international friends come. The following are examples:

"_Operation World, The Definitive Prayer Guide to Every Nation_," by Jason Mandryk, [revised 7th ed. IVP 2010 hardback, 978 pgs.] is the most thorough reference with prayer guides for all the countries of the world. This great reference includes a daily prayer calendar plus maps, prayer needs, and religious, political, economic, and people group information for every country in the world. Individual copies are also available in paperback with CD-ROM and other formats. Call 1-800-MISSION for a special discount for mission workers (case of 10 paperback copies went for $10 each + $21 shipping); mention Mission Frontiers magazine and pay by credit card. Another book re prayer is _Worldwide Journeys in Prayer, 101 True Stories from..._ (all the continents) (IVP 2002 paperback, 417 pgs.) Over 35 years ago Wentworth Pike started collecting stories of people from all walks of life, miracles to disappointments. From these, he compiled 101 true accounts from all over the world.

Demographics:

The Canadian government has put together a website listing all 208 countries of the world, with specific information of interest on each country's history, geography, religions and culture. This is an invaluable tool for ISM workers in learning about the background of an international student while welcoming and befriending them: www.intercultures.ca/ cil-cai/overview-apercu-eng.asp

Country Profiles – The CIA's "World Factbook" contains a lot of information about countries of the world at: www.cia.gov/library/ publications/the-world-factbook Press "the world factbook," then select a continent and country using your mouse. Finally, scroll down the page for that country to find out almost any factual data you'd like for data on the recent History, Geography (including a map at the top), People (religion percentages), Government, Economy, Communications, Transportation, or "Trans-national issues."

For a more narrative (including photos) coverage of Country Profiles visit the BBC website, which has less data but presented in more interesting style with brief commentaries, particularly focusing on recent history, the country's leaders and the types of media in operation. Go to:

http://news.bbc.co.uk/2/hi/middle_east/country_profiles/default.stm (then select a country).

ISI also has a few excellent country profiles: www.isionline.org/ Resources/FreeMaterial.aspx as do other mission groups (eg: www. asianaccess.org/ministry/profiles.html - 20 Asian countries)

Identifying International Student Ministry locations:

An updated list of over 1,000 ISM-relevant websites in 38 countries of the world is also featured on the ACMI website: www.acmi-net.net! The non-North American (worldwide) list is on the "public" side:

www.acmi-net.net/index.php?module=documents&JAS_Document Manager_op=viewDocument&JAS_Document_id=37

The North American (only) list is on the "private" side of this website. This private password-protected side is for ACMI members only, and includes a list of current and past ACMI members plus a "calendar" for posting notices of ISM-related events and announcements.

The ACMI website is located at: www.acmi-net.net It includes a contact list of many ISM workers (incl. volunteers) in all the major organizations and churches in USA and Canada (1,300+ on the "ISM Worker Directory database"!), a list of important future ISM-related events, and a new description of ACMI, (including its purposes, its affirmation of the NAFSA code of Ethics, requirements for <u>membership in ACMI and an online or printable membership application</u>).

Find out how many <u>international people are living in your area</u> and where they're from! Go to <u>www.peoplegroups.info</u>. It will give you some statistics for Canada (by province) and for the USA (by state) using the U.S. census of the year 2000. Press the location of your interest on the map and you will be able to access an ethnic breakdown of information on your local city, county or zip zone, as paired with nationalities, languages spoken, ancestries and religions within that location! You can also access a list of "people groups" within a particular country of the world, but you have to register (no cost) as a user to access people groups in your locale.

Bibliographies, Books and booklets on ISM:

An "<u>International Student Ministry Reading and Resource List</u>" was put together and updated periodically by Ms. Katie Rawson, InterVarsity ISM staff director. This last update was in 2001, with a few updated address changes by Ned Hale in 2007. An earlier version of this can be found on the web at: <u>www.intervarsity.org/ism/download.php?version_id=955&article_id=147</u> and as a Word doc at: <u>www.intervarsity.org/ism/cat/42</u> under "Basic Bibliography and Resource" lists.

"<u>INK Bibliography</u>" is a bibliography designed specifically <u>for Christian international students</u> – This is a list of about 25 books on the themes "Guidance, Decision Making & Transition" and "Spiritual Warfare and Temptation." Order from the national IV office, ISM Dept., 6400 Schroeder Road, Madison, WI 53707-7895. It was given to Christian internationals in the "Internationals for God's Kingdom" (INK) training conferences in recent years. For full description of a former INK Conference, including videos clips, see: <u>www.intervarsity.org/ism/event/1297</u> and <u>www.inkusa.org</u>

"<u>Crossing Cultures Here and Now</u>" is a terrific booklet by Lisa Espineli Chinn (first pub. in 2006). It shares foundational attitudes and practical steps on developing friendships with international students. Information on how to order this 24-page booklet ($5 for a bundle of 5) is found at: <u>https://store.intervarsity.org/catalogsearch/result/index/?x=0&y=0&q=ISM&department=13</u> or <u>https://store.intervarsity.org</u> (click on "International Student Ministries").

"<u>The World At Your Door</u>" is ISI's foundational publication on the essential things one needs to know to have a ministry among internationals.

It was authored by Tom Phillips (then ISI President), Robert Norsworthy, and Terry Whalin and was published in 1997. It is available from ISI, P.O. Box C, Colorado Springs, CO 80901. See www.isionline.org

Similarly, the book "*God Brings the World to Your Doorstep*" or the earlier 1984 version "*The World at Your Doorstep*" by Lawson Lau is available from lawsonllau@gmail.com Dr. Lau (originally from Singapore) got his MA and PhD on Illinois campuses as an international student. He is still pastor of "All Nations Baptist Church" in Champaign-Urbana.

Grete Shelling says her new book, "*In Love But Worlds Apart*," has been published and appeared for the first time in the "Show and Tell" at the ACMI 08 conference! It is being offered at ACMI 2010 to all fellow ACMI members and their associates at a special price of $11.75 incl. shipping. Contact her directly: grete@iface.org She and her husband, Ted, work with InterFACE Min. in Austria. To order online: www.authorhouse.com/BookStore/ItemDetail.aspx?bookid=51338 then write the title into the SEARCH window (or **ISBN#: 978-1-4343-8116-3**). A review of it is posted on the ACMI E-Network incl. how it can be ordered:

www.acmi-net.net/index.php?module=documents&JAS_Document_Manager_op=viewDocument&JAS_Document_id=27 **Resources for Returnees**: *Back Home* (IF in UK) and *Think Home* (ISI) by Lisa Espineli Chinn, *Home Again* (Navigators) by Nate Mirza, and a returnee booklet (ISI) by John Eaves are some individual ISM workers' contributions to provide training for reentry/returnees:

For Lisa Chinn's recent booklet *Back Home*: info@friendsinternational.org.uk

For Lisa Chinn's workbook *Think Home*; https://store.intervarsity.org/think-home.html

For Nate Mirza's book *Home Again*: www.navpress.com/Product/9780972902304/Home-Again

For John Eave's booklet: "**Preparing Your International Friend for Life Back Home**" http://store.isionline.org/products/Preparing-Your-International-Friend-For-Life-Back-Home-%252d-PDF.html

Publications on religions and regions of the world: World Religions: Gene Congdon points to "ISI's excellent book," The Compact Guide to World Religions by Dean Halverson: http://store.isionline.org/products/The-Compact-Guide-To-World-Religions.html IV Press has a good pocket dictionary on world religion: www.ivpress.com/cgi-ivpress/book.

pl/code=2705 Note also ISI's "religion profiles": http://store.isionline.org/categories/Religion-Profiles

Brian Rightler says "The best pocket guide I have found is put out by Baker Pub. *The Pocket Guide to World Religions*: http://tinyurl.com/63nco7 For a thorough treatment you can get *Neighboring Faiths*: www.ivpress.com/cgi-ivpress/book.pl/code=1524 Patricia Durst says to look at *Christianity, Cults & Religions* English Pamphlet pub. by Rose Publishing (CA) www.amazon.com/s/ref=nb_sb_noss?url=search-alias%3Daps&field-keywords=Christianity%2C+Cults+%26+Religions also available on CD as a power point presentation: www.rose-publishing.com/Christianity-Cults-Religions-pamphlet-P14.aspx

World Regions: Instant newspapers worldwide (!) – View the front page of current daily newspapers in most of the major cities of the world (about **580 newspapers from over 80 countries**) at: www.newseum.org/todaysfrontpages/flash This could be helpful to you or international in keeping up with the news in a particular country or city and talking points for conversation on current issues/events. **Chinese:** *Ambassadors for Christ, Inc.* bookstore, as well as *Chinese Christian Literature*, Inc. and *Overseas Missionary Fellowship*, each have one of the largest collections of apologetic literature (in Mandarin and some English). EG: the book "*Go Back To China*" by Fan Xuede is available in Mandarin at www.afcresources.org/bookstore/contents/en-us/d167.html#p29932 (about ½ way down the page) or call: 717-687-8564 at 21 Ambassador Drive, Paradise, PA 17562. Ambassadors for Christ's *Song of a Wanderer* is an innovative way of sharing Christianity with Chinese students and Scholars, in both English and Chinese, says Shaun Rudolph. *Go Back to China* is basically a dialogue on various subjects, geared to target non-believers and serving as a guideline of what questions people usually ask in China - available in Mandarin (simplified script), but not (yet) in English. The author, Fan Xuede, was a professor in a Communist Party school and then became a Christian. He is well known to Mainland Chinese Christians. This book is perhaps the second most popular for non-Christian intellectuals, next to *Song of a Wanderer*. His other book "*Why I Would Not Become a Christian*" could *not be legally published in China*. Get all these at AFC's website: www.afcinc.org

South Asians: The "Reaching South Asians" issue of InterVarsity's *Internationals on Campus (IOC)* magazine is now available. This issue includes articles such as "Reaching Indians Looks Different than Reaching

Other Internationals" and "Training Students to Reach Hindus." Other articles offer practical suggestions on reaching international students from Muslim and Hindu backgrounds as well as examples of outreach events and situations you may face in this ministry. Find at: www.intervarsity.org/ism/go/ioc (download about 1/2 way down the page, "Growing International Student Leaders - Fall 2007 issue") where you can view individual articles or download a PDF of the entire issue. You can also order printed copies as well as a separate issue on "**East Asians**" from the InterVarsity Store (scroll half-way down at): https://store.intervarsity.org/catalogsearch/result/index/?x=0&y=0&q=ISM&department=13&limit=15

For working among **Muslims**, Carmen Bryant recommends the book, *From Seed to Fruit*, by J. Dudley Woodberry, published by the William Carey Library. In 2011 a Revised and Enlarged edition was released with new chapters and updated information. For more info see: http://missionbooks.org/williamcareylibrary/product.php?productid=702&cat=0&page=1 Browse other books on missions there at: www.missionbooks.org *Two Messiahs: The Jesus of Christianity and the Jesus of Islam* by Jeff Morton (Biblica Pub 2011,161 pg. pbk. – see: www.Biblica.com). "...as a method to instruct Christians about Islam, (this) is ...ideal, especially for those uninitiated Western Christians who have little or no knowledge of this subject," says Bassam Madany, Middle East Resources.

The tests of holy books are helpful: "*Walking on Jesus (Isa) Street*" is a YouTube presentation of the gospel (4 min.), comparing points of the gospel in the Quran with the same points in the New Testament.

See: http://bit.ly/IzJeQr or www.youtube.com/watch?feature=endscreen &NR=1&v=pW4VvZ0FGfg

The Bible and Islam authored by Bassam Madany is "a gold mine and still one of the best and most insightful books on understanding Islam and the Muslim ever written," says one worker among Muslims in North America." Jochen Katz points to his website article of Madany for a summary of his views: www.answering-islam.org/authors/madany/scriptural_principles.html

RE understanding **South Americans** "*Thirty Books That Most Influenced My Understanding of Christian Mission*" is an article by Samuel Escobar which can be found by registering online (free) with the "International Bulletin of Missionary Research" website of the Overseas Mission Study Center (OMSC) in New Haven, CT: See: www.internationalbulletin.org/files/html/2010-02-contents.html (April 2010 issue)

Western Civilization: *The Book that Made Your World: How the Bible Created the Soul of Western Civilization*, by Vishal Mangalwadi is reviewed in an 8-minute interview with Dr. Mangalwadi on Fox News in March 2011 at: www.revelationmovement.com/instructors/blog_post/23 This is an outstanding look at the Christian roots of Western culture, why the "West" has moved away from its roots under the influence of the "Enlightenment" and all from the perspective of a Christian from India. Order from amazon.com.

Similarly, "*Forgotten Foundation – how the great ideas of the Christian faith became the foundation of the western world*" by Russ Stevenson (Reformed Press, 2009, 161 page paperback) is written in layman's language and is a case for the ways in which ideas that are Christian have helped shape Western culture. Chinese, enamored with democracy, for example, will find his chapter on democracy a helpful study of how the checks and balances of modern-day democracies were inspired by Christian ideals. To order see: http://books.google.com/books/about/Forgotten_Foundation. html?id=ClhnPgAACAAJ

Various Visual and Electronic Media:

Flags of the World T-Shirts: Visionwear has an International Flag and multi-flag-T-shirts with flags of the world on them. www.visionwear.us/cart/index.php/wearables/shirts/t-shirts-1/multi-flag-t-shirts.html Ordering in large numbers may reduce cost:

Films: List of films to use with internationals: Liz Godwin in a January 2009 email assembled a 4-page long list of films that have been used successfully with international students over the years: Contact Ned Hale for a copy of that list in MS Word or PDF format: acmiemail@gmail. com In March 2012 Brian Hart shared with the ACMI e-network "you can watch *the Jesus film online in 1,120 languages* at: www.jesusfilm.org/film-and-media/watch-the-film The many language choices, use of the book of Luke for the script, and focus on historical accuracy are positive, but students expecting a Hollywood blockbuster may be distracted by the lower-budget 1979 video and effects."

DVDs: Suggestions for DVDs to show internationals – Contact ACMI member Kurnia Foe, President, Global Student Friendship Old Dominion University, Norfolk, VA: kurniafoe@gmail.com

"*The Hope*" video/DVD, subtitled "*The Story of God's Promise for all People,*" is a Mars Hill Production. It takes one all the way through the Bible to show how God's plan spans the Old and New Testaments. For those whose first language is not English, the clearly-speaking narrators and pictures are excellent. Check out www.mars-hill.org for more info. (or call 1-800-580-6479 if you have questions). You can watch it at: www.thehopeproject.com and find a "study guide" here to go with it (press "Resources").

A website that sells *resources/scriptures/songs in over 80 languages*, Christian books in 45 languages, the "Who Is Jesus?" tract, Bible-based ESL materials, the JESUS DVD in over 1000 languages, plus foreign-language Christian DVDs. You can order these at: www.multilanguage.com

Videos: A new (2010) training video "*International Friendship Program*," (27 min.) produced by Rice University & the Institute of International Education (IIE) as an orientation and training video which facilitates a friendship program between newly-arriving international students and North American community volunteers. It includes information on how international students impact and enhance US campuses, provides guidelines on cross-cultural expectations for US volunteers, and contains easy suggestions for successful initial interactions. View segment online at: http://oiss.rice.edu/content.aspx?id=1100

Testimonies of over 100 Muslim Background Believers (MBBs) are in online video format at: www.muslimjourneytohope.com/watch.asp (and) www.youtube.com/user/Muslims4Jesus

Radio station broadcasts worldwide are also listed at: www.muslimjourney tohope.com

Power Points: International Friendship Inc. (IFI) has a very full list of 36 power point (PPt) presentations on a variety of topics for use with internationals posted online by Shaun Rudolph in August 2009 - topics such as "Overview of the Bible," "Uniqueness of Christ," "Science Track using *Song of Wanderer* - for Chinese students & scholars only," and many more! These are listed at their website: www.ificincy.org/oneonone.htm Check them out!

A very simple Gospel PPt presentation of "The Bridge Illustration" is given on the following website: www.lifebpc.com/resources/pps/**Bridge%20of%20 life%20(auto)2.pps** This illustration is used extensively in as an evangelistic tool by many student ministries in the past (especially by some in Campus Crusade and The Navigators). A simple (slide) illustrative presentation is also available at: www.cometocalvary.org/thebridge/con.html YouTube has a brief (3 min.) talk-drawing on this at: www.youtube.com/watch?v=VzHgzVgVnQc and animated: www.youtube.com/watch?v=SnXTo8W2ZoQ

Audios: _Android and iPhone/iPad users_ can download _Free apps_ at www.bible.is/resources These apps, once downloaded, enable you to listen to audio Bibles in 634 languages, read the text from most versions, and see clips from the _Jesus film_ in many languages _on your phone_.

Articles, especially on Ethnic groups: _"Why Are Americans Like That?"_ (Enculturation Books, pub. 2005) is a simple and humorous book by Stan Nussbaum, designed to help newly arrived international friends understand American culture. It includes the table of contents, the entire preface and first chapter of the book for review online, and a final chapter on Christianity – an ideal gift for American friends to give to an inquiring international. To order copies see: www.business-connect.net/product/ BK001 A similar (brief but equally good) online statement _"Why Do Americans Act Like That?"_ by a different author is given at: http://10ib. pbworks.com/w/page/696312/Why%20Do%20Americans%20Act%20 Like%20

NAFSA (secular assoc. of professional foreign students' advisors, counselors and community volunteers) has a publishing wing with several titles designed to help new internationals get oriented to North American campuses. See: www.nafsa.org/interactive/core/orders/category. aspx?catid=4

"Who is Jesus? The most influential life ever lived" is a recent addition to Campus Crusade's evangelistic websites, this one giving a thorough description of who Jesus is. It features everything from "highlights" of His life to his miracles, teachings, relevance to you and a way to "investigate" Him for oneself. See: www.church-webs.com/whoisJesus/index.html

Many campus ministries are responding to the "spike" in numbers of Chinese students and scholars coming to North American campuses (30% increase in 2009-2010). A well-written news article on Chinese scholars coming to Christ has appeared online in a March 2010 website at: http://abcnews.go.com/US/chinese-students-choose-christianity/ story?id=13086190&page=1 A special article on Chinese students arriving in North America was published by The Chronicle of Higher Education in May 2011, entitled: _"Colleges Adapt to New Kinds of Students From Abroad: Younger, sometimes less-experienced students require more academic and social support."_

http://chronicle.com/article/Colleges-Educate-a-New-Kind-of/127704 "This changing profile presents challenges both academic and cultural to colleges across the United States." it said.

In April 2012 Leiton Chinn emailed a Word document on the Japanese government's recent decision encouraging more Japanese to study abroad. See the article by Mizuho Aoki, a Staff writer for the Japan Times online April 20, 2012: www.japantimes.co.jp/text/nn20120420a2.html

European and Middle Eastern traditions for forgiveness and reconciliation are different from the "West's" because of the different place for the teachings of Jesus in the respective cultures. In European tradition, the ideal reconciliation flows from forgiveness and repentance. In Middle Eastern tradition the ideal reconciliation flows from retribution and restitution. For a more detailed analysis on this, see: www.oprev. org/?s=biblical+rationale+for+delayed&x=10&y=4 (scroll down to "Biblical Rationale....")

COMMA, a "Coalition Of Ministries to Muslims in (North) America," has launched (in 2011) its first phase of a public website: http:// commanetwork.com Its target audience is the Christian community. You can check it out and then recommend it to your church as a resource. They have kept the articles short and simple, and would like your feedback/ comments at: feedback@commanetwork.com

In April 2012 Nate Mirza reported in an email: "Over the last two years I have been contacting people about the possibility of conducting a one-question-survey to identify the yearnings of Muslims. My desire is two-fold: 1) To open doors for you into the hearts of your Muslim friends, and 2) To get their responses so I could demonstrate to our Muslim friends how Jesus Christ most completely satisfies our deepest longings. I hope to do this through small booklets and videos for those who can't or won't read." Contact nhale@intervarsity.org for further information on this survey and its results.

There is increasing backlash to the new "Insider" movement (IM) on how to reach out to Muslims.See: http://tinyurl.com/yfgolo9 Articles like this one by Bassam Madany on the "New Maghrebi Christians" of North African countries are showing that missionary efforts of prior centuries to the Muslim world did not necessarily fail in their methods and that this "insider" movement is actually a "western construct." A 17-minute sample video on "Insider Movements: A Critical Assessment" can be found at: www.i2ministries.org (see "downloads") includes clips of three testimonies from former Muslims discussing their thoughts on "IM" and experiences with Western "IM" missionaries. An example of one controversial area is recent efforts in scriptural translation to substitute "Allah" for

"Father" - one take on this issue: http://husseinwario.com/blog/2012/04/19/wycliffe-sil-and-frontiers-translation-controversy-and-the-ahmadiyya-sect

Is the Arab Spring a movement leading to more freedom and equal rights? "Not for women," according to Amal al-Malki, a Qatari author of *Arab Women in Arab News* who is very concerned about the rights of women in the Arab world. She is largely skeptical of recent developments and says, if anything, the Arab Spring has only highlighted the continuing "second-class citizenship" of women in the region Listen to her interview on *"Talk to Al-Jazerra"* in English online at: www.aljazeera.com/programmes/talktojazeera/2012/04/201242111373249723.html

The story about the shrinking population of the Palestinian Christians in the Holy Land was broadcast on *"60 Minutes"* Sunday, April 22, 2012 at 6pm (Central USA time). You can watch the story on the CBS website: www.cbsnews.com/sections/60minutes/main3415.shtml An added feature called *"60 Minutes Overtime"* is at: www.cbsnews.com/60minutesovertime?tag=hdr;cnav

Examining Worldviews: Paul Champoux has put together a set of audio and video presentations introducing the Christian worldview and comparing it to others. See: www.sciencegodandlife.com Simple apologetics: brief answers to common questions asked about Christianity - Henry P. Poetker of Edmonton, Alberta Canada has constructed a website with numerous questions and answers given in simple English: http://henrysanswers.info/qanda.html#Q5 (press: "Questions and Answers" at top of menu). Other topics are considered more in depth.

www.answering-islam.org is one of the best websites for a wealth of apologetic material on Islam, A list of new (in 2012) additions are at: www.answering-islam.org/New/new.html managed by Jochen Katz in Germany (former international student PhD candidate in the States who felt called full-time to this website work). It has most of the questions that you'll ever ask answered, plus many testimonies of MBBs (Muslim Background Believers). For example, there are 3 studies here on "Love" in the Koran and in the Bible at: www.answering-islam.org/Index (under "L" find Love, then scroll down to the bottom three articles).Similarly, a good presentation of the Gospel for Muslims is there entitled "Heartfelt Fasting and Repentance" with much common ground commending it to Muslim readers, and a sharp edge at the conclusion by which the Spirit can penetrate to the core issue of our sinfulness and need of a Savior – See: www.answering-islam.org/authors/clarke/fasting.html (also now a 4-page tract). Also a 5-page article by Roland Clarke answers a commonly asked question: "Do Muslims and Christians worship the same God?" See: www. answering-islam.org/authors/clarke/worship_same_god.html

Reasons to Believe is an organization founded by a Canadian astrophysicist, Dr. Hugh Ross. It's website features articles, books and numerous apologetic materials aimed at showing the wealth of information on the created universe pointing to a Creator (and accepting an "old earth" view but not a macro-evolutionary view). There are articles on Geophysics, Cosmology, Evolution, Biochemistry, Particle Physics, Worldview Apologetics, Comparative Religion, Molecular Evolution, Creation Design [EG: it deals with arguments from other movements like Creation Science (older - focusing from geology for "young earth") and the re newer Design/Designer movement]. There are many books as well as articles available. Reasons to Believe is both evangelical and scientific in its commitment. This is an excellent resource for internationals in the sciences or those wrestling with evolutionary ideas. Location: 731 East Arrow Hwy., Glendora, CA 91740. 800-482-7836. In Canada: 250-245-0012. Website: www.reasons.org

Training for International Student Ministries: Manuals and Publications for Cross-cultural workers:

InterFACE Ministries has posted an excellent "*International Student Ministry Handbook*" by John Eaves, former staff of IFACE Ministries, (pub. 2001) at: https://reports.iface.org/staffonly/handbook3.1.pdf

(id: *friend* password: *ofgod*). This 63 page handbook is designed primarily to inform local church people interested in cross-cultural friendship and to give them tools to work with (e.g.: understanding "culture shock"). It is filled with ideas, checklists and suggestions for activities, all with good humor and simplicity. Also the document "*Putting the Bible to Work in our Culture,*" by John Eaves, can be found at: www.intervarsity.org/ism/article/2044 (scroll to the bottom for this MSWord doc.)

Conversation Partners - suggestions for getting started and improving conversations with internationals can be found at the following:

- helps on "Hospitality" and "Hosting": www.intervarsity.org/ism/articles.php
- ideas for first conversations: www.intervarsity.org/ism/article/29

- beginning friendship through conversation: www.intervarsity.org/ism/article/6
- resource guide: www.intervarsity.org/ism/article/2045 (and) www.intervarsity.org/ism/download.php?article_id=2045&version_id=3160
- putting the Bible to work (some issues to discuss in depth, especially with/for Christian
- int'ls.): www.intervarsity.org/ism/download.php?article_id=2044&version_id=3159
- *The Complete Book of Questions* - *1001 Conversation Starters for Any Occasion* (Zondervan) *possible topics for conversation:* http://earlyrain.org
- hundreds of good questions to use: http://iteslj.org/questions
- Julie Arant has produced a book called *"Discussion Topics for Internationals"* where she has discussion questions on 48 topics. To purchase go to www.multilanguage.com and look for this title, or item number ENG-L253 – or contact JulieArant@hotmail.com
- **Cross-cultural training games for use with internationals**:
- Over 25 online sources!: www.wilderdom.com/games/Multicultural ExperientialActivities.html

Bartow Wylie (U.K.) says: "There are LOTS of ideas here. I skimmed through them and found them very varied - I think that some of these would be useful for our specific situation, but others are less relevant. You need to invest time in working through them to find the best ones." Includes a large bibliography of books and materials as references (scroll down for this), also the well-known "Bafa Bafa."

Selected Future ISM-related Events

NAFSA: Association of International Educators (formerly National Assoc. for Foreign Student Affairs) is primarily for Foreign Student Advisors (administrators on all campuses) in North America, counselors of international students and others involved with internationals in higher education. For more info on this and future conferences see the NAFSA website: www.nafsa.org/annualconference/default.aspx?id=3204 or www.NAFSA.org For info. on Christians at the conference invited to NAFSA's *"Specific Interest Group"* (SIG), see Jack Burke's article on ACMI's homepage at: www.acmi-net.net (center, at bottom, entitled "NAFSA's Christian SIG"). **NAFSA Conferences are held in different locations each year.**

"Legacy Conference" will be held in Detroit, Michigan (with opportunity to visit the Arab International Festival, Dearborn, MI). http://dearbornlegacyconference.org

International Students Inc. (ISI) has its annual *National (training)* Conference. For info. see ISI's website: www.isionline.org/AboutISI/ISIEvents.aspx or call 800-ISI-TEAM. In the past ISI has extended an invitation to ACMI members to participate in these annual national conferences. *3-6 month Internships for Christian internationals* are offered starting in June or August by "International Friendships" (IF) in Columbus. Ohio. "The internship focuses on development of character, calling, ministry skills, foundational Bible knowledge, and work as ministry," says Rich Mendola. "If you have Christian international students who you would like to recommend for an internship, you can write to me for further information or put the student in touch with me. We are looking to add three interns this year." rmendola@ifiusa.org

(Most summers) – the Zwemer Institute for Muslim Studies seminars & courses are offered. For more information re registration go to: www.ciu.edu/muslimstudies/register.html. every year - *Christmas Season annual Conferences (e.g.: "houseparties") for International Students* were held. These "houseparties" are open to Christian volunteer workers coming and bringing Christian and non-Christian international friends, and are open to other organizations and churches full participation. The following were the locations in the USA and Canada for these *Christmas holiday events*: •Cedar Campus, Cedarville, MI USA. For more info and to register for future Cedar Campus events, see: www.intervarsity.org/cedar/info.php?id=3714 and www.intervarsity.org/cedar/info.php?id=2945

For information on one of the Canadian internationals holiday conf. events, email: ian_elliot@telus.net Any new locations in Canada may be available at: http://ivcf.ca/ivcf/myweb.php?hls=10090

InterVarsity's URBANA Student Missions Convention will be held at St. Louis, Missouri [ed. note URBANA is held every 3 years]. This is a gathering of over 20,000 students and young adults from all over the world, including 1,000 in the International Students Track: The central focus is the worldwide mission of the church. For info on URBANA 12 and a glimpse of the previous URBANA 09 (with various blogs and videos of the main sessions) see: www.urbana.org/home and https://urbana.org/urbana-12/whats-urbana for future announcements. 12 Videos of past Urbanas are given at: http://urbana.org/urbana-12/whats-urbana/videos-and-photos *The International Students Track* will provide *a place for international participants to connect, pray, process, and personalize the messages at URBANA 12* See the Facebook tracking of this event: www.facebook.com/events/121226528001976 International students are urged to attend and can often find some financial assistance for both travel and conference costs.

Coalition Of Ministries to Muslims in (north) America (COMMA). This is a "by-invitation" conference, open only to workers among Muslims in North America. COMMA exists: For more info, contact the Muslim Ministry Dept. at the Billy Graham Center: mmd@wheaton.edu

"Upcoming Events" of Ambassadors for Christ, Inc. (AFC), are published at www.afcinc.org (note rotating list). AFC is dedicated to "Reaching Chinese Intellectuals for Christ," and is located at 21 Ambassadors Drive, Paradise, PA 17562 Phone: 717-687-8564. Also important for Chinese students - a major Chinese Missions Convention is held every three years in December (usually one year after Urbana) sponsored by AFC in cooperation with a sister organization, InterVarsity. In December - a major *Chinese Missions Convention* is held every three years in December sponsored by AFC in coop. with a sister organization InterVarsity. (It is usually held one year after the "Urbana" student missions convention of InterVarsity. . . Other "Upcoming Events" of Ambassadors for Christ, Inc. (AFC), are published at www.afcinc.org (note rotating list). AFC is dedicated to "Reaching Chinese Intellectuals for Christ." AFC: 21 Ambassadors Drive, Paradise, PA 17562 Ph: 717-687-8564.

Late December (every year) – *"Equipper Conference"* ("ec"), of the Japanese Christian Fellowship Network (JCFN). The most recent one was held . . . at Murrieta, CA – designed for Japanese Christians who met Jesus "overseas" for their eventual return to their home country as ambassadors of Christ. Look for future announcements at their JCFN (English) website: (press "Japanese" for change of language).

<u>Recommended addition to Ned Hale's list</u>:

Most recent book providing "A Case for ISM" Dr. Jack Burke's book, <u>Paradigm Shift: Why International Students Are So Strategic to Global Missions,</u> WestBow Press, Bloomington, Indiana, 2018.

AUTHOR: LATE BREAKING NEWS – New Frontier — increasingly expanding number of international students enrolling in American high schools.

<u>Expanding high school international student enrollments open new opportunities for the love of Jesus to be shared with international high school students through hospitality and parental care. This is what churches should be doing as strategic partners of those in global missions.</u>

Author advises the reader to check the internet for information on mounting number of high school international student arrivals from many countries who are registering in American high school classes. Opportunities for Christian service and witness abound for Christians who open up their homes to high school internationals who are looking for a "home away from home." You will find information by checking "Foreign High School Students in the U.S" on the internet. You will find such titles as "International Students Flock to U.S. High Schools," "Chinese Students Flood Christian High Schools." "New Report from IIE Looks at International Students at U.S. High Schools: Students Enrolling Directly for Diplomas Outnumber Exchange Visitor Students."

ENDNOTES

1   Yohannan, K.P. (Nov. 2013) "Revolution in World Missions: One Man's Journey to Change a Generation", gfa books, a division for Gospel for Asia. Carrollton, TX, p. 160-161

2   Ibid, p. 160-161

3   Farrugia, C.A. & Bhandari, R., Open Doors 2015, Institute of International Education, p. 39

4   Ibid, p.39

5   Open Doors, Institute of International Education, Nov. 2017

6   Cultural Globilization, Courtesy of Wikileaks, Nov. 2017

7   Globalization101.org, an internet resource offered by the Levin Institute, a graduate institute of international relations associated with the State University of New York

8   Shaw, Douglas, "The Gospel and International Studies: Can We Make the Connection?" Lausanne World Pulse Archives Issue, May 2010, www. LausannWorldPulse.com/perspectives – php

9   Ibid

10 Bisagno, John R., "Jerusalem First," Houston's First Baptist Church, CD #944, 11/17/85

11 Yohannan, K.P. (Nov. 2013), What International Christian Leaders Are Saying About Gospel for Asia," Revolution in World Missions, gfa books, A Division for Gospel for Asia; introductory pages & back cover

12 Blackaby, Henry T. & King, Claude V., Experiencing God: How to Live the Full Adventure of Knowing & Doing the Will of God, Lifeway Press, Nashville, TN, p. 55

13 Ibid, p. 55

14 Ibid, p. 123-124

15 Institute of International Education, (2015) "International Student Enrollment Trends, 1948-/49-2014/15. Open Doors Report on International Educational Exchange, Retrieved from http://iie.org/opendoors

16 So Wing-chi [Patrick So], "The Transformation of an Atheist" p.35, Heart Publishers Ltd., Hong Kong, www.heartpro.hk, Sept. 20, 2011

17 Ibid

18 (Unknown writer, presumed to be the book's author, Dr. T.E. Koshy, inside book jacket, 2003, or an unnamed colleague)

19 Ibid, p. 19

20 Ibid, p. 20

21 Ibid, p. 22-23

22 Ibid, p. 24

23 Ibid, p. 22-23

24 E-NEWS, 2012 AFRICAN ENTERPRISE, "FOUNDER – MICHAEL CASSIDY, africanenterprise.org

25 Ibid

26 International Student Guide to university and higher education in the USA. www.usastudyguide.com

27 Ibid

28 CATO POLICY REPORT: "Dangerous World? Threat Perception and U.S. National Security," from conference sponsored by Cato Institute, October 25, 2013 printed from CATO.ORG, 1/25/14, CATO Policy Report, January – February, 2014.

29 Lindsey Graham's speech to the Senate, shown on C-SPAN, 6/10/15

30 "First Thought - Who will send them?" Msg; Weekly Message from Gregg Matte...at Houston's First Baptist Church, 11/19/2015

31 Farrugia, C.A. & Bhandari, R. Open Doors, 2016, Report of International Educational Exchange, New York; Institute of International Education Open Doors, p. 14

32 Number of higher education institutions in the United States from 1980 to 2014, Statistica-The Statistics Portal

33 Excerpts from email received from Wichit Maneevone, Escondido, CA, affiliated with International Students Inc. (ISI) to Jack Burke, 1/18/2015. Wichit and Miriam are ICF sponsors

34 Farrugia, C.A. & Bhandari, R. (2015) Open Doors 2015 Report on International Educational Exchange, New York: Institute of International Education p. 39

35 Ibid, p. 40

36 Farrugia, C.A. & Bhandari, R. (2016) Open Doors 2016 Report on International Educational Exchange, New York: Institute of International Education, p. 142

37 Ibid, p. 12-13
38 Ibid, p. 143
39 Marketing Sales and Customer Service, Market Research, Sumaira85, 8/4/14
40 ACMI Conference Plenary Address by Sam Tin, Houston, TX 6/1/2012
41 Michelle Vu, Christian Post Reporter, THE CHRISTIAN POST, 5/18/2010. HTTP:/WWW.CHRISTIANPOST.COM/NEWS/MISSION-LEADERWHY-SO-FEW-CHRISTIANS-IN-JAPAN-45217
42 Ibid
43 Stiller, Brian C., "The Difficulty of Evangelizing in Thailand," Huffungton Post, The Blog 05/08/2013/updated July 8, 2013, www.huffingtonpost.com/brian-c-stiller/the-difficulty of-evangelizing in Thailand
44 Ibid
45 Yohannan, K.P., Revolution in World Missions, Nov. 2013, p. 166

CPSIA information can be obtained
at www.ICGtesting.com
Printed in the USA
FFHW020711221119
56119798-62212FF

9 781973 656852